Screenwriting is Rewriting

Screenplays aren't written. They are rewritten and rewritten and rewritten.
Alexander Mackendrick, Writer/Director,
The Man In The White Suit, The Ladykillers

The experience of writing Cider House *has confirmed what I've always believed as a writer, that the most important and essential element of writing is rewriting.*
John Irving, Screenwriter/Novelist,
The World According to Garp, Cider House Rules

As a kid I was a terrible writer. I was inarticulate and made C's on my writing papers, until I transferred schools in the tenth grade and suddenly starting getting's A's. Why? Two reasons. One, because I started reading fiction with a passion. Two, I learned the value of revision—the rewrite.
Tom Schulman, Screenwriter,
Dead Poets Society, Honey I Shrunk The Kids

I'd write it to the end and go back and write it all over again, go back and write it all over again, go back and write it all over again. I think I probably wrote, without exaggeration, about twenty drafts of A Few Good Men.
Aaron Sorkin, Screenwriter/Playwright,
A Few Good Men, West Wing, The Social Network

Screenwriting is Rewriting

The Art and Craft of Professional Revision

Jack Epps, Jr.

BLOOMSBURY ACADEMIC
NEW YORK • LONDON • OXFORD • NEW DELHI • SYDNEY

BLOOMSBURY ACADEMIC
Bloomsbury Publishing Inc
1385 Broadway, New York, NY 10018, USA
50 Bedford Square, London, WC1B 3DP, UK

BLOOMSBURY, BLOOMSBURY ACADEMIC and the Diana logo are trademarks
of Bloomsbury Publishing Plc

First published in the United States of America 2016
Reprinted 2016, 2017 (twice), 2018 (three times), 2019, 2020

Library of Congress Cataloging-in-Publication Data
Epps, Jack.
Screenwriting is rewriting: the art and craft of professional revision/Jack Epps, Jr.
pages cm
Summary: "A step-by-step guide that takes the mystery out of rewriting and
leads the writer through a series of focused passes which address the core
fundamentals of screenwriting resulting in a polished, professional screenplay"–
Provided by publisher.
Includes bibliographical references and index.
ISBN 978-1-62892-739-9 (hardback) – ISBN 978-1-62892-740-5 (paperback)
1. Motion picture authorship–Handbooks, manuals, etc. I. Title.
PN1996.E66 2016
808.2'3–dc23
2015025733

ISBN: HB: 978-1-6289-2739-9
PB: 978-1-6289-2740-5
ePub: 978-1-6289-2738-2
ePDF: 978-1-6289-2736-8

Typeset by Deanta Global Publishing Services, Chennai, India
Printed and bound in the United States of America

To find out more about our authors and books visit www.bloomsbury.com
and sign up for our newsletters.

For My Family
Cynthia, Liza, and Kerri

Contents

Part 3 Screenwriters on Rewriting

Part 4 Examples

Introduction

Writing is creating something out of nothing. Rewriting is creating something out of what is there.

Robert Towne, Writer/Director,
The Last Detail, Chinatown, Mission Impossible II

Many writers find rewriting to be a mysterious process and flounder around aimlessly playing musical words. They have a love-hate relationship with the task and would rather run barefoot over hot coals than face a rewrite. But it doesn't have to be that way. Rewriting, when done right, can be satisfying and rewarding. It demands a great deal of deconstruction and reconstruction, reconfiguring and reconceiving. To succeed you need a plan of attack: to analyze, organize, problem-solve, and execute. There can be no wasted lines or pointless scenes in a screenplay. It is not about just changing words; rewriting is about stripping away all the dead and irrelevant parts, and finding the heart and core of your characters and story. Everything has to contribute to the whole. There is a famous quote attributed to the renowned sculptor, Michelangelo: "Every block of stone has a statue inside of it and it is the task of the sculptor to discover it." Let's rewrite the quote for screenwriting: "Every screenplay has a movie inside of it and it is the task of the screenwriter to discover it."

It's my firm belief that rewriting made my career. While I was an undergraduate at Michigan State University, I had an intimidating creative writing instructor, Virgil Scott, who drilled the importance of rewriting into my head by demanding I rewrite a short story over and over again. Scott was a published author and someone I didn't want to disappoint. After initial resistance (the normal reaction of all writers), much to my surprise the story got better, and the importance of rewriting was hammered home. When my remarkable partner, Jim Cash, and I began to work together, we spent over two years and five major drafts getting our first spec script into shape to send out to the town. From my experience as a production assistant and a reader, I realized there was only one way to enter the business, and that's at the top with a professional seamless screenplay. No one says "nice try" in Hollywood.

The screenplay form is very conducive for rewriting. It's not a novel and not read as literary material. A screenplay is part stage play and part blueprint. A screenplay can be broken into many component pieces and is malleable in a way that novels and plays are not. Individual scenes can be swapped out with relative ease, and entire characters can disappear and new ones appear in their place. Unlike a novel, the focus of a screenplay is not on the writing, but on the characters and their stories, the visual images and the driving narrative—in other words, storytelling. A screenplay is a guide for directors, actors, cinematographers, set decorators, production designers, visual effects artists, and an entire crew of creative people who use it to focus and coordinate their work. Filmmaking is a collaborative art, and the screenplay is a statement of the shared vision of what the final film should be.

Rewriting makes everyone a better writer. To rewrite successfully, you must understand how all the screenwriting elements work together to form a cohesive script. Rewriting also teaches you what you *must* know before you start your next screenplay. Rewriting is always a challenge, but there is a great deal of satisfaction when you see how far you have taken your screenplay, and how much closer it is to your original intention. If you are serious about becoming a professional screenwriter, then you must become a diligent rewriter. There are no successful screenwriters who are not good at rewriting. They may not like it, but they know how to do it, and they spend more time rewriting then they do writing first drafts. Screenwriting *is* rewriting.

Author's Note: Singular Pronoun Usage

After much thought and consideration, I have decided to use the pronoun "they" as the singular pronoun in place of the traditional "he." The usage of "he or she" would be clumsy to read over the course of an entire book. I hope as writers we can easily understand that favoring one gender over another throughout this book would be objectionable. Male and female writers should feel the ideas and concepts put forward in this book apply to everyone without favoring one sex over the other. So, I choose inclusion rather than exclusion.

Traditionalists may be uncomfortable with usage of the pronoun "they," but after doing a bit of research, it appears our culture is in a transitional period where the use of "they" as a singular pronoun is becoming more common and acceptable. Here is a quote from *Fowler's Modern English Usage*, Edition 3, 1996.

> *Over the centuries, writers of standing have used they, their, and them with anaphoric reference to a singular pronoun or noun, and the practice has continued into the 20c. to the point that, traditional grammarians aside, such constructions are hardly noticed any more and are not widely felt to lie in a prohibited zone.*

That's good enough for me, and hopefully, it's good enough for you too. Let's get on with it. You've got a screenplay to rewrite.

How To Use This Book

No two rewrites are the same, and there is no one way to rewrite. Talk to ten different screenwriters and they will describe ten different approaches to rewriting. There is not a right way or a wrong way. But I do believe there are more effective and efficient ways to approach rewriting. As a professional screenwriter, in order to deal with the constant need to rewrite quickly *and* successfully, I developed a way to categorize notes and organize rewrites to bring order to a chaotic and confusing process. In addition, as a professor and chair at the University of Southern California's Writing for Screen and Television Division, I created the Bachelor of Fine Arts and the Master of Fine Arts rewriting classes and have taught my approach to rewriting to hundreds of students. There are ways to bring order to chaos, but you have to do your part. You have to be 100 percent committed to the work both mentally and physically. Rewriting is blue-collar hard work and the only way to do it is to spend long hours working your screenplay. There are no shortcuts or formulas to rewriting, but there is a way to analyze, organize, problem-solve, and execute your rewrite efficiently.

Be Flexible

This book is meant to be flexible. *Screenwriting is Rewriting* was not written to be followed chapter and verse. Unfortunately, there is no one-size-fits-all approach to rewriting. Generally, every set of notes is different, and therefore, every rewrite is different. Also, each writer has their strengths and weaknesses, and must tailor each rewrite accordingly. Every rewrite I have ever done has had its own unique notes and priorities. Depending upon where you are in the rewrite process, you will also need to figure out which passes are appropriate for your specific rewrite. This is what makes rewriting so challenging. But there are common areas that *always* need addressing like character, theme, plot, structure, and scene work. In addition, there is also a logical order in which these areas should be addressed. I have structured the book in the order that I believe is the best way to structure your rewrite. Think of this as a guide book you will use to pick the best route for your journey.

Customize and Combine Passes

In trying to make this book cover a wide range of rewriting possibilities, I have created eleven separate passes which focus on different essential elements of screenwriting. To address a note on character you may have to combine a Character Pass with a Plot Pass or a Story & Theme Pass. Only you can determine which passes are best suited for your needs. One of the things you should strive for in your rewrite is to work across your entire screenplay to link and connect your characters and their stories. A great screenplay has many interdependent layers that affect and influence each other. One of the hardest lessons in screenwriting is learning how to juggle multiple stories while complicating and advancing each story at the same time.

But . . . Start With Character

Once you create a game plan, and know how you want to approach your rewrite, there is no one place you must begin. But, the main character must drive the screenplay, and until you know your main character's story, you will not be able to create a coherent focused screenplay. So, I advise you to start with character. Character is ridiculously hard to grasp and even the most successful screenwriters struggle with character. Unless you understand how this inner life affects all the important areas of screenwriting, including plot and relationships, you will not be able to take full advantage of what this book has to offer, nor will you be able to do much with your rewrite. But character does not exist in a vacuum. Character revisions also involve addressing plot, structure, theme, and relationships issues—virtually every aspect of your screenplay is affected by your main character's story.

We Must Be on the Same Page

For this book to be of any value, we must be on the same page. You need to watch the movies I reference throughout the book. You can find a list in the chapter: "Movies You Must See." Even if you saw them a while ago, watch them again. In addition to the chapters devoted specifically to rewriting, please read the general screenwriting chapters such as "Character," "Plot," and "Structure." I do not know what you know, and unless we have a shared working knowledge of the fundamentals of screenwriting, you may not make as much progress in your rewrite as you would like.

Rewriting is not just about changing words, or switching scenes; rewriting is about applying and reinforcing the fundamentals of screenwriting and storytelling to your existing screenplay. Even the most experienced screenwriters—present company included—lose sight of the fundamentals and make critical mistakes when writing their screenplays. I look back at several of my produced films and wince at some of the fundamental mistakes I made writing them. If I could, I would rewrite most of them one more time. As writers, we are often lost in the fog of writing and do not always have perspective and distance from our work. Reviewing and reinforcing the fundamentals will help you gain perspective and insight about the craft, and will inform your rewrite immensely. When teaching students rewriting, I spend a great deal of time reviewing fundamentals before they embark on their rewrites. Don't be impatient or in a hurry. Take time to learn the craft. Even if you think you know it, it's always good to review the fundamentals.

Write In This Book

Write in this book, underline—use a yellow maker. When something strikes a chord with you, mark it. Makes notes on the margins. Even write down thoughts about your screenplay. Use this as a reference guide you can go back to again and again. In addition to helping you plan and organize your rewrite, the book should also help you jump-start ideas. So, if you get an idea while reading the book, write it down.

Read the Interviews

Beyond the theory and craft chapters, there are also three interviews with influential screenwriters: Robert Towne, Frank Pierson, and Susannah Grant. These screenwriters have written some of America's greatest screenplays, and have had long and active careers. Towne and Pierson each won an Academy Award® for best original screenplay, and Grant was nominated for an Academy Award® for her work.

Although the interviews are stashed at the back of the book, please read them as you work through your rewrite. In fact, before you begin your rewrite, you should read an interview, and then as you work through your rewrite, read another. I interviewed these screenwriters to give you a broader understanding of how professional writers rewrite. As you will see, each writer has a different approach to rewriting. Over time, if you do a lot of rewriting, you will develop an approach that works best for you.

Final Thoughts

Rewriting does not have to be a chore or something to be dreaded. I grew up playing puzzles, and to me, a rewrite is one giant puzzle. I take great satisfaction when the pieces come together. Try not to be impatient. Rewrites usually get worse before they get better. There is always a great deal of deconstruction before there is reconstruction, and that space in the middle is usually messy and disconnected. Not every idea you have will be brilliant or successful. But, if you are patient and diligent, then eventually, over many passes, you will persevere and emerge with a much stronger screenplay.

Let's Talk About Rewriting

The truth is that writing is rewriting. I am by no means the first person to say this, but let me be the latest. And I go over and over and over, scene by scene, then act by act, then sequence by sequence, until it's as tight and clean as I can possibly make it.

Akiva Goldsman, Screenwriter,
Batman Forever, A Beautiful Mind, Insurgent

Facing the blank page is always difficult. Getting a story up on its feet and then writing an entire screenplay is an incredible accomplishment. Sometimes it goes fast and other times it's like pulling teeth. For the most part, writing a first draft is fueled by the passion and excitement of discovering the characters and the plot. Rewriting, on the other hand, is like being a detective at a crime scene trying to figure out what all the clues mean. Like a good mystery, the clues don't always lead in a straight line. Rewriting is hard work. It's deconstruction and demolition, and then precise surgical repair. It's easy to lose your objectivity and know if something is working or not. This is why rewriting is so challenging. But if you want to be a screenwriter, you must learn to rewrite. You really should think of yourself not as a writer, but as a rewriter. Rewriting is what you will be doing most of your professional writing career, so it is essential that you learn to rewrite successfully and efficiently.

I've never written a perfectly formed first draft in my entire professional career. I've had some good drafts and some horrible drafts, but every screenplay I've written was greatly improved by doing a series of focused rewrites. That is "rewrites" with an "s." Rewriting is a never ending process because everything can always be improved. Eventually, either the screenplay is produced or it's abandoned. Throughout my career, my rewrites were driven by producer, studio, and director notes. In most cases, I was trying to make changes the studio wanted, but I was always rewriting the notes that I felt actually improved the screenplay. You can't write anything well if you don't believe in it.

The Idiosyncrasies of Rewriting

Rewriting is a beast of its own. No two writers approach rewriting the same, but there are some idiosyncrasies of rewriting that are universal. Here are a few.

The Never Ending Rewrite

No matter how much work you have done on a draft, and how much everyone likes it, there is always more work to do. My writing partner, Jim Cash, and I were hired to write *Dick Tracy* for one director, and ended up going through four directors and three different studios before the film went into production nine years later. Each new director wanted their own imprint on the project, so we did numerous drafts. There are often rewrites on the set, and sometimes reshoots during editing. Learn to love rewriting because you are going to do a lot of it.

Scripts Don't Always Get Better

It may seem counterintuitive, but during the rewrite process screenplays don't always get better. In fact, usually they get worse before they get better. Once you figure out *what* needs to change, then you have to figure out *how* to make it better. Not every new idea or solution will be a good one. There is a great deal of trial and error in rewriting, and that's as it should be. In rewriting, you want to take some chances and be open to discovery. Sometimes the notes are misleading or dead wrong, or your solution is not the right one. Often, the original idea was better than the new idea, but maybe the execution was lacking. There are a million different variables. Over the long haul, if you stay at it, it *will* get better. But you will have to work through it to get there.

Rewriting is Messy

Rewriting is like working in a construction zone where the deeper you dig the more you are surrounded by rubble. It's hard to have clarity when you're in the trenches digging away at the concrete. Often in trying to fix one thing you create a new problem somewhere else. Rewriting is also like remodeling a house of cards. At some point you realize you have to remove one of the bottom cards and hope the entire house doesn't collapse. You have to learn to live with the mess and track the loose ends. For me, one of the pleasures of rewriting is tying up all the loose ends and seeing the whole screenplay finally come together.

Notes Are Often Confusing

Notes are the bane of every screenwriter's existence. They are often confusing, contradictory, or don't say what they mean, and are sometimes dead wrong. If you follow the notes exactly, they will probably lead you and your screenplay off a steep cliff. You have to learn how to interpret notes, and learn which suggestions to listen to and which ones to ignore. Another fact of life is, as a professional, you will be rewriting to satisfy a wide range of people who are sometimes at odds with each other. The producer wants to sell the project to the studio, the director wants to put their stamp on the screenplay, the actor wants their character to be someone else, and the studio has notes for marketing. Trying to satisfy a wide range of demands is extremely challenging. Even the most experienced of us gets overloaded and confused by the process. Professional rewriting is a compromise, but it's important to know how each compromise will affect the whole. You can lose a few battles if, in the end, you win the war.

P.S. If you don't believe a note and you write it anyway, and it doesn't work— it's now your idea. No one will ever say, "Sorry, my mistake." You write it—you own it.

You Are Emotionally Attached to Your Screenplay

One of the hardest things about rewriting is that as writers we get emotionally attached to our work. It takes a great deal of time and energy to write a first draft of a screenplay, and it is really hard to let go of those pages. Your attachment to your pages makes it extremely difficult for you to think clearly about whether those pages are the right pages for your screenplay. They may be really good writing, but they may not be relevant anymore and are actually holding you back. There is often a mourning period the writer has to go through to be able to face the fact that all that work needs to be cut or substantially rewritten. It's sort of like breaking up with your pages—divorcing them. Your characters, pages, and scenes are fixed in your mind, but you have to let them go. Until you can detach from all the effort it took to write them, your rewrite will be stuck in neutral, and you will not be able to make forward progress. You need to get to the place where it is as if you are not actually rewriting your screenplay, but are rewriting someone else's screenplay. It takes time to come to terms with letting go. But once you detach from your work, it's like a weight has been lifted from your screenplay, and a new world of possibilities begins to open up.

Odd-numbered Drafts are Better than Even-numbered Drafts

There is also a saying that odd-numbered drafts are better than even-numbered drafts. Even-numbered drafts, such as the second draft, are often based on big new ideas that don't always work. There may be too many cooks in the kitchen, so a lot of the ideas are at odds with one another. As a professional screenwriter, you feel pressure to make the executives happy and try things that your heart may not fully believe, but you want to be a team player. On the odd-numbered draft, such as the third draft, it's usually much more obvious what doesn't work, so you tend to have better clarity and perspective. On my third draft, I may go back to my first draft and put in scenes, characters, or dialogue that were working. I've learned to mine my previous drafts for good ideas that, for one reason or another, got discarded. Never throw anything away—you never know when you will need it.

Rewriting is Challenging

The point of all this is not to dissuade you from rewriting, but to communicate that rewriting is challenging in many different ways. To succeed at it you've got to have a systematic approach to the material, a thick skin, a lot of determination, and a great work ethic. You've got to be able to hang in there even when the work is going south. You've got to believe you can do it, you will make it better, and you are going to work until you've got it right. You need to have a long-term perspective and a lot of passion for your work.

Doing hundreds of passes made me a better writer. I learned what I must have in my screenplay before I begin writing. The best way to avoid a lot of notes is to write a solid first draft, and the best way to write a solid first draft is to ask the right questions before you begin. Starting out on a journey in the dead of night without a road map is not a good way to reach your destination. Your odds of getting lost are pretty good. To analyze, organize, problem-solve, and execute is the best way to achieve your goals, but you do have to have patience and endurance to succeed. Screenwriting is hard work and you've got to love it. Or else, why do it?

The Pass Method

Layer By Layer

Writers will finish a script and think, "God, this is perfect. They should film it just the way it is." That's not how, in my experience, screenwriting works. It's an endless process. I go through draft after draft after draft before I show it to the first person, and then I go through more. You have to commit to the ride and not to the destination.

William Broyles, Jr., Screenwriter,
Apollo 13, Cast Away, Flags Of Our Fathers

The Pass Method is an organized, systemic, strategic way to approach rewriting that evolved out of years of my professional experience writing and rewriting hundreds of drafts. Because I worked for a long time with a writing partner, Jim Cash, we had to discover a way to communicate about how we were going to approach our rewrites. We wrote long distance and never worked in the same room together. We needed to coordinate the process, be on the same page, and find a point of attack. What emerged after doing literally hundreds of passes for studios and directors was an organized approach to rewriting. We learned very quickly the benefit of knowing exactly what we were going to revise, and figuring out scene by scene, character by character, line by line, how we were going to address the notes in a way that worked for the studio and us. With the director and the studio breathing down our necks, and with a production start date staring at us in the face, we could not afford to flounder around and hope we wrote a better draft. We had to know exactly what we were going to do and execute it quickly and efficiently. We had to hit the marks and make everyone happy, including ourselves. Not an easy task.

Over the course of many rewrites, I found we could be more effective if we broke our rewrites into several focused passes, rather than trying to fix every note in one giant pass. I approach rewriting as if I am adding thin layers of paint to a canvas. With each layer that is applied, the characters become richer, the stories become deeper, and all the essential elements become interconnected and cohesive. As a professor, I taught this approach to hundreds of aspiring writers. I've seen it work for them, and I know it can work for you—if you are patient and willing to put in a lot of time.

Pick Four or Five Notes To Accomplish

The Pass Method is not a formula and you can't just fill in the blanks. The goal is to identify problems, find creative solutions, and execute the revisions. With the Pass Method, you focus on four or five notes that you can accomplish, rather than trying to fix everything in one gigantic draft and end up fixing very little. I learned early that starting all over and doing a page one rewrite usually yields a "different," but not usually a "better" screenplay. The "new" draft is often a less inspired screenplay than the original, but still has a lot of the same problems.

There is something special about a first draft that is very important to protect. That initial spark of inspiration and that first blush of getting to know your characters and their stories is something to be celebrated and protected. A lot of things don't always work in a first draft, but a lot of things are also magical. It is my firm belief that in rewriting you must learn what is working before you begin tearing things apart. There is always gold to be mined in a first draft that can be used to build upon in your rewrite. There is a popular saying in Hollywood: "Don't throw the baby out with the bathwater." One of the hardest things about rewriting is getting a perspective and being able to recognize what is working, and what needs to be revised or discarded.

What You Want To Accomplish With Your Rewrite

Your rewrite will be more successful if you have a clear understanding of what you want to accomplish. Here are some of the specific goals:

- A screenplay that fully reflects your original intention.
- A great read from page one to The End.
- A screenplay that moves readers emotionally.
- A compelling main character with identifiable flaws and a strong character arc.

- A screenplay filled with crisis and conflict.
- A screenplay populated with interesting characters that actors want to play.
- Complicated and dysfunctional relationships.
- A plot that continues to surprise and reveal.
- A cohesive screenplay that links and connects each dramatic element.
- A tight efficient structure that supports intriguing plot and character development.
- Consistent characters, stories, plotlines, and theme from beginning to The End.
- A strong second act that builds to a high point at the end of the second act.
- Stakes that continue to rise until the third act climax.
- An ending that is unpredictable but satisfying.
- A screenplay that gets passed up the executive ladder and gets you work.

Create a File Management System

The way I do drafts, I do them like software updates because I'm a geek. So I'll do 1, and then minor adjustments to them I'll do 1.1, 1.2. And then when I make the first major rewrite where I feel a lot has changed I'll go to 2.0. On Looper *I got up to 4.2. So, all said and done, probably in the twenties. Twenty five or so drafts to it. I really tried to discipline myself to rewrite more than I ever have on this one.*

Rian Johnson, Writer/Director,
Brick, The Brothers Bloom, Looper

A quick housekeeping note. File and folder management is very important for successful rewriting. Use a simple file naming system. Dates can be a helpful way to name files as dates clearly show the progression of your work. Also, create a separate slug file and dump any old writing into the slug file for future reference. You will be surprised how often you will go back and check an older version of a scene. Eventually, the rewrite process becomes a blur and you will not remember where you put that one brilliant scene you suddenly must have. Also, back up everything. Eventually, every computer crashes.

Final Thoughts

Screenwriters who succeed work incredibly hard and put in long hours. Screenwriting is our life, and everything else is secondary. The people who succeed love movies, and have a deep drive and passion to see their screenplay on the big screen. It's got to be about the writing and the stories you want to tell.

This is the major leagues; there is no room for good enough. I can share my approach to rewriting to help make your script better, but you have to do the work. And it is work. The key is to find a way to enjoy the process. If it's not fun, it's torture. And if it's torture, then you are not doing it right. It should be challenging but rewarding. But the rewards come in small doses. Don't look for people to pat you on the back. Get over it. You need to be your own cheerleader. It's about process over product. If you enjoy the process, you will end up with a great screenplay.

Movies You Need To See

Making a film means, first of all, to tell a story. That story can be an improbable one, but it should never be banal. It must be dramatic and human. What is drama, after all, but life with the dull bits cut out.

Alfred Hitchcock, Director,
The 39 Steps, North By Northwest, Psycho

Movies are the language of Hollywood. You need to be able to reference a wide range of movies including independents, internationals, big budget Hollywood spectaculars, and the classics. A good place to broaden your film literacy is the AFI's "Top 100 Movies . . . 100 Years" list. There is always something to learn from every movie—including what *not* to do.

Over the course of this book, I repeatedly reference the movies listed below. Please watch them. Movies come and go, but these have important classical elements that transcend time and trends. They are well written and references to these films are easy to grasp. It's not a matter of whether or not they are your favorite movies. These movies teach well, and that's why they are used so often by writing instructors. There is a tendency in younger students to dismiss classic films. Yet, I strongly encourage you to watch these films and learn all you can from them. Great screenwriting is timeless.

Crazy Heart
    Based on the Novel by Thomas Cobb
    Screenplay by Scott Cooper
Die Hard
    Based on the Novel by Roderick Thorp
    Screenplay by Jeb Stuart and Steven E. de Souza
Erin Brockovich
    Written by Susannah Grant
50/50
    Written by Will Reiser
Glory
    Screenplay by Kevin Jarre

Good Will Hunting
    Written by Matt Damon & Ben Affleck
Little Miss Sunshine
    Written by Michael Arndt
On The Waterfront
    Screenplay by Budd Schulberg
One Flew Over The Cuckoo's Nest
    Based on the Novel by Ken Kesey
    Screenplay by Lawrence Hauben, Bo Goldman
Tootsie
    Story by Don McGuire, Larry Gelbart
    Screenplay by Larry Gelbart, Murray Schisgal
Top Gun
    Written by Jim Cash & Jack Epps, Jr.
Toy Story
    Original Story by John Lasseter, Pete Docter, Andrew Stanton, Joe Ranft
    Screenplay by Josh Whedon, Andrew Stanton, Joel Cohen, Alec Sokolow

Part One

Foundations and Fundamentals

Notes

Receiving and Organizing Notes

I am very aware having worked in TV for so many years that other people can have other ideas and a lot of time they're going to be better than mine, and it's just going to make it work better and that's what's really important.

Alan Ball, Screenwriter,
American Beauty, Six Feet Under, True Blood

You've finished your first draft, and you are probably feeling like the entire script is a disaster. You are not alone. We all feel that way. No one writes perfect first drafts. The best screenwriters in the world will tell you their first drafts are a mess. So, help yourself out and admit to yourself there are flaws that need to be addressed. First drafts are sort of like first dates. Sometimes they work out, but most times they are a train wreck.

The point of getting notes is not to validate you as a screenwriter, but to make your screenplay better. If you are looking for validation then you will be disappointed. The very nature of getting notes is to be criticized, so you need to get a tough hide as soon as possible. Notes sting. No one likes getting notes, but there is no avoiding it if you want to be a working screenwriter. The art to getting good notes is to be able to listen and find the note behind the note.

Getting good notes is essential to having a successful rewrite. The entire process can be disorienting and confusing for the writer. The more systematically the writer can approach the process, the less confusion and the better the results. Your job as the screenwriter is to listen and look for the areas you need to address that will improve your screenplay. If you are resistant to criticism or you feel you must defend your screenplay, you will not get good notes, and the process will not be productive. You *need* to get good notes, and it's in your best interest to make sure you get the best notes you can.

Create A Touchstone

Before you embark on your rewrite, take a second to reconnect with what inspired you to write your screenplay in the first place and use it to create a touchstone. It can be an image, a title, a scene, a character, a song—whatever it is that inspired you to write your screenplay. Once you are deep into your rewrite, it's not unusual to find yourself unsure of what you are even writing about anymore. A touchstone can help you stay centered. When you feel lost, go back to your touchstone and reconnect with your original spark of inspiration.

With *Top Gun*, my original inspiration was a photograph of a pilot in an F-14 with his reflective face mask, and two F-14's on either side of him. Modern day warriors at 28,000 feet in sleek jet fighters. My goal was to capture the excitement of that photograph in a screenplay. I continually went back to that photograph for inspiration and guidance. As you go deeper into the rewrite process, stay connected with the touchstone that inspired you to write your screenplay.

Choose Your Readers Carefully

Try to get notes from at least three different people, but limit the feedback to five sets of notes. Any more than five sets of notes will drive you crazy and drain your creativity. People will be telling you what you did wrong and too much negativity becomes overwhelming. Three good reads will help you identify the main problems you will need to address on your next pass. You are looking to find consistent notes that need to be addressed. If several people say you have a character problem or a plot problem, then that is a problem that needs to be addressed.

Pick and choose the people you give your first draft to very carefully since their reactions will play a huge role in your revision process. Your parents, siblings, girlfriend or boyfriend are not good sources for story advice. They love you and want to support you. They don't want to hurt you, and even if they hate it, they won't tell you. If they do tell you they hate it, it could impact your relationship. Keep your professional life and your private life separate.

There is an art to reading a screenplay and it does take practice. After you read about fifty screenplays, you have a pretty good idea of how they work, and how a good one should read. Lay people usually don't know how to read a script and their notes will probably not be valuable—in fact, they could be counterproductive. Find thoughtful, experienced readers to give you notes. Their comments and criticisms will affect every aspect of your next pass. You need to trust the people giving you notes.

Writers Group

You should be in a writer's group. If you are not, then you should find a writer's group or create your own. Trying to give yourself notes is like doing surgery on yourself. It's going to be painful and not very effective. A good writer's group will offer a lot of creative and moral support, and help you stay in the game. There are many successful professional screenwriters that are still in their writer's groups twenty years later. You want to surround yourself with likeminded people who understand the challenges of screenwriting and have good critical skills. There is a brotherhood and sisterhood between writers. We all share the same challenges of the blank page and the difficulty of writing compelling screenplays. Be part of a writing community.

Paying for Notes

There are many online sources that will read scripts and give notes for a fee. If you are going to pay for notes, make sure you know what they are offering. Ask to read a sample of their notes so you will understand what you will get for your money. Find out if their service includes a phone consult. It is always better to have a conversation with the reader so you can put the notes into the proper perspective.

Don't Talk—Listen

Do not argue with the people giving you notes and do not try to defend your work. You are there to *listen*. You cannot talk someone into liking your screenplay. Either they get it or they don't. The reader doesn't care how long it has taken you to write this draft or how hard you have worked on it. They only care about whether it works or not. The rest is none of their concern, and in the room, none of that can be your concern either. Your job is to figure out *why* they are interpreting your screenplay a specific way, and *what* you need to do to get it closer to your original intention.

Readers can sometimes be reluctant to give tough notes. You want to assure them you have a thick skin and can handle tough notes. You need tough notes. Do not take it personally. *They are not criticizing you.* If you project a defensive attitude, the reader will hold back and just give you notes they think you want to hear. That will not help you. Keep your blood pressure down and your ears open.

Record Your Note Session

During a note session, make sure you are taking notes. It's a sign of disrespect if you do not take notes. You will not remember them, and the person giving you notes knows that. So, if you are not taking down notes, you are basically saying: "I don't really care about what you have to say."

Better than taking notes, record your note session. As a courtesy, always ask permission to record the session. You want to be part of the meeting and not just a note taker. You want to make eye contact, listen, and interact with the reader, and you can't do that with your head down taking notes. You want to be able to follow the reader's logic, and ask pointed questions to help you better understand and clarify a note.

After the meeting, transcribe the notes. You will be surprised how much you will pick up by transcribing the notes. Often in the room, you react emotionally and may be unable to see the wisdom in a note. Later, once your adrenaline has gone down, you might be able to hear a difficult note more clearly. When I review the notes, if I missed the original context of the note, it helps me put it into a larger context.

What Worked?

At the very start of any note session always ask the person giving the notes, "What did you like about the script? What worked for you?" This is very important. Just as you want to know what is not working, it is essential to know what *is* working. You may think you know what is working, but you really need to hear from your readers what they liked. If you don't ask, they may not tell you. People are so intent on critiquing that they often forget to give positive feedback. One of my basic tenants of rewriting is to make sure you know what is working and to protect what works. Build on what is working and strengthen what is weak or unclear.

Limit The Note Session

Keep the note session to about forty-five minutes. Do not let it go much over an hour. After an hour, the notes usually get too detailed and counterproductive. You'll feel like a zombie and shut down. In your first draft note sessions, you want big overview notes about character, plot, story, theme, and structure. You don't need individual scene or dialogue notes because your screenplay is going to undergo a great deal of change over the course of your rewrite.

At a certain point, end the discussion and thank the reviewer for their time and thoughts. I read a lot of screenplays, and it takes me several hours to read a script properly and write out notes. Be positive and genuinely thankful. You want to be able to go back to these people again, so make sure they know how much you appreciate their effort on your behalf.

Organize Your Notes

To solve a problem, you first have to identify the problem. Break your notes into separate groupings and categories so you can begin to see the patterns. Create a master note list. Even if you do not agree with a note, put it down. Your next step will be to prioritize your notes, but for now make your master list as comprehensive as possible. You want to get a sense of the big picture.

Here is a list of suggested categories. You may not have a note in each category. Feel free to create your own categories that best reflect your notes.

- What Works
- What Needs Work
- Big Picture Overview Issues
- Surprising Suggestions
- The Main Character
- Supporting Characters
  - Create a heading for each supporting character

- Major Relationships
  - Create a separate heading for each important relationship
- Antagonist—Main Opposition Force
- Multiple Opposition Forces
- Plot
- Structure
- Theme
- Subplots
- Stakes
- Tone
- Genre
- World
- Scenes
- Dialogue

Do not edit the notes at this stage—just get them all down. By drawing all your notes together and organizing them, you will give yourself a chance to think and begin to see patterns. Repetition of the same note is a pretty good indication there is a problem in the screenplay. You will also see contradictory notes, and even notes you do not agree with. Put them down too. This is gathering, not refining.

Let the notes percolate a little bit. I firmly believe in letting your subconscious do a lot of the work. But, if you get a thought or an idea on a potential fix, definitely write it down immediately. Do not depend on your memory—there is a lot going on and it's hard to keep it all in your head.

If you are feeling overwhelmed, you are not alone. At one point or another, all writers get overwhelmed by notes. Part of the process is learning how to see the big picture, choosing the critical notes that you want to address in your first pass. You are *not* going to fix every note on your first pass. You will pick four or five things you can do a great job on with each pass. Over a series of successive passes you will address all the important issues. It's better to do a few things well instead of trying to fix everything at once and ending up with a mediocre draft. Organize—Analyze—Problem-Solve—Execute.

Circle of Confusion

After receiving a tough set of notes, it is not unusual to become confused and maybe a bit demoralized. Months of work have been ripped to shreds and you may find yourself spinning in what I call the "Circle of Confusion." The creative mind is spinning in circles searching for something to hold on to, but each thought gets negated by the next thought until the writer is totally lost and nothing makes sense. To make matters worse, the writer then internalizes this circle of confusion and begins to doubt themselves. The way to stop the circle of confusion is to take action and begin to plan your rewrite. Make it real—write it down. Making lists of notes and putting your thoughts on paper will help stop the circle of confusion.

Resist A Page One Rewrite

After getting notes, everything in the screenplay suddenly becomes suspect and there is a tendency to want to throw the entire draft away and start all over on page one. Don't throw the baby out with the bathwater. There must be *something* worth salvaging from all that work. I've read a ton of first drafts and there is always something valuable to build upon. The challenge is finding the gems and knowing how to build from there.

The idea is to improve what you have—not write something different. *Different is not always better.* If I am going to change something, I want to make sure that I am changing it for the better and not changing for the sake of change. Your first draft has a lot of raw inspiration and is closer to your original intention. Even if you missed by a mile, there is good work to protect. If you start all over again, you will probably write a less inspired imitation of the first draft. At the end of your second draft, you will have two entirely different screenplays, neither of which will be polished or ready to show to anyone. You will also be burned out by the process and not a step closer to actualizing your initial intent.

Final Thoughts

Rewriting is about growing as a writer. The less experienced you are, the more valuable the process will be. After several passes, you will look back on your first draft and be amazed at how much progress you have made. But first, you have to do the hard manual labor. Impatience will be your worst enemy. There are no shortcuts in screenwriting. Shortcuts lead to dead ends.

Writing a screenplay is a marathon—not a sprint. Pace yourself for the long haul. It takes many passes to get a screenplay working on all cylinders. With each successive pass, you will focus on what specifically needs to be addressed and write more effectively and efficiently. Efficiency is critical to your success as a writer. You need to be productive to be successful. Being efficient does not mean sacrificing quality or integrity; being efficient means using your time more effectively and having more clarity and focus in your writing.

What is most important is to dedicate yourself to the work. Make sure you have the mental and physical strength as well as the *passion* to do the work. Part of the preparation process is getting *excited* about the project again, and enjoying the creative process. You've got to fall in love all over again. Getting started on the rewrite is always hard, but at some point you become re-energized. But first, you've got to pedal uphill—and it's a bit of a steep climb until you get your rhythm.

2

Interpreting Notes

Reading Tea Leaves

You're the doctor, I'm the patient. I may be wrong with the solution, but I'm giving you a symptom. These pages are sick, they're not well. Please don't ignore my symptoms. You may ignore my remedy—you're the doctor, so figure it out. But what I don't like is when the doctor just ignores my symptoms.
Bob Cooper, Former Head HBO Pictures, President Tristar Pictures, President of Production, Dreamworks, CEO Artisan Pictures

Not all notes are equal. Some notes are extremely helpful, and some notes hijack your screenplay and take you on a meandering tangent. It is important not to take every note literally. You have received a note because something isn't working for the reader. Look for the note behind the note—try to decipher the *intent* of the note. What is the note really saying, and where might the solution lie? For big notes, look beyond the quick surface fix for something deeper such as character motivations or the nature of key relationships. A note may say one thing on the surface that seems simple but in reality it points to a deeper systemic problem the reviewer is unable to articulate.

Their Solution May Not Be The Solution

It's not the reader's job to figure out how to fix your screenplay. Your job is to interpret the notes and figure out where the real issues lie. The reader's ideas may not be the right ideas, but you can use them to point you in the right direction. On the other hand, you should not dismiss the reader's ideas automatically. Consider all ideas to see if they have merit. You have to be careful not to just pick the ideas that are easy, or quick band-aid fixes. You have been face down in your computer writing your screenplay, and it's really hard to suddenly come up for air and see the big picture. Don't be in a hurry and make snap decisions. Let it percolate for a bit. Over time, as you gather your notes and put them into categories, things will become much clearer.

Common Notes

The biggest challenge is being objective about your work. Readers cannot always articulate the problems with your screenplay. Here are some examples of notes you might get, what they may be saying about your screenplay, and areas that may need some attention. This is by no means a comprehensive list of possible notes. Notes are like snowflakes, no two are exactly alike, but they do have similarities. These are some common notes and possible solutions.

1. I just wasn't involved in the story. I wasn't that concerned about the main character.

The reader is essentially saying they were not emotionally involved in the main character's struggle and journey. Either the main character does not have an internal story with flaws, or there is not enough personally at stake for the main character. The aspiring writer often misinterprets this note to mean they need to add more plot. If the reader is not involved in the story, then adding more plot elements will not address the lack of emotional empathy between the characters and the reader.

- First, look at your main character's internal story. Is their story committed and clear? Have you created scenes that reveal the main character's personal issues? You might consider adding a supporting character, like a best friend, to help articulate the main character's issues.
- This note could also be saying the stakes are not high enough. Is there a personal stake for the main character besides solving the main plot problem? The most effective way to raise stakes is through a key supporting character that is important to the main character. This is often the love interest relationship. If the main character fails to resolve their internal issues and resolve the external main plot problem, the supporting character will also face dire consequences. What is the price the main character will pay if they fail to resolve their *internal* character issues?

- This note also suggests the motivation for the main character to begin their journey may be weak or unclear. Have you created a clear external goal for the main character to accomplish by the third act? Is the goal stated near the end of the first act?
- You may not have specific plot moments that pressure the main character's internal story. The plot events may be too episodic and need to be written so each plot event pressures the main character's flaws. The plot needs to continue to pressure the main character's emotional wound.

2. It felt familiar. I feel I have seen this movie before.

A mistake aspiring writers often make is to base their screenplay on a film they admire. They write a version of their favorite film mimicking the story elements beat for beat. This can lead to a screenplay that feels familiar, predictable, and formulaic. While you may be inspired by a favorite film, it is essential that you bring your voice to your screenplay.

- When you hear the note "it feels familiar," look at your main character. In fact, look at all your characters to be sure their stories are personal, honest, and original. If your characters are clichés borrowed from movies you admire, then you are writing a generic copy and not an original screenplay. Professional writers spend a lifetime learning how to write great characters. They do it by writing draft after draft until their characters start to speak for themselves.
- Your plot maybe too predictable. There needs to be reveals and reversals, and unexpected surprises. You need obstacles and complications that are difficult to overcome.
- Your main antagonist may feel too predictable, familiar, and one-dimensional. Good antagonists have personal stories and don't see themselves as wrong or evil, they see themselves in the right. Their ethics may be different, but they have rationalized their actions. It makes sense to them.
- Your originality comes from your own personal emotional experiences and from the unique way you see the world. The best way to make it your own is to put something of yourself into the main character. What are you afraid of? What are your secrets and lies? How do you think the world works? If you can be honest on the page, your screenplay will take on its own unique voice.

3. I don't believe the character would do this.

To address this note you need to consider the root of the problem: character motivation. The reader is saying they do not believe your character or your story. This is a serious problem. You need to go back to the basics and ask: Who is my character? What is their internal character story? What do they want? What do they need? You must have a clear understanding of the main character's central emotional issue and make sure this issue is the basis of the main character's arc.

- You may be emphasizing plot at the expense of character. By basing your screenplay on solid character stories that *force* the action, you will create a dynamic connection between character and plot.
- Character consistency is critical to a believable and credible screenplay. A character's attitude, behavior, and want must be consistent scene by scene. The audience wants to know how *this* character will react to *this* situation. The character must act consistently until something monumental forces them to change. This change should not happen until the third act and completes the character arc.

4. I don't really get the main character. I'm not really sure who they are.

The note suggests there is nothing unique or original about the main character. You will get this note when your main character lacks an emotional internal story and a distinct attitude.

- To solve this note you will need to commit your main character to an emotional internal story and then consistently complicate their story.
- In addition, your screenplay is probably too plot driven and the main character is a cardboard character going through the plot paces. There may be nothing personally at stake for the main character and there may be no significant relationships that add dimension to his life. Use your major relationships to help flesh out the main character's personal issues as well as to complicate their relationship problems.

5. The Main Character is not likable.

The audience has to emotionally identify with the main character. The main character must have a goal the audience understands and supports. If the main character is mean or cruel they will be unlikable. The mistake in addressing this note would be to remove the main character's flaws which in turn would make them one-dimensional. Movies are not about happy people. Movies are about lives in crisis, with the main character in the midst of a life-altering crisis.

- Instead of trying to make the main character "nicer," work on making the main character more *relatable*. Nothing is more relatable than a flawed character going through a personal crisis. The audience understands pain and empathizes with the underdog. Messy lives are more interesting than saintly lives.
- You also need to show the main character's good side, moments they are trying to do the right thing, but just can't quite get there. If someone is trying to do the right thing, but making bad choices, or just can't catch a break, then the audience will root for them.
- Do not make the main character mean or cruel—audiences never forgive cruelty. The audience must believe the main character is redeemable.

6. The best friend is more interesting than the main character.

Is the reader saying you should change the screenplay and make it about the best friend? No, what the reader is saying is the best friend is more interesting because the best friend probably has faults and flaws. Often, we tend to hold our main character too dear and not dirty them up enough. As a result, the main character is the least interesting character in the screenplay. This is a common problem with many aspiring screenwriters' scripts.

- This note does not mean you should make the best friend less interesting. You have a good character that is working, so now you need to bring up the main character's vitality by adding relatable flaws. To address this note, your main character needs to be struggling with an internal emotional issue.
- In addition to adding dimension to the main character, work on your main character's major relationships. Relationships help dramatize the main character's problems. The main character must have multiple relationships that pressure them. Is there a love interest you can use to show another side of the main character? How can you use the relationships to explore another aspect of the main character's emotional life?

7. The love interest in the story isn't interesting or essential to the screenplay.

Most films have a love story, and often the love interest is not essential to the plot or the main character's journey. Love interests are often cardboard characters.

- To address this note, the love interest needs a strong committed emotional story with their own hopes, dreams, and fears. Their actions and dialogue must come out of the character—come out of who they are and what they want.
- In addition to creating a dimensional character, there needs to be an authentic relationship where each character brings their emotional baggage to that relationship. What is the arc of their relationship? How does the relationship change each character for better or for worse?
- Do not base your key relationships on "movie relationships." Base your relationships on your personal experiences and observations. Bring truth to your screen relationships and your entire screenplay will be elevated to another level.

8. I got lost. I got confused.

This note suggests your plot may be too complicated and probably is over written. There is a misconception by aspiring writers that they need to make their plot complicated. Too many plot twists and turns, and too many action sequences can render the reader brain dead. The reader may have gotten lost because they may have gotten bored.

- Dial back plot intricacies while adding more character and relationships. A little mystery and misdirection can go a long way in making a good plot, but an overtly complicated plot can be confusing and hard to follow. You want twists and turns the reader can follow. Walk the reader through your screenplay yet keep it exciting and unpredictable.
- If your screenplay is all plot twists without an engaging main character, the reader will quickly skim the script to the ending. The best complications are characters and their entangled relationships, which in turn become further complicated by the plot.
- Refrain from introducing too many characters in the opening pages. Set up your significant characters early but not all at the same time. Spread out your major characters and relationship introductions. Don't confuse the

reader by naming nonessential characters. Name characters that are only important to the story. The cabdriver doesn't need a name unless they are important to the screenplay.

9. I didn't care about anyone in the story.
I didn't like anyone in the screenplay.

This note suggests the characters lack depth and personal stories. The reader did not get emotionally invested in the characters. The screenplay may be too plot heavy without enough emphasis on character development.

- All major characters need to have dreams, hopes, fears, agendas, and attitudes.
- Creating empathy for your characters is a top priority as a screenwriter. The audience must identify with your main character and root for them to achieve their goal.
- There must be something at stake other than just solving the main plot problem. Someone or something personal for the main character is also at stake should they fail in their journey. There must be dire consequences if the main character fails in their quest and those consequences are usually best personalized through a supporting character.

10. I don't understand what your screenplay is about.

When working with aspiring writers, I am surprised how often they are unable to articulate what their screenplay is about—even after they have written a complete draft. You should be able to reduce your screenplay to one word, or at the very least, one sentence.

- First, you must know what you are writing about and be able to state it succinctly. If you are writing a redemption story then your plot and your characters must revolve around redemption stories. Your plot must present the main character with opportunities for redemption which they fail to take advantage of until the third act.
- Review your theme and make sure you are restating your theme consistently through the characters and the plot events. Like a musical score, your theme should repeat again and again to help unify your screenplay. Look for ways to weave your theme into the fabric of your screenplay.

- Check that the main character's personal story is clear and committed and that the plot pressures the main character's personal issue. While the plot events may be interesting, they may feel random and unrelated to the character stories, and therefore the screenplay will lack cohesion.
- Examine whether your main character's want is clearly stated early in the screenplay. If the reader does not understand why the main character is pursuing their agenda, the screenplay will lack focus and direction.
- Your stakes may not be high enough. What is at stake for the main character if they fail to resolve the major plot problem?

11. The dialogue doesn't seem real.

Write the best dialogue you can, but resist doing a major dialogue revision until the final stages of your rewrite. Much of your dialogue will change during your rewrite, so focusing on dialogue too early will be a waste of time. In the early passes, use your dialogue to help you know your characters better. Eventually, you will do a Scene Pass where you will focus on improving your dialogue.

- In many ways, dialogue is one of the easier aspects of a screenplay to improve. A little judicious editing can work wonders on dialogue. Less is definitely more. Many times what is left unsaid is more powerful than a line. The space between the lines can say more than a page of dialogue.
- Your speeches are probably too long. People speak in fragments, bits and pieces of dialogue. The characters may speak too formally in complete sentences. There needs to be a natural rhythm and flow to good dialogue.
- If all your characters talk about is the plot, then your screenplay will read very flat. Your characters should be primarily talking about their personal and relationship problems. Your dialogue maybe too expository and you are telling rather than showing through action.

12. All the characters sound the same.

A character's language and voice are a reflection of how they see the world.

- To address this note, assign each character a specific attitude and philosophy. An optimist would always be cheery and upbeat in how they see the world. A pessimist would be negative and see the sky falling. Put them together in a scene and not only do you have immediate conflict, but also you have two very different voices.

- Your characters must be consistent in their actions as well as their voices and dialogue in each scene. Once you establish a character's attitude, it must be consistent in each scene unless their change is motivated by events.

13. Not much seems to happen.

The note suggests there is not enough conflict and crisis in your screenplay. To address this note, first look at your main character's story.

- Your main character must be going through a life-altering crisis. In addition, they need to have relatable character flaws. Each aspect of their life must be under siege and on the verge of falling apart. The main character's relationships need to be filled with tension and resistance, if not completely dysfunctional.
- There also needs to be an external plot crisis that is pressuring the main character's flaws. The external plot crisis must be of significant magnitude to throw the main character's entire life into chaos and cause the main character to scramble to find equilibrium.
- Many times the narrative story line is too straight and direct. You may not have enough subplots and significant obstacles to complicate the main character's journey. You want to have just enough subplots to keep it interesting but not too many to make it overly complicated.
- Your antagonist, or opposition force, may not be strong enough, or actively blocking the main character's want. Your main character can only be as strong as the opposition they face to achieve their goal.

14. The screenplay seemed to slow down near the end.

This note implies the story lost momentum and the reader lost interest. The solution to this note usually involves revising and reinforcing several elements across your entire screenplay from the first act to the third act.

- You may not have established enough story and conflict in your set-up. Read the chapter on "The Set-Up" to see how you can strengthen your third act by creating a strong set-up.
- The main character's internal story is probably not clear or significant. You should make sure your main character has a clear arc and that pays off in the third act.

- The stakes may not be personal or high enough. The stakes cannot be the same on page 25 as they are on page 90. The stakes must continue to rise throughout the entire screenplay.
- Your main antagonist, or main opposition force, may not be formidable. The antagonist must continue to gain in strength and become even more of a threat the closer the main character gets to the climax.

15. The ending didn't work for me.

This is a good example of not taking a note literally, but looking for the intent behind the note. Be a screenplay detective to figure out *how* you fix the note, and *where* you fix the note. Your initial response might be to make the ending bigger, but that is probably not where the problem lies.

- If there are problems with your third act, look to the first act for the root of the problem. The first act must set up the third act. The second act must complicate the main character's personal issues and flaws. The third act climax should force the main character to face their fears and flaws, and be transformed.
- You can only resolve in the third act what you set up and establish in the first act. If your main character's internal story is weak or uncommitted, then you will have nothing to resolve. The third act will suffer from a feeling that the screenplay has not come full circle.
- In the third act, the main character completes their character arc. The main character should satisfy their need, not their want. To satisfy their need, the main character must face the truth, grow, and transform. They might have to pay a price for their growth and insight.
- The problem at the end of the screenplay must be difficult to resolve. The main character must earn the ending by going through challenging obstacles and setbacks that test them every step of the way until the final test—the third act climax.

Final Thoughts

Do not look for the notes to tell you *where* or *what* to fix. Listen to the notes and interpret them, then decide how best to address them. The reader is not the writer and their solutions may not be helpful. Address the critical issues of character, story, structure, and theme first. Don't get caught up in trying to please everyone and fix every little note. Once you have built a solid foundation, in later passes you can begin to work on the smaller issues of dialogue, scenes, and text. Even when working on these issues, character will still be the major issue you will be addressing. I have *never* seen the note: "There is too much character in this screenplay."

3

The Annotated Draft

A Reference Guide To Your Rewrite

Give yourself that chance to put together the eighty, ninety pages of a draft and then read it in a nice little ceremony when you're comfortable, and you read it and you make good notes on it. What you like, what touched you, what moved you, what's a possible way. And then you go about on a rewrite. I'll rewrite a script a trillion times. So rewriting is just the middle name of writing.

Francis Ford Coppola, Writer/Director,
The Godfather, Apocalypse Now

At this point, you should have collected and categorized your notes into lists. Clear patterns should be emerging along with a general sense of the larger issues that need to be addressed. In addition to getting notes from people you respect, it is also essential that you sit down and read your draft cover to cover in one sitting, undisturbed. It is always better to get some distance from the writing so you can read your draft with fresh eyes, and react to your screenplay as a reader and not the writer.

As you read, you need to annotate your first draft. To annotate is to write critical comments alongside a written work. You will use this annotated draft as a guide to help you create a game plan for your rewrite. Do not skip this step. It is critical to read your screenplay from cover to cover and react to your screenplay as a whole.

Print A Hard Copy

Print a single-sided hard copy of your draft. This is not negotiable. Do not read your draft on your computer. It is too easy to skim on a computer and you also may be tempted to make little fixes which are counterproductive at this stage in your rewrite. The reason you need to print a single-sided draft is that the back of each page is perfect for writing notes and ideas. Use that blank page to write notes to yourself, sketch out dialogue, draw arrows, and track emotional beats.

You are creating an essential document that will act as a road map for your revision. You need to be able to pick it up and reference your hard copy notes. Don't be cheap and try to save a few dollars reading your draft on your computer. You've spent an enormous amount of time and effort on this draft, so spend a few dollars on a hard copy.

Read Your Screenplay In One Sitting

Find a comfortable place and set aside several hours where you will be undisturbed. Do not check your email, don't tweet, and don't answer the phone. Lock yourself away from any distractions. The challenge is to read *every* word you have written from the beginning to The End in one setting. You are reading for character development, story, plot, and narrative flow. You need to *experience* your screenplay as a reader not the writer.

If you read your draft over a series of days, you will lose the feeling for the overall flow and emotional connections. You have one good read in you and you must take full advantage of it. Do not let anything or anyone take you away from your read. If your house is on fire, just sit there and let it burn down around you until you have gotten to The End. Then run like hell.

Give Yourself Notes

Mark up every page of this draft. Draw arrows, circle things you like, cross off things you hate, jot down quick thoughts, but keep reading. React to your screenplay. Trust your instincts. Do not filter your immediate reactions and impressions. Write them down. Stay in rhythm to get a sense of the flow and the development of the character and story. Don't just read it, feel your screenplay.

You will get a ton of ideas on how to improve your script as you read through it. The flaws will be painfully clear and the process can be demoralizing, but don't let it weigh you down. This is about engaging your screenplay as a reader and tracking the emotional and narrative flow. Make sure to take note of what is working. If you like something give yourself a pat and write: "Great stuff." "This is a really strong moment!" "More of this." These are the DNA strands you will be using to build upon throughout your rewrite. Remember, it's a first draft, so give yourself a break. You will make it better, but it's going to take time. See Part Four: "Examples," Annotated Pages.

Read for Flow and Story

As you read, listen to what you are feeling. Trust your instincts and your initial reactions. Take note of your thoughts and feelings as you read your screenplay. It is important to react as a reader to the power of the narrative. The questions below are intended to stimulate your instincts about areas to consider as you read your draft.

- Is your screenplay a good read, page by page?
- Do you have enough peaks and valleys?
- Is the main character on a roller coaster?
- Are the obstacles the main character faces formidable and challenging?
- Is the screenplay unpredictable with unexpected surprises?

Character

Film is an emotional journey. As you read, you want to emotionally experience your main character's journey.

- Are you emotionally involved in the screenplay?
- Do you care about the main character?
- Does your main character have a relatable internal character story?
- Does your main character have an internal crisis?
- Does your main character have a clear character arc?

If your screenplay is too plot heavy, then look for places to add character beats. If your screenplay is all character and no plot, then look for ways to add plot beats that pressure the main character's internal story. Character and plot must work together to make a great screenplay.

Structure

Structure is how you tell your story. Always be looking for ways to tell your story more effectively and efficiently.

- Can you trim your opening scenes and start your screenplay later?
- Is this the best order in which to tell your story?
- Do the scenes flow into each other in logical and believable ways?
- Are you introducing obstacles and reversals at strategic moments?
- Does your second act build to a strong conclusion with unresolved character and plot problems?
- Does the third act resolve events set in motion in your first act?

Relationships

A major portion of the main character's story is told through relationships. Look at the nature of your relationships and the bonds that tie them together. Relationships should be filled with conflict and tension.

- What is the nature of each relationship?
- Is there a tension in each relationship?
- Does the nature of the relationships change throughout the screenplay?

Supporting Characters

Pay attention to the supporting characters in your screenplay. Each character should be distinct with a specific attitude and a clear agenda.

- Have you populated your screenplay with interesting supporting characters?
- Does each supporting character have a distinct attitude?
- Does each supporting character have an essential role to play?

Don't Sweat the Small Stuff

Don't stop to edit description or dialogue. If something needs to be edited, make a note: "Edit," or "Trim," and read on. If a description or a dialogue speech feels too long, then write: "Cut" in the margins. Draw a line through dialogue or description that is unnecessary. You will go back and address these notes later. This read is about the overview and not details. If there are scenes that are dead, put a line through them. Write a note explaining to yourself why the scene doesn't work. Do not trust that you will remember why you felt that way.

Read Every Word

If you find yourself skimming your screenplay, make a note: "Dropped out." If you are bored with your own script, imagine how a producer or agent who reads stacks of scripts is going to feel. The idea is to make each and every page hold the reader's attention. If you start skimming, go back to the head of the scene and reread every word you skipped. Make notes on why you skimmed the pages and how to make it better.

After Your Read

Immediately upon completing your read open a page on your computer or grab a legal pad, and let your thoughts come tumbling out. This is critical to your rewrite. React to your screenplay. React to the emotions you felt about the story and the characters. Don't try organizing your thoughts—that will come later. Just get your immediate reactions down on your computer. You are in a highly charged creative state of mind and must take full advantage of it. Be selfish. *Do not allow anyone or anything to distract you.* Stay in the moment and write until you have nothing more to write. If you wake up in the middle of the night with new thoughts, rush to your computer and continue to get them down. Trust your subconscious and get out of its way.

Add Your Notes to the Master Note List

Once your explosion of thoughts and ideas has passed, it's time to begin to organize your thoughts. Just as you organized your notes from your readers, begin to organize your thoughts and ideas into categories and columns. Go through your annotated draft and read your comments. Pull out the best ideas and thoughts, and combine them into the appropriate columns. Once again, patterns will emerge. In the next chapter, "Game Plan," you will draw everything together, and begin to prioritize and organize your approach to your entire rewrite.

Final Thoughts

By stepping back and getting a perspective on your first draft you will be able to make objective decisions on what needs to be addressed, and in what order. Your first read is essential because you will react instinctively to what you actually have on paper. These are important reactions to capture, and you will use your annotated draft as a reference guide throughout your rewrite.

All writers struggle to get the story and the characters they envision onto the page. If it were easy, everyone would be able to do it. Telling a story dramatically, creating living, breathing, three-dimensional characters, and developing a working plot, is extremely difficult. So much of screenwriting depends on the writer's attitude toward their work. Frame your rewrite as a challenge, as something you *want* to do and your rewrite will be much more successful and interesting.

4

Game Plan

Creating the Road Map for the Rewrite

I don't think people spend the amount of time necessary to rewrite a script and all the detail work you need to really understand the characters.

Eric Roth, Screenwriter,
Forest Gump, Munich, The Insider

To rewrite successfully, you need an organized plan of attack—a game plan. Pinpoint the most pressing problems, find solutions, and then execute the changes throughout the screenplay. Haphazardly slogging through your screenplay will not yield great results. Like taking a road trip, it's always better to plan out your route before you hit the road. You may not know how you are going to accomplish your revisions, but you must know what you want to revise, and in what order. Otherwise, you will be driving in the dark without headlights. You will spend some of your time on the road, but you may spend most of your time in a ditch. To make things even more challenging, you will be working on many different areas of your screenplay at the same time. This is not easy to do, and it means leaving some tasks unfinished until later passes. That is precisely why you need a clear game plan to help you stay on track.

You are well on your way to creating your game plan. You have drawn together your notes into categories. The next step is to prioritize your notes, decide what you want to accomplish first, and consider potential solutions. Your game plan is a guide you will use for many passes to help you stay focused and on track. See Part Four: "Examples," Script Notes and Game Plans.

Statement of Intent

Start creating your game plan by writing a statement of what you want to accomplish with your rewrite. Writing this statement will help focus your rewrite and give you a clear direction. For example:

Generally, people did not think that Jason was very clear as a character and they did not know what he wanted. He seemed at times to be unmotivated. His personal story was unclear. He needs a strong want to help motivate him to action throughout the screenplay. In addition, there needs to be more plot events that pressure his story. The plot feels episodic and needs to be directly connected to Jason.

Notes & Solutions Chart

Creating a chart is one of the best ways to visually organize your notes and solutions. Be selective and list the notes that resonate with you that need to be addressed first. You will not address all your notes in your first pass, but you want to get a sense of the big picture and look for solutions that may solve several issues at the same time. Tackle the bigger notes that will have the greatest overall effect on your screenplay first. The foundational elements such as character, structure, plot, and theme should be the areas you want to address in your first series of passes. Leave dialogue, scene work, and text until later passes.

Across from each note, list possible solutions. You may not have the exact solution worked out, but you know generally what needs to change. As you review your game plan, you can develop more detailed solutions. You will discover that a fix in one area may also create problems in another area, or may point to a potential solution for another problem. Continually update your game plan with new ideas and solutions. Since you will be working across your entire screenplay, look to link and connect your dramatic elements together to create a cohesive screenplay.

The Main Character

Address notes about the main character first. Your screenplay is about one person's journey so *who* that person is and *what* motivates them must be established before you can begin to work on the other foundation elements.

Without a strongly committed main character, it will be hard to move ahead since ultimately everything must service the main character's story. While you might be tempted to jump into another note because it appears easier, do the hard character work first. Solving your major character's issues first will serve you well throughout the rest of your revision.

Build plot and structure around a character; do not shoehorn a character into a plot.

Notes: Main Character	Solutions:
Jason feels unmotivated in the screenplay. People are unsure of what he wants.	*Jason's story is about a man who is afraid people won't like him for who he really is so he pretends to be someone else. Jason needs to let go, be himself, and let the chips fall where they may. He needs to be happy in his own skin.* *Jason's story is about identity. Create scenes where we see who Jason really is and scenes that show him covering up his true self.* *Show more of Jason's flaws. Also show what's good about him too.*
Jason's story got lost and disappeared.	*Jason's story is inconsistent and needs to be a bigger part of the screenplay. Retrace Jason's character arc to show him struggling against change.*
Jason goes on a big journey but I'm not sure why.	*Give Jason a clear goal. He has to be strongly motivated.* *Create a best friend character for Jason so he can share his true feelings, and the audience can learn more about what he is thinking and feeling.* *Find places where Jason can reveal what he really wants.*
The story happens around Jason. He doesn't seem to be directly involved in the story.	*Make Jason proactive rather than reactive.* *Too much of the plot is episodic and random.* *The plot events need to be connected to his story.*

Expand Your Game Plan

You are creating an overall game plan for many passes, not just one pass. Use your note categories to expand your game plan. By categorizing your notes into subject areas such as character, structure, plot, and theme, you are also creating a game plan for future passes in each major category. There is no set length for your game plan. Every rewrite is different and the length of your game plan will depend on the amount of work that needs to be done.

It is important not to try to fix everything in one big pass. You will be more successful focusing on specific areas and solving specific problems, rather than trying to fix everything in one giant draft and ending up with a mediocre screenplay. Think of this approach as layering, and that you will craft each layer. Eventually, all the loose ends will be tied together, and the good work done on each pass will add up to a strong focused cohesive screenplay.

Continue to expand your game plan:

Notes: Structure	Solutions:
It takes a long time for the screenplay to get started. It really doesn't pick up steam until the middle of the second act.	*Consider trimming or cutting the opening scenes and starting the screenplay later. Also, the inciting incident may not be strong enough. There needs to be a stronger obstacle earlier in the second act.*
The antagonist doesn't show up until late in the second act.	*Move the antagonist introduction scene earlier in the second act. All the action in the second act needs to be moved earlier.*
The screenplay seems repetitious.	*Develop more subplots. The "A" plotline is carrying too much weight. Expand the subplots, and bring them in earlier.*

The Ripple Effect

Everything in a screenplay should be there for a reason. To have a successful rewrite, you cannot change one element without considering the effect it will have on all the other elements of the screenplay. Change one scene or character, and you will have to make adjustments throughout the entire screenplay. Part of the challenge of rewriting is recognizing the ripples of change, and tracking those ripples throughout your screenplay. Tying elements together into a cohesive screenplay is one of the major goals of your rewrite. When you make a change, use your game plan to help keep track of the change and the effect on characters and scenes.

Feedback on Your Game Plan

If you have someone you trust, maybe one of your readers or your writer's group, you might like to review your game plan with them and get feedback. Make sure you organize your thoughts in a way that other people can understand. Verbally discussing your game plan will help cement your goals in your mind. There is nothing wrong with getting feedback at this point—just as long as the feedback doesn't turn into another note session. Keep the discussion focused on your game plan. You might also get some help on solutions for your notes. It's easier to adjust your game plan now, rather than later on and having to rewrite entire scenes and sequences.

Reevaluate Your Game Plan

All this prep work is critical to the success of your rewrite. Keep your game plan and annotated draft on the desk next to your computer and refer to them often. Also, check off each item you address on your game plan so you have a sense of accomplishment. You're creating a road map that will help you reach your destination. But do not be rigid. Part of rewriting is staying open to surprises and new ideas along the way. New ideas and solutions can have a huge impact on your overall screenplay so you must continually check in and reevaluate your game plan.

Final Thoughts

Rewriting can be confusing. Being confronted with a long list of notes can be daunting. It is easy to get lost and lose perspective. This is precisely why you must create a game plan. The process of organizing notes and developing solutions will help you take control of your rewrite and build your confidence. But take it one day at a time, one page at a time, and one pass at a time, and eventually you will end up with a stronger, more cohesive screenplay that represents your original intention.

5

Character

Writing from the Inside Out

I always look at a character from the inside. So, everyone, rightly or wrongly, is a person to begin with. And then they're informed by their class, their childhood, their occupation, their gender, their race.

Matt Weiner, Writer/Director,
Mad Men, Sopranos, You Are Here

The emotional core of all great writing is character. Unless a writer has a strong understanding of how character works, as well as how to use character to strengthen other aspects of their story, their rewrite will not be successful. It all begins and ends with character, and with rewriting, character work is never done. This chapter is a review, from the writer's point of view, of what goes into creating great characters. The ideas and theories expressed in this chapter will be referenced throughout the book. While you maybe chomping at the bit to get started with your rewrite, please read this chapter to better inform your rewrite.

It's Not What but Who

Movies are about *people* not events. It sounds simple and obvious, but I find most aspiring writers focus almost entirely on plot events at the expense of their characters. Even veteran writers lose sight of their characters while struggling with the demands of plot. It is easy to become caught up in *what* happens rather than *who* it happens to. Plotting is not easy and writers often shoehorn their character into the plot rather than building the plot around the character.

Movies are predominately about one person's journey. There can only be *one* main character for each story. The story has to be about this *one* unique individual, and they are the *only* person in the universe that this story is happening to at this very moment in time. As a writer, it is your job to discover *who* this one and only person is, and *why* this story can only be about them. If you can grasp this simple principle, then you will take a huge step in understanding the basis of character.

What Is Character?

A character in a screenplay is a representation of a human being. As human beings, we are all flawed and stumbling through our lives trying to do the best we can—under the circumstances. We have flaws and failings, weakness and fears. We have a voice inside us that at times we use to mask our true feelings. We are duplicitous, heroic, deeply flawed, and magnanimous. We achieve great things and also do horrible things to each other. We can be conniving and sinister like Amy Dunne in *Gone Girl*, or we can change the world like Martin Luther King, Jr. in *Selma*.

So, what is a character? A character is a person with dreams, hopes, fears, insecurities, and deeply hidden emotional secrets. They have something they want to prove, or something they are trying unsuccessfully to run away from. The permutations are endless, but what is most important is that they have an active emotional inner life. It is this inner life that is motivating them and controlling their behavior. A character is someone who is having a personal life crisis and must come to terms with it before it consumes them. In addition to their personal issues, the character is also in a terrible situation—plot—that pressures them to make a decision and act, or suffer dire consequences—stakes. While most of our lives are boring and undramatic, screen characters must be in the eye of the hurricane with the outcome in doubt.

- In *The Imitation Game*, Alan Turing is a brilliant cryptographer working to crack the German Enigma cipher machine, but he is tormented by an inner secret. He is a homosexual at a time when homosexuality was illegal, and if discovered, he will be imprisoned. Turing has to live a lie and is caught in a web of deceit which costs him everything he holds dear, and eventually contributes to his untimely death.

What Makes Interesting Characters?

Great characters need to be flawed. They represent the best of human nature and the worst of human nature. They must have rich emotional inner lives.

They need to have a personal emotional crisis they must come to terms with in order to move forward in their lives. Characters must have something they desperately want, and must be willing to go to great lengths to get it. Great screen characters are active, not passive. They must be unpredictable and surprise the audience. But they also must be consistent and logical in their actions. They must project a strong attitude through their actions and deeds.

Your characters need a committed personality which makes them "larger than life" screen characters. It doesn't matter if they are loud or quiet, insecure or frightened. What matters is that they have a specific personality that is consistent throughout the screenplay. The audience must be able to relate to them as real people. For the main character, the audience doesn't need to like them, but they do need to be able to sympathize and relate to their plight. They will forgive the main character for their misdeeds if they believe the main character will eventually do the right thing.

Character is best revealed through a character's actions. The audience draws conclusions about a character by how they act in any given situation. Like peeling an onion, you should reveal character one layer at a time over the course of the screenplay. The challenge to screenwriters is in creating interesting dramatic situations that pressure the characters' stories. There is a remarkable emotional transference that goes on between the audience and screen characters. They become emotionally involved in the plight of the main character and deeply care how it turns out for them. Audiences will laugh and cry, gasp and cringe, but only if they care about the main character. And they will only care about the main character if they identify with the main character emotionally.

Lives In Crisis

Movies are about lives in crisis. Your main character must be in a crisis—in fact, they must be in two crises: a personal emotional crisis, as mentioned above, and a plot crisis. While these two crises are different, they must work together to pressure the main character to eventually resolve their internal and external crises. Most aspiring writers have a good understanding of the external plot crisis, but are weak on the internal character crisis. The heart of all great screenplays comes from the internal crisis.

- In *On the Waterfront*, when Terry Malloy was younger, he threw a boxing match for the mob, and now lives every day filled with regret and shame.

Terry tries to act tough and pretend that everything is alright, but Terry is deeply wounded and motivated by regret. He keeps his regret buried deep inside, but it's eating him alive. This is Terry's internal crisis. Terry's external crisis is when he inadvertently sets up a hit of a fellow dock worker who testified to a Crime Commission investigating crime on the dock. Suddenly, Terry is involved in a murder and is hounded by the Crime Commission to testify against the mob. Ultimately, the external plot crisis forces Terry to face his internal emotional crisis, and move forward with his life.

Your main character must be battling two crises in your screenplay—the internal and the external.

Internal Character Story

The phrase I use to describe a character's internal emotional crisis is "The Internal Character Story," or "Character Story." The character story is that private, secret, hidden *emotional* problem that is driving, haunting, torturing, and motivating the main character. A character is like an iceberg. Only a small portion shows on the surface, but the depth, complexity, and truth of the character is hidden from view. Most characters are in denial about their emotional issues, and either cover them up with a mask, or refuse to acknowledge they have a problem. A character's internal emotional struggle motivates their external behavior. The only way to know how a character will act in a given situation is to understand *who* the character is and *what* is motivating them.

Once you understand what is motivating a character, then it becomes clear how they must act. Their behavior must be consistent throughout the entire screenplay. Characters often hide behind a mask and do not reveal their true emotions. A character may be defensive but tries to hide their problem by being aggressive. It's up to you to determine how a character's emotional issue affects their external behavior.

- In *Good Will Hunting*, Will is in denial about the source of his anger and his deep insecurity. He has a feeling that he is not good enough, and although he has many exceptional talents, he is self-destructive and his own worst enemy. His internal crisis motivates his exterior behavior. But as we peel back the layers, we also see that Will's behavior is motivated by much darker physical abuse he received as a child. He must first come to terms with his emotional issues, before he can move forward with his life.

A character without an internal story is just a rat going through a plot maze. Without an internal character story, the only question is whether the rat will find the piece of cheese at the end of the maze. Add the internal emotional issue and suddenly you are telling a story about a rat that has something personal at stake and a compelling reason for getting to the end of the maze.

- In *Ratatouille*, Remy has a dream to be a world-class chef but no one believes in him. He has to believe in himself, overcome his fears, and prove he has a rare gift. Remy maybe a rat, but he runs the maze to prove he can be a world-class chef.

It's The Story About A Man/Woman Who . . .

In rewriting, it is essential to have a clear concise understanding of your main character's emotional issue. You should be able to distill your character's internal story down to a single sentence. It is virtually impossible to write a focused screenplay, or take your character development to the next level, if you do not know your main character's emotional issue. During your rewrite, you must use the main character's internal story to unify your screenplay. Virtually everything revolves around it.

In my classes, I use a paradigm to help students identify the main character's story. On first glance it may appear to be relatively easy, but I know from teaching students, it's much harder to grasp than it appears. To help clarify your character's internal story, complete the following sentence: *It's the story about a man/woman who . . . .* The sentence must describe the main character's emotional issues, not the plot.

- *Casablanca*: *It's the story about a man who* had his heart broken by a woman he believes deserted him, and now he's turned his anger and bitterness against himself and the rest of the world.
- *On the Waterfront*: *It's the story about a man who* sold out his dreams for pennies and now he's living a life filled with regret and shame.
- *Erin Brockovich*: *It's the story about a woman who* in the face of two hungry children to support and no job prospects, has lost faith in herself and in her belief that she could make a difference in the world.

In the sentences above, the key words are: "anger and bitterness," "regret and shame," and "lost faith." These are words that describe emotional states.

Next, write a sentence that explains what the character needs to do to resolve their emotional issues. Usually, it involves facing a truth about themselves which leads to growth and transformation. This is also a statement of what the main character must do to complete their arc. *He/she needs to . . .*

- *Casablanca*: *He needs to* forgive, let go of his bitterness, and realize there are more important problems in the world than his own hurt feelings.
- *On the Waterfront*: *He needs to* stop living a lie, and face the truth about himself, before he loses his last chance for happiness.
- *Erin Brockovich*: *She needs to* believe in herself again, and fight for her voice and place in the world.

Now, combine the two sentences together. These two sentences distill the essence of the internal character story and the main character's arc.

- *Casablanca*: *It's the story about a man who* had his heart broken by a woman he believes deserted him, and now he's turned his anger and bitterness against himself and the rest of the world. *He needs to* forgive, let go of his bitterness, and realize there are more important problems in the world than his own hurt feelings.
- *On the Waterfront*: *It's the story about a man who* sold out his dreams for pennies and now he's turned into an aimless shell filled with regret and shame. *He needs to* face the truth about himself, before he loses his last chance for happiness.
- *Erin Brockovich*: *It's the story about a woman who* in the face of two hungry children to support and no job prospects, has lost faith in herself and in her belief that she could make a difference in the world. *She needs to* believe in herself again, and fight for her voice and place in the world.

These examples describe the inner turmoil and crises of the main characters. The inner world of the main character should be fraught with heartbreak, insecurity, anger, self-criticism, doubt, and regret. The best screen characters have personal emotional issues they must face, and the arc of the story is how they eventually come to terms with their issues.

Practice writing these two sentences for movies you admire before you write one for your screenplay. It is more difficult than it appears to distill the main emotional arc into two sentences. Beware of just writing the plotline. Here are examples of the same films, but with two sentences only about the plot and not the main character's personal story.

- *Casablanca*: It's the story of a man who has to find the letters of transit so he can leave Casablanca with his old girlfriend. He needs to find the letters.
- *On the Waterfront*: It's the story of a man who helps fight corruption on the docks. He needs to testify.
- *Erin Brockovich*: It's the story of a woman who holds a huge power company responsible for ecological damages. She needs to find evidence to win the case.

Write your characters from the inside out. Have their actions, motivations, and attitudes come from a place deep inside them. Once you know what is going on inside your characters, they begin to write themselves.

Character Arc

A Character Arc is the trajectory of a character's emotional journey. A character at the end of the screenplay should be different than they were at the beginning. The main character should undergo some sort of an emotional transformation. A character arc means a character goes from selfish to sharing; fearful to brave; resentful to supportive; self-absorbed to giving; angry to joyful; bitter to positive; self-loathing to acceptance. The list is endless.

For a character arc to be effective, the arc must be based on the main character's internal story. If there is no link between the internal character story and the character arc, the arc will feel arbitrary and unfulfilling. Changing a character for the sake of change does not work. To change, a character must go through a life-altering crisis which forces them to look deep inside and face the truth about themselves.

- In *Toy Story*, Woody and Buzz both have strong character arcs. Woody goes from being jealous and insecure to open and sharing, and Buzz goes from being egotistical and selfish to humble and respectful. They both reach their lowest point trapped in Sid's room on the brink of their imminent destruction. Their personal growth and transformation allows their relationship to change. They go from being distrustful adversaries to best friends.

Without their character arcs, what would the screenplay be about? The heart of the story is about each character's personal growth, and the effect it has on their friendship.

Resistance to Change

Resistance to change is critical in creating strong and vibrant character arcs. People change kicking and screaming. It is the main character's denial and resistance to change that helps the audience believe the character's transformation at the end of the story. If the character changes too soon, the air goes out of the balloon, the conflict dies, and the movie is over. Denial and resistance to change creates plot and relationship story opportunities as well as a more vibrant second act.

- Terry Malloy in *On the Waterfront*, resists facing the truth about his brother's betrayal and his own shame and regret. He is living a lie, pretending he was a top boxer, when in reality he knows he threw a fight for the small money. If Terry Malloy does not face the truth, he will lose out on his one opportunity to find happiness in his relationship with his girlfriend, Edie. But Terry resists until his brother Charlie is murdered. This event forces Terry to see Johnny Friendly for who he really is—not a father figure, but a ruthless coldblooded killer. Terry doesn't change because he wants to change—he is forced to change because of the emotional impact of his brother's murder.

Genre Often Determines Degree of Personal Issues

Depending upon the genre, not every character must be deeply scarred or in an emotional crisis. The degree to which a character has emotional issues often depends on the genre and topic. The more dramatic the screenplay, the deeper the emotional issues.

Independent films are character driven and therefore character development is usually the focus of the screenplay. Action films are less character driven and therefore tend to have less character development. It would be a serious mistake for a writer interested in working in the action genre to disregard character development entirely. Inside every big action film should be a smaller story that humanizes the action hero to make them a human being, and not just a fighting machine.

- In *Kingsman*, agent Harry Hart is filled with remorse over for the death of a member of his team. Hart desperately wants to make amends by helping the deceased agent's son, Eggsy, straighten out his life. Eggsy must overcome the chip on his shoulder to assume his rightful place as a top secret agent.

The Antagonist

The more you can humanize the antagonist, the more dangerous and sinister they become. Evil for evil's sake does not make a great antagonist. For the antagonist to be effective, they also need a personal motivation for their actions. Therefore, the antagonist also needs an internal character story. The one important difference between the main character and the antagonist is that the antagonist does not have a character arc and does not change. It is also important the antagonist believes they are in the right and that the main character is wrong. The antagonist must see their mission as the correct way and will stop at nothing to achieve their goal.

> *Writers must be fair and remember even bad guys, most of them anyway, see themselves as good. They are the heroes of their own lives. Giving them a fair chance as characters can create some interesting shades of gray, and shades of gray are also a part of life.*
>
> Stephen King, Novelist/Screenwriter,
> *Stand By Me, The Green Mile*

In essence, every character in your screenplay must be a flesh and blood person with a rich emotional inner life.

Character is Not . . .

Character is not a personality trait. Whether someone is happy, sad, angry, or funny is not character. These are examples of personality traits and behavior. Personality traits and behavior should be a reflection of the internal character story. But character has to come from the inside out.

- In *Casablanca*, Rick Blaine is bitter and cynical because his heart is broken.

- In *On the Waterfront*, Terry Malloy is glum and sullen because of his lost dream.
- In *Erin Brockovich*, Erin is loud and profane because of a deep need to be heard and validated.

Each of these character's external personalities and attitudes is a reflection of their internal story.

You may initially come to your character because you want to write a story about a cynical character. Fine, but your next question must be *why* are they cynical? *What* made them this way and *what* is going on inside of them emotionally? Spending time describing a character in great detail does not create a character. Reveal character through behavior and action based on the character's internal crisis and character story.

Final Thoughts

Writing from the inside out means writing the character's emotional journey. To write from the inside out, you must understand the *why* of your characters. Each major character must have an internal struggle that makes them act or react consistently scene by scene. Because of their internal character stories, they can only act one way. Once you know your characters' internal stories, you can put them into any situation and their internal character stories will write the scene for you. They almost don't need you anymore. The characters know their stories and are better at telling them than you are.

Character is a person in the midst of a personal emotional crisis. Find each of your characters' internal stories and let those stories be your guide. Stay committed and consistent with your characters' stories, and ride those stories to the conclusion of your screenplay. Write the emotional journey. Write from the inside out.

6

Foundation Pass

Strengthening the Core

The most important decision I have to make: What is this movie about? I'm not talking about plot, although in certain very good melodramas the plot is all they're about. And that's not bad. A good, rousing, scary story can be a hell of a lot of fun. But what is it about emotionally? What is the theme of the movie, the spine, the arc? What does the movie mean to me?

Sidney Lumet, Writer/Director,
Dog Day Afternoon, Network, The Verdict

One of the primary goals of your rewrite is to bring the four pillars of screenwriting into alignment. The four pillars are: character, theme, plot, and structure. This is the foundation that holds up your entire screenplay. Just like building a house, if you build upon a faulty foundation, your house will collapse. Your plot needs to support the main character's story. You must have an understanding of your theme and it must resonate throughout your screenplay. The main plot problem needs to be clear, consistent, and drive the story. You also want to ensure your structure is telling the main character's story the best way possible. Over the course of your rewrite, these four pillars will support the majority of the work on your later passes.

This is a deconstruction pass where you separate the script into its basic elements to see your screenplay's foundations clearly. Your goal is not to fix these areas in one huge pass, but to bring them into alignment so they begin to work together. As you continue with more specific passes, you will build upon a strong foundation. It is the nature of rewriting to leave a lot unfinished. Write notes to yourself about future work to track the loose ends that will eventually be tied up in a later pass. **Bold** your notes so they are easy to see.

Objectives of Your Foundation Pass

- Build a solid foundation.
- Use your theme to unify your screenplay.
- Strengthen and focus the main character's internal story.
- Unify the elements of character, theme, plot, and structure.
- The main plot problem must be consistent, consequential, and difficult to solve.
- Focus on the four pillars of your foundation and do not get distracted by details.

Foundation Draft Notes

The purpose of this pass is to bring your four pillars into alignment. Your goal is to get each element working together and not necessarily fix every note in each area. Consult your game plan to identify the essential issues to address first. You should be looking to address issues that deal with the main character's story, the main plot problem, the central theme, and the general structure. Look for overall notes such as not enough conflict, or the main character is vague.

Foundation Notes

Common Notes:	Potential Solutions:
I'm not sure what the script is about.	What is Your Screenplay About?, Theme, Internal Character Story, Main Character's Want
I'm not sure whose movie this is.	Internal Character Story, Main Character's Want
I don't really care about the main character.	Internal Character Story, Main Character's Want, Stakes*
I don't know what the main character wants.	Internal Character Story, Theme, Main Character's Want, Stakes*, Key Relationship*
The main character is unmotivated.	Internal Character Story, Main Character's Want, Stakes*, Key Relationship
There isn't enough conflict in the screenplay.	Internal Character Story, Main Plot Problem, Stakes*, Central Dramatic Conflict*, Antagonist's Plan*

Foundation Notes (Continued)

Common Notes:	Potential Solutions:
The story feels plot heavy.	What is Your Screenplay About?, Internal Character Story, Theme, Main Plot Problem, Key Relationship*, Stakes*, Structure
The plot feels episodic.	What is Your Screenplay About?, Internal Character Story, Theme, Main Plot Problem
I can't follow the plot. I keep getting confused.	What is Your Screenplay About?, Internal Character Story, Main Plot Problem, Structure, Theme
The screenplay takes a long time to get started.	Structure, Ticking Clock*, Four High Points*

*See index: concept found in other chapter.

What is Your Screenplay About?

Is your screenplay about redemption? Second chance? Living in the moment? You should be able to reduce your screenplay to a single word, or simple phrase. It should be that clear to you. If not, then you probably do not know what your screenplay is about. If you are unsure about it, look to your main character's journey and character arc. What consistent problems are they facing? What does the main character want, and what do they fear the most? Understanding what your screenplay is about is the first step to discovering or creating your central theme.

- In *One Flew Over the Cuckoo's Nest*, McMurphy has problems with authority figures and he is strongly antiestablishment. *Cuckoo's Nest* is about power, control, and authoritarianism.

What you are writing about does not have to be complex or original. But as the writer, you must know exactly what you are writing about, and tell your story in your voice.

- What is your screenplay about?
- What does the main character want?
- What does your main character fear the most?
- What are consistent problems the main character faces time and again?

Theme

Theme unifies your screenplay. Some writers start with theme, and others find their themes as they write. Before you begin this next pass, you must settle on your theme and use it to draw your screenplay together. If you are unsure of your theme, it can probably be found in your first draft—you may not have recognized it yet. Your characters may have stated it in a line of dialogue, or you may have several scenes that revolve around themes of second chance, sacrifice, redemption, or commitment. You may have many themes, but you want to choose a main theme to unify your screenplay.

- In *On the Waterfront*, the theme is redemption, and each major supporting character either helps or hinders Terry's struggle for redemption. In the end, Terry makes an unselfish decision, takes action, and is redeemed. In addition to Terry's redemption, many other major characters are also redeemed. Edie's faith in the power of good over evil is confirmed—her faith is redeemed. The Priest comes out from hiding in the church and is redeemed by his activism on the docks. Terry's brother, Charlie, has deeply betrayed his brother, but he makes a last ditch attempt to redeem his past mistakes, and pays the ultimate price—death. On the opposite side of the ledger, Johnny Friendly and his hoodlums remain corrupt and unredeemed.

What makes *On the Waterfront* such a compelling film is that the major characters and the plot are thematically linked together which makes the story tight and cohesive. Each major character story or action should in some way reflect an aspect of your theme. Your theme must be consistent and resonate throughout your screenplay. If your theme is redemption, then your characters should either be seeking redemption or trying to block redemption.

- What are you saying about the human condition and about life's journey?
- What is your point of view and perspective as a writer?
- What truth do you want to share?
- Is there an overarching question about humanity you are asking?
- Is your theme repeated consistently throughout your entire screenplay?
- Do your scenes and characters test and retest your theme?

Character

Your main character is the audience's emotional entry into your movie. If the audience does not care about the main character, they will not care about your movie. In the Foundation Pass, you must clearly establish the main character's internal personal story early in your screenplay. The main character must have an internal emotional crisis that is negatively affecting their life and their ability to find happiness. The internal problem should also negatively affect their important relationships. Usually, the main character is in a state of denial about their personal issues. They believe they are in control of their emotions, when in fact, their emotions are in control of them. Throughout the screenplay, the main character fights against facing the truth until they reach their lowest point where they are forced to see the truth, which in turn causes them to grow and transform. The main character's internal story must also echo your theme. During their journey, the main character's personal trials must question and/or reinforce your theme.

Establish the main character's internal story firmly in your mind and on the page. Use on-the-nose dialogue or consider adding voice-over narration to help you clarify the main character's story in your mind. In addition, consider creating both an accusatory and/or a confessional scene to further reveal your main character's story. In later passes, you can remove the voice-over and delete some of the on-the-nose dialogue. Action is always better than words, and less is more. But for this pass, do not worry about anything other than committing your main character to an internal story, that is consistent throughout your entire screenplay.

- What is your main character's internal story?
- Is the main character's story consistent throughout your entire screenplay?
- Does the main character's internal story echo your theme?
- Does your main character have a clear consistent character arc?

Main Character's Want

The Main Character must have something, or someone, they desperately want and they must actively pursue their want throughout the screenplay. Their want should be difficult if not impossible for them to achieve. The main character's pursuit of their want plays an important role in tying the main character's internal story and the plot together. The action the main character takes to achieve their want is the central plot.

- In *Cuckoo's Nest*, McMurphy is a selfish individual who is out for himself. He wants to gamble, cheat, have sex, and not be held accountable for his actions. McMurphy's pursuit of his want puts him into direct confrontation with Nurse Ratchet and hospital regulations. McMurphy's actions to achieve his want determine the plot.

Make sure you establish the main character's want early in your screenplay so the reader/audience clearly understands what is driving the main character throughout your screenplay.

- What does your main character want?
- Who or what stands in the way of their achieving their want?
- How do you use the main character's want to create obstacles, complications, and plot events?

Plot

Most aspiring writers approach plot as a series of random episodic events instead of a series of physical and emotional challenges the main character must overcome. One goal of your Foundation Pass is to tie your plot to the main character's personal story. Do not force the main character into the plot; build the plot around the main character's story. If you change the main character, then you will need to change the plot. Your plot must be a series of obstacles and roadblocks that complicate and hinder the main character from achieving their goal. In addition to entertaining the audience, these obstacles and complications must also pressure the main character's emotional issues and flaws.

- In a big action film like *Die Hard,* the plot is there to mostly entertain, but there is just enough of a personal story to make the audience care about the main character. While the major focus of big action films are the exciting set pieces, all action films are better if the main character has an emotional stake in the outcome. *Die Hard* is just as much the story of a marriage that is falling apart as it is about a high stakes robbery.

- In independent films like *50/50*, the main character's personal emotional journey is more prominent and important than the plot twists and turns. The focus of independent films is usually on the main character's emotional issues and dysfunctional relationships. In either case, there must be balance between plot events that entertain and plot events that pressure the main character's story.

If you are getting notes that your screenplay is too plot heavy or the plot is too episodic, work on the major plot events to pressure the main character's personal story. Have the main character's emotional issues complicate the plot. Identify two or three critical plot moments and make these affect the main character's internal story. In this pass, don't be afraid to sacrifice plot for character. It is easier to add exciting complications and obstacles in a later pass than it is to add more character. Remember, the goal of your Foundation Pass is not to fix all your plot notes, but to draw the plot and main character into alignment, and get them working together.

- Why *this* character in *this* plot?
- How is your plot unique to the main character's story?
- Do your major plot events pressure the main character's story?
- Is the main character's personal journey at the center of your plot?
- Why does the audience care?
- Are you using the main character's story to create and tailor the plot?

Main Plot Problem

Your screenplay must have a main plot problem that needs to be resolved by the end of the screenplay. The main plot problem must be introduced in the first act and be consequential, difficult to solve, and a consistent problem throughout the screenplay. The main character should be sailing into an ever-increasing headwind in your entire screenplay. To continue the analogy further, the closer the main character gets to the third act climax, the stronger the wind, the bigger the waves, and the greater the danger. Depending upon the type of film, this danger can be physical, emotional, or psychological.

- In *Little Miss Sunshine,* the main plot problem is getting Olive to the beauty contest on time. The fixed deadline creates a great deal of tension and pressure on the main characters and their personal stories. The main plot problem is complicated by Grandpa's death and the van breaking down.

- In *Die Hard*, the main plot problem is that the "terrorists" have taken over Nakatomi Corporation and will kill the hostages unless their demands are met. Over time, the antagonist's actual plan is revealed, but the main plot problem remains the same—the lives of the hostages are still at stake.

The main plot problem is the spine that binds everything together and allows the writer to branch off and explore characters and relationships as the screenplay sails at an increasing pace in a rising sea toward the climax. The main plot problem should also be linked to your theme.

- Do you have a main plot problem that the main character must resolve by the third act?
- Is your main plot problem consequential and difficult to resolve?
- Are you using your main plot problem to create complications and obstacles for the main character?

Structure

Structure is about storytelling: where you begin, what order you tell your story, and when you resolve your story. Structure is not just about three acts, eight sequences, or "plot points." As the writer, you must know *whose* story and *what* story you are telling before you can determine the best way to structure your screenplay. Structure should never determine character or story. Structure serves character and story.

Structure is also how time is used in a screenplay. Time can be compressed or time can extend over many years.

- In *Little Miss Sunshine* there is a limited amount of time to get Olive to the beauty pageant which creates a great deal of tension and conflict.
- Time can be extended as in Lee Daniels' *The Butler* which follows one man's life journey as a butler in the White House.
- In *Stand By Me*, the story is told through a series of flashbacks as the main character reflects on a life-changing event.

In your Foundation Pass, your major concern should be whether your structure supports the main character's personal story, and creates a sense of urgency and tension throughout your entire screenplay. Examine how you are using time and consider ways to enter your screenplay later to create a greater sense of urgency. Often events can be moved up and opening scenes can be cut to create a greater sense of immediacy. Look for ways to compress time to add more pressure on the main character.

- Does your structure support the main character's internal story?
- Is your story best told in a linear manner or through a flashback?
- Can you begin your screenplay later to create a greater sense of urgency and crisis?
- Can you compress time to create more conflict and tension?

Dialogue

Do not worry about dialogue at this early stage in your rewrite. Let your characters talk to you and tell you their stories. As you write new scenes, and add depth and dimension to your characters, you will inevitably change a lot of dialogue—probably most of it. You are still discovering critical information about your screenplay. You do not want to restrict your imagination. Don't worry about the length of your speeches or scenes, or even the length of your screenplay. You will have many opportunities to trim, tighten, and sweeten later.

Final Thoughts

Keep the scope of your foundation pass limited to working on the four pillars of screenwriting: character, theme, plot, and structure. Resist tinkering with details. You are building a foundation not decorating a room. Foundation work is heavy construction. You are not trying to fix all your issues in this pass, but to bring these elements into alignment so they support the main character's journey and eventual transformation. No matter whether you are writing a Hollywood tentpole movie or a small independent film, you must solidify the main character's emotional story before you can move forward with your screenplay.

Have a long-term perspective on the entire rewriting process. You will be doing multiple focused passes to build your screenplay one pass at a time.

Do not become impatient and hurry the process. Follow your game plan and execute your ideas. Do not second guess yourself. Be disciplined and work through the material. Some of it will work, and some of it won't. Not everything you try in your rewrite will be successful. Anyone can write a screenplay, but very few people, however, can successfully rewrite a screenplay. If you want to be a professional writer, learn to enjoy rewriting—you are going to be doing a lot of it.

7

Character Pass

The Emotional Core

To me, truth is the big thing. Constantly you're writing something and you get to a place where your character could go this way or that and I just can't lie. The characters have gotta be true to themselves. To me a character can't do anything good or bad, they can do only do something that's true or not.

Quentin Tarantino, Writer/Director,
Pulp Fiction, Inglorious Basterds, Django Unchained

Every rewrite is unique: different problems—different needs—different solutions. But if there is one constant note to all first drafts, it is that there are problems with the main character. Character is the most challenging element for any writer to master and is central to a successful rewrite. If the audience does not identify with or emotionally care about the main character, they will not care about the movie no matter how brilliant the plot.

In the Character Pass, your primary objective is to solidify the main character's personal story. You have many characters in your screenplay but it is ultimately one person's story. It is essential to that you tell your main character's story *consistently* from beginning to end. The main character's internal story must track through every scene, and each character interaction, with a clear traceable character arc. The main character must be active, and drive the action and momentum of the screenplay. Movies are about lives in crisis and you must have a character that has both an external crisis *and* an internal crisis.

Objectives of Your Character Pass

- Clarify and strengthen the main character's internal story.
- Create a strong emotional through-line.

- Reveal the main character's story through behavior and dramatic action.
- Make the main character consistent throughout the screenplay.
- Create scenes and moments that pressure the main character's flaws.
- Use want and need to drive the main character's story.
- Create a strong unpredictable character arc.
- Make sure the character is active and forces the action.

Character Notes

Review your game plan and choose three or four major character issues to address in this pass. Issues such as vagueness, motivation, story, wants, and needs should be addressed first. Placing your main character at the center of your screenplay is your primary goal. Stay with your game plan for this pass and do not enlarge the scope of your rewrite.

Character Notes

Common Notes:	Potential Solutions:
I don't know whose story this is.	Internal Character Story, Lives in Crisis*, Want, Need, Sounding Board Character, Pressure the Flaws, Active vs. Passive
The main character is vague and unmotivated.	Internal Character Story, Defining Scene, Want, Need, Attitude Adjustment, Active vs. Passive
I don't like the main character.	Internal Character Story, Character Flaws, Personal Stakes, Sounding Board Character, Relationships*, Active Character
I don't know what the main character wants.	Internal Character Story, Lives in Crisis*, Defining Scene, Want, Need, Sounding Board Character, Active vs. Passive
The main character doesn't seem to grow or have an arc.	Internal Character Story, Character Arc*, Defining Scene, Consistency, Want, Need
The main character feels predictable.	Internal Character Story, Want, Need, Character Arc*, Reveals*, Reversals*
I have a hard time rooting for the main character.	Internal Character Story, Lives in Crisis*, Want, Need, Personal Stakes*, Sounding Board Character, Relationships*

Character Notes (Continued)

Common Notes:	Potential Solutions:
I like the best friend more than the main character.	Internal Character Story, Defining Scene, Pressure the Flaws, Attitude Adjustment, Want, Need
The main character keeps changing.	Internal Character Story, Consistency, Pressure The Flaws, Attitude Adjustment, Want, Need

*See index: concept found in other chapter.

Internal Character Story

In your character pass, you must be able to complete this sentence: *It's the story about a man/woman who . . ..* There must be a clear traceable character arc that weaves through the entire screenplay. Every scene does not have to focus on the main character's emotional crisis, but each scene should reflect the main character's emotional DNA. The internal character story is the key to adding emotional dimension to your screenplay, and makes the screenplay about the character and not just about the plot.

Look for places in your screenplay where you can add scenes, moments, and character interactions to dramatize the main character's personal issues. Make sure the main character's internal story is reflected in their behavior. Identify five key scenes that emphasize the main character's emotional story. Small moments and interactions can have a significant effect on the entire screenplay—a single line of dialogue can change an entire screenplay.

- It's the story about a man/woman who . . .
- What is the main character's internal story?
- What he/she needs is . . .
- Why *this* character in *this* story?

State Of Denial

The main character should be in a state of denial about their problems. If they weren't in denial, they would be facing their issues and there wouldn't be a reason to tell their story. But it is precisely because they are unwilling, or unable, to face their personal shortcomings, that they have a serious crisis. Denial is a coping mechanism. The main character has suppressed and ignored their problems until—because of an external inciting incident—they can no longer ignore them. Either the main character will deal with their internal crisis, or it will destroy them.

Throughout your screenplay, the main character must resist even acknowledging that they have a problem. Have scenes that show the main character resisting facing their issues. Show the effect of their resistance through their many relationships. Resistance to change creates conflict and tension throughout your screenplay. If you are getting notes that there isn't enough conflict in your screenplay, then see how you can use your main character's resistance to change to generate more conflict and tension.

- Is your main character in a state of denial?
- Are they consistently resisting facing their issues?
- Are they blind to their bad behavior caused by their personal issues?
- Is their bad behavior causing problems in their relationships?
- Are you using the main character's resistance to change to create tension and conflict?

Defining Scene

A strong defining scene establishes the main character's attitude, behavior, and issues early in the screenplay.

- In *Good Will Hunting*, Will has two strong defining scenes. Early in the screenplay, Will gets into a playground brawl which established Will's anger and propensity for violence. Then, as a janitor at Harvard, Will solves a difficult math equation. These two scenes establish two sides to Will's character and establish Will as an enigma. These scenes makes the audience ask: "Who is Will and why is he acting this way?" You do not need to supply the answer quickly.

Holding back revealing the secrets of the main character's internal story until later in the screenplay will make the audience want to know more. Characters are only willing to face the truth about themselves when they hit bottom.

- What is the defining scene that establishes your main character's behavior?
- Are you withholding the details of the main character's issues until later in the screenplay?

Consistency

Character consistency is the cornerstone of all great screenplays. Once you have committed your main character to an emotional story, check to see that you are telling that story *consistently* from page one to The End. One of the most common problems in developing a character is keeping that character's story, attitude, and behavior consistent through the entire screenplay.

- In *Good Will Hunting*, Will gets in fights, drinks a lot, lies to his girlfriend, and solves complex math equations. Will reveals his character through his behavior, but why he acts this way remains a mystery until it is revealed late in the story that he is a victim of physical child abuse. Will's behavior is consistent throughout the movie until he finally confronts his demons.

The main character's behavior must be consistent until they are motivated to grow and change. A good exercise is to pull out your main character's major scenes and read them back to back. Read for character consistency in story, attitude, dialogue, and behavior.

- Is the main character's behavior consistent with their internal character story?
- Is the main character's behavior consistent throughout the screenplay?

Pressure The Flaws

Character should be revealed primarily through action and behavior. The way the character acts reveals a great deal about them. Use plot scenes and conflict situations to pressure the main character's flaws. It's like pressure testing a piece of metal. Every metal has a breaking point, and so does your main character. Your plot should be testing the main character's breaking point. How will *this* character react in *this* situation? The character's internal story *determines* how they should act.

If you have notes that you have too much plot and not enough character, then rewrite your plot scenes into character/plot scenes by making the plot moments pressure the main character's story and flaws. In addition, create new scenes that test the main character's determination and mettle. Determine your main character's emotional weaknesses and flaws. Then attack them. What's the worst thing that can happen to your main character? Do it to them.

- Are you using your plot events to pressure the main character's flaws?
- Are you taking your main character to the breaking point?
- Can you rewrite your plot scenes into character/plot scenes?

Attitude Adjustment

If you are getting notes that your main character is vague or unclear, they may not have a distinctive consistent attitude. Strong characters have a strong attitude. They step into a scene and their attitude permeates the air. Just by attitude, the audience can learn a lot about a character. They can be cynical, optimistic, pessimistic, sarcastic, condescending, or defensive—the list is endless. But their attitude must be motivated by their internal story.

Often, a writer will establish a character's attitude in opening scenes only to drop their established attitude in later scenes. This creates an inconsistent character, and causes the character to lose their voice and presence in the screenplay. A character's attitude is like their fingerprint. Once you establish an attitude you must use it consistently in each scene. A cynic cannot suddenly become an optimist—unless motivated to change.

- In *American Beauty*, Lester Burnham's cynical attitude is consistent scene after scene until he is motivated to change because of what he has experienced and learned in his journey.

Go through your screenplay and list the main character's attitude in each scene. Then go scene by scene to check if the main character's attitude is consistent throughout the screenplay.

- Does your main character have a clear specific attitude?
- Why do they have this attitude?
- How does their attitude tie into their character story?

- What does the main character's attitude reveal to the audience?
- Do you hear the character's attitude when you write their dialogue?

The Want

In your rewrite, your main character must actively pursue something they desperately want. Their want motivates and drives the main character to the third act conclusion. If you are getting notes that your main character is passive or unmotivated, then your main character may not have an active want. If the main character's want is not clear or consistently pursued, the entire screenplay can feel unfocused and aimless.

While it might seem counterintuitive, the want can change. If the main character satisfies their want, then a new want must be quickly established.

- In *Tootsie*, Michael Dorsey's want changes six times. Initially, he wants to be hired to work as an actor. Once that want is satisfied, he then wants to be taken serious as an actor, then he wants off the show, then he wants to bed his co-star, Julie, then he finds he's in love with her and wants Julie to love him in return.

First, make sure your main character has a clear want. Second, the character must be actively and consistently pursuing their want throughout the second act. In addition, use the main character's want to define your plot events and heighten conflict in your screenplay.

- Is your main character's want clear?
- Does the main character's want and internal story work together?
- Does your main character actively pursue their want?
- Are you using your main character's want to create plot and conflict?
- Does the antagonist stand in the way of the main character achieving their want?

The Need

The main character is driven by something they want. They believe if they can obtain their want, their life will be better. But, what they think they want is not what they really need. What they need is to have an insight about themselves so that they can let go of their past, fulfill their life, obtain true happiness, or heal a deep emotional wound. Once the main character embraces their need, they resolve their internal story, complete their character arc, and grow and transform. While the want can change throughout, the need cannot change.

If your screenplay feels predictable, it may be that the main character gets their want instead of their need. The audience expects the main character to achieve their want, but must be surprised when the main character embraces their need instead. It is essential the audience does not see the need coming. Like a magician, the audience must be misdirected by the main character's active pursuit of their want. It is less predictable if the main character pays a price, or sacrifices something important to them, once they accept their need.

- Is the main character's want and need connected to their internal character story?
- In the third act does your main character satisfy their want or their need?
- Is the main character's need unexpected but satisfying?
- Does the main character's need complete their character arc?

Sounding Board Characters

An easy way to help clarify and state your main character's issues is to use a sounding board character, such as a confidant like a best friend. Since the main character is at ease with and trusts their best friend, they can confide in them. These characters are truth-tellers and can confront the main character about their flaws and bad behavior which helps the reader understand the main character's issues. Best friends are great for accusatory moments. Other useful sounding board characters can be parents, siblings, a love interest, or ex-love interest. In many ways, the sounding board character is the voice of the audience.

- In *Tootsie*, Michael Dorsey's roommate, Jeff, gives Michael an opportunity to express his insecurities and hopes. Jeff listens to Michael but also challenges him.
- In *Good Will Hunting*, Chuckie is Will's best friend and sounding board.
- Goose in *Top Gun* gives Maverick someone to confide in as well as confront him about his flaws.

If you do not have a sounding board character, consider creating one to help you define and strengthen the main character's story. Look for places to weave this character into your screenplay.

- In *Tootsie*, Jeff was added in a last minute rewrite, yet is seamlessly woven into the screenplay. He is so integral to the story that it is hard to imagine the movie without him.

You may also have an existing character you can convert into a best friend character. Look to create a moment where the main character opens up to the sounding board character, or the sounding board character confronts the main character about their flaws and bad behavior.

- Do you have a sounding board character?
- Does your main character open up to the sounding board character?
- Does your sounding board character confront the main character on their flaws or bad behavior?

Active vs. Passive

A frequent note is that the main character is too passive. The main character must drive the action and momentum of the screenplay.

- In *Little Miss Sunshine*, Richard actively pursues his want by going to great lengths to get to his agent and pressure him about his book deal.

Go through your screenplay and list where the main character is active or passive in each scene. If you have an excess of passive scenes, rewrite those scenes so the main character aggressively pursues their want.

- Is your main character active or passive?
- Is your main character actively pursuing his goal?
- Is the action coming to the main character or is the main character forcing the action?

Final Thoughts

Whether you are writing a Hollywood blockbuster or a small independent film, your main character must be the central focus of your screenplay. Once you have a clear understanding of your main character's story, you will be able to bring all your other screenwriting elements into line. It is essential once you establish your main character that they be consistent throughout your screenplay. An inconsistent character undermines the entire screenplay.

Anyone can create a plot. Developing strong screen characters is a constant challenge, like quicksilver through your hands. You have to always keep the main character's story in mind when making important decisions about structure, plot, and theme. With enough practice, writing from character becomes second nature. Learn to write from the inside out—learn to write from character.

8

The Set-Up

Establish—Complicate—Resolve

If you have problems in your third act, the real problems are in the first act.
Billy Wilder, Writer/Director,
Double Indemnity, Sunset Boulevard, The Apartment

The first forty pages are the most important pages of a screenplay. Aspiring writers often focus too much attention on the ending of a film without realizing there can be no ending without a solid beginning. I call the first forty pages of a screenplay the Set-Up. It is where and when the writer establishes the major characters, their interior and exterior story problems, key relationships, subplots, opposition forces, and the main plot narrative.

The Set-Up includes the first act, but also extends beyond the first act to approximately page forty. There are no rules to say a writer cannot continue to add new characters, but generally, it is better to establish your story elements early, and then use the rest of the screenplay to develop and complicate the characters, relationships, and situations you have created. The audience likes to know who the players are and then settle into the story. There are always exceptions to the rule, but you want to get your characters and story elements in place quickly and efficiently.

Aspiring writers often have trouble writing third acts that resolve both the main character's internal issues and the main plot problem. It is easy to get carried away and turn the third act into a huge plot extravaganza while completely missing essential character stories. Unless the writer establishes the characters and their personal stories properly in the Set-Up, the writer will have nothing to resolve in the third act other than the plot. While plot is important, plot without character is just an empty sequence of events.

The Elements of the Set-Up

The Set-Up is where the screenwriter must establish the important story and character elements to be developed and complicated in the second act, and resolved in the third act. A flawed setup produces a flawed screenplay. Here are the elements that must be established during the Set-Up:

- The World
- Rules of the World
- Status Quo
- Genre
- Tone
- Main Character
- Internal Character Story
- Main Character's Goal
- Want and Need
- Main Antagonist
- Opposition Characters
- Main Plot Problem
- Theme
- Stakes
- Key Relationship
- Supporting Characters
- Subplots

While this may seem like a lot of information to "cram" into the opening pages, many of these elements can be combined in a scene. The key is to organically weave them into many scenes, and spread them out over the first forty pages. A common mistake is to create one big scene and establish everything at once.

- In the opening scene of *Erin Brockovich*, the genre, tone, main character, main character's goal, stakes, and theme are all expertly established. As an experienced writer, Susannah Grant knows instinctively she must establish a great deal about the main character right from the first line of dialogue.

Read the first forty pages of *Erin Brockovich* and see how much care and craft goes into establishing all the elements listed above.

The World—The Setting of the Story

The world of your screenplay is the environment of your story. *Glory* is set in the Civil War; *The Verdict* is set in the dog-eat-dog world of tort law; *Tootsie* is set in the world of daytime television. Your screenplay should be set in a very distinct world. The audience wants to get out of their monotonous day-to-day world and escape to some place interesting or magical. Use the world to take the audience to a place they have never been before.

Top Gun is very world dependent and based on a specific subset of naval aviation—Top Gun fighter pilots. When I got the assignment to write *Top Gun*, I did a great deal of research which included traveling to Naval Air Station Miramar; interviewing scores of fighter pilots; going through pilot training exercises; and taking a jet ride in an F-5—all to better understand the world and discover stories. Before I could write about the world, I had to have a working knowledge of their world so I could depict that world accurately. Also, if you look deeply enough, the world will supply you with characters, stories, plot, scenes, complications, and opposition forces.

Research and The World

Do just enough research to understand the world but not too much so that you are overwhelmed. Ultimately, you are writing fiction, not making a documentary. It's important to take dramatic license whenever necessary to tell a great story. Never write your story for the expert; write it for the uninformed audience. Use the "truth" of your research to help create a good story, but do not be a slave to your research or feel beholden to the people you have interviewed.

Rules of The World

It is important to establish the rules of your world from the very first line of your screenplay. Nothing is more annoying than a writer making up rules as they go along. If the rules change at will, then it seems convenient or capricious, and the reader/audience will drop out. Part of the fun of unique worlds is seeing how the character solves problems and plot events within the tight constraints of the world.

If there is a fantasy element to the story, it is essential to establish the rules during the Set-Up. This is one of the reasons fantasy and science fiction stories are so hard to write. The writer usually has to spend so much time creating the rules of the world that often their characters get lost in the process.

- The original *Star Wars: Episode IV* is a great example of a unique world with a clear set of rules and great characters.
- *Back to the Future* is another example of a great world with memorable characters.

In the end, you may remember the great visuals, but it is the characters that ultimately stay with you. It's not the hardware, it's the heart that counts.

Establish Status Quo—Then Destroy It

One of the first tasks of your screenplay is to establish the status quo of the main character in the world. Status quo means the existing state of affairs. Even before the main story problem is introduced, establish the world in which the main character feels secure and safe—the status quo of the story. Then something happens which destroys their status quo and thrusts them into unfamiliar territory.

When confronted with a new world order, the main character struggles to return to their original status quo. Throughout the second act, the main character fights against the new status quo, trying to return to their prior status quo, but fails time and again. Eventually the main character faces their internal story issues, transforms, and creates a new status quo that is better and more fulfilling for them.

- In *Cast Away*, as a FedEx supervisor, Chuck Nolan is someone who is always working against a deadline. Time and seconds are everything; Nolan doesn't have a minute for himself. Nolan survives a plane crash and is stranded on a desert island—his status quo is destroyed. Suddenly, he is confronted with a new status quo, and as much as he tries to fight it, he has to learn to adjust to his new world. When Nolan returns home, a lot has changed, but he learns to accept one day at a time.

Genre

Are you writing a thriller, an action film, a comedy, a character study, or a slasher film? The reader needs to know what genre they are reading right from the opening page. You can combine genres such as an action-thriller or comedy-thriller. But what you should not do is change genres mid-story. Nothing destroys a screenplay faster than starting with one genre then switching to another midway through the screenplay. Once you establish your genre, you must be consistent throughout the screenplay.

- In *Zombieland*, the writers primarily worked in the horror genre, but they also had elements of comedy, romantic comedy, and thriller genres. All these genres were established in the Set-Up so the reader understood right from the start that the screenplay was a composite of several genres. At its very core *Zombieland* stays in the horror genre, but flirts with other genres to bring a fresh and humorous take on zombies.

Tone

Tone is the feeling or mood of your screenplay. Is it light and carefree, or dark and brooding? Is it a serious drama or a campy send-up? Establish tone early to let the reader know what to expect. Once you establish your tone, the tone must be consistent from the beginning to The End.

- The tone of *Nightcrawler* is a creepy, dark, noir drama; *Groundhog Day* is a light comedy punctuated with dark moments; *The Big Lebowski* is an absurdist satire. The tone for each of these films is established from the first frame and is consistent throughout.

Tone can shift if motivated. A movie can start light and get serious, but it cannot go the other way. A comedy can get serious but a drama cannot turn into a comedy. In general, a comedy should become slightly more serious because the closer the main character gets to the ending, there should be more at stake for them personally. When you raise the stakes, a screenplay usually takes a more serious turn.

- In *Top Gun*, in the first half of the film, the tone is light comedic banter combined with action. After Goose's death, the tone markedly shifts to a more serious story, almost a drama. This tone shift was motivated by the loss of Goose and the effect it had on Maverick. The conceit was to make the audience feel the loss of Goose so they would emotionally empathize with Maverick and his loss of confidence.

Tone can only change when something happens that raises the stakes and suddenly makes things more serious.

The Main Character

Establishing the main character's internal story should be a high priority in the Set-Up. Resist telling the audience everything about the main character. Hold back "why" the main character is troubled. Use the "mystery of motivation" to keep the audience curious. Show, but don't tell, until there is sufficient motivation for the main character to reveal their inner demons near the end of the second act.

Create a defining scene that cues the audience into the main character's personality, behavior, and flaws. You can use the device of a sounding board character, such as the best friend, to reveal the main character's problem. If you understand your main character's personal issue, you can consistently motivate them in each and every scene. Unless you establish the main character's internal problem in the Set-Up, you will not have an emotional issue to further complicate the second act and resolve in the second act. Remember: Establish— Complicate—Resolve.

- In *As Good as It Gets*, writer James L. Brooks took great pains to establish Melvin Udal's neurotic character from the opening image. In the first frame of the film, a smiling woman opens her apartment door and then suddenly frowns. The audience quickly sees who she is frowning at. It's Udal. She shuts the door rather than have to deal with him. Next, when a small dog in the hallway pees on the wall, Udal drops the dog down the garbage chute, and then lies to his neighbor, Simon Bishop, about the whereabouts of the dog. As Simon heads into his apartment, Udal calls after him:

UDAL
Hope you find him. I love that dog.

SIMON
You don't love anything, Mr. Udal

Brooks uses his supporting character to reveal the essence of Udal's personal problem. He then continues showing scenes of Udal incapable of love or empathy. Udal's character is established in one scene and then stays consistent throughout the screenplay. His character flaw complicates his relationships and his life throughout the second act, and then is resolved in the third act.

Main Character and The World

Your main character's place in the world is important to establish in the Set-Up.

- In *Toy Story*, Woody is in charge of his world and is respected by all the toys.
- In *Groundhog Day*, the main character is initially established as a big city weatherman but is forced to leave his world to go somewhere he hates: small-town America. Phil Connors becomes the outsider and fights his new world until he learns to adjust and appreciate small-town America.

What is your main character's place in the world?

- In *On the Waterfront*, Terry lives near the docks and is a lowly longshoreman without purpose in his life; in *Whiplash*, Andrew is a new student at a highly competitive music school struggling to be the number one drummer; in *Erin Brockovich*, Erin makes a job for herself as a clerk at a small law office struggling to feed her family.

In each case, the main character inhabits a unique world with a specific place in that world. In your set-up, use the world to help define your main character and make them three-dimensional.

Main Plot Problem

It is important to establish the main plot problem in the Set-Up. The main plot problem is the major physical or emotional problem the main character must resolve by the third act. The main plot problem can be introduced in the Set-Up, but the full effect might not be revealed or complicated until later in the second act.

The main plot problem can be a physical problem.

- In *Cast Away*, Chuck Nolan is trapped on a desert island surrounded by crashing surf without a means to escape. Nolan must figure out a way to overcome the physical difficulties of wanting to escape.

The main plot problem can also be an emotional issue.

- In *As Good as It Gets*, the main plot problem is Melvin Udal's emotional problem which prevents him from being able to connect with the waitress, Carol Connelly, or any human being for that matter. While Udal doesn't have a physical mountain to climb, he does have an emotional mountain to conquer.

The main plot problem should be a formidable obstacle confronting the main character. They must harness both their internal strength as well as their external fortitude in order to overcome the obstacle. While overcoming it, the main character must be tested along the journey to prove they are worthy of defeating the problem. In independent films, the main plot problem is usually a personal flaw, dysfunctional relationships, or even further plot problems.

- In *Crazy Heart*, the main plot problem is Bad Blake's alcohol addiction. The plot is secondary to Blake's personal and relationship problems.

In the Set-Up, establish the problems confronting the main character so that you have multiple issues challenging them throughout the second and third acts. In the second act, use the plot problem to pressure and test the main character's internal story. The main plot problem also provides the scenes and situations which force the main character to confront their flaws and weaknesses.

Want and Need

The main character's want must be established in the Set-Up. Seeds of the main character's need should also be planted in the Set-Up but not fully revealed until late in the third act. To help a screenplay remain unpredictable, the need should come as a surprise to the audience. If the need is signaled too early, the screenplay will feel predictable and the ending will be an anticlimax. Often there is a price the main character must pay to obtain their need.

- In *On the Waterfront*, Terry wants respect but he needs to earn it by taking a stand against corruption.

- In *Casablanca*, Rick wants to be left alone wallowing in his self-pity, but he needs to stop feeling sorry for himself and join in the fight for freedom.
- In *Top Gun*, Maverick wants to be the best, but he needs to be a team player.

The need and internal story are linked together. By realizing their need, the main character must take action and resolve their personal issues. The need is the action the main character takes to resolve those issues. Realizing their need is ultimately what satisfies the main character's internal character story.

Theme

Establish the theme in your set-up through characters, scenes, subplots, and dialogue. Theme is the unifying idea that binds a screenplay together. The theme is tied to the main character's internal story. The main character's journey must revolve around the central theme. The main character then tests and challenges the theme. The main character can push against the theme, and even rebel against it, but in the end they confirm the theme.

Once established, the theme needs to repeat throughout your screenplay. Once you find the theme, support it through your characters and their actions. Theme is something the audience feels and reacts to, but is not conscious of. If they are aware of your theme, you are laying it on too thick.

- In *Top Gun*, the theme is: No man is an island. Maverick consistently tries to defy the theme, but ultimately finds he cannot live only for himself. In contrast to Maverick, the supporting characters work together which echoes the theme, and further emphasizes Maverick's selfishness.
- *Casablanca* has the same theme: No man is an island. Rick tries to ignore the world around him and retreats into his shell. But ultimately events and relationships cause Rick to reengage as a citizen of the world. Rick realizes there are bigger things at stake than his own hurt feelings.

Antagonist/Opposition Force

If you are writing a Hollywood film, it is essential to establish the main antagonist in your set-up. The main character must push against someone or something which makes their journey to discovery and transformation increasingly difficult. The main character and the antagonist both want something, and both stand in each other's way of getting what they want.

- In *Die Hard*, Hans Gruber wants the bonds, and John McClane wants to free his wife and the hostages. In addition to a battle of egos, the main character and the main antagonist have a battle of competing agendas.

Many films tend to be more gray than black and white. The line between good and evil is blurred. In independent films, there often is not a "bad guy," but instead dysfunctional relationships that provide the major conflicts. In addition to relationship issues, the central conflict can revolve around an idea, such as racism; or a physical force, such as a escaping from a desert island.

- In *Cast Away*, Chuck battles against isolation and nature.
- In *Crazy Heart*, Bad Blake is his own worst enemy. The conflict is generated by Blake's alcohol addiction.

But in all cases, the main character must be struggling against someone or something. All great screenplays have a strong central dramatic conflict.

Opposition Characters

Not all screenplays have antagonists, but all screenplays have opposition characters that challenge and threaten the main character. These opposition characters supply the majority of conflict and tension in your screenplay. It is essential to set the opposition characters in motion in your set-up so that you can develop and complicate them throughout your second act, and eventually confront and resolve them in your third act. You cannot complicate what you do not establish.

- In *50/50*, Adam is diagnosed with cancer. Cancer may be the catalyst of change for Adam, but cancer is not the antagonist. In fact, there is no central antagonist in *50/50*. There are many opposition characters that make Adam's struggle more complicated and difficult. Cancer is an opposition force which causes Adam a great deal of fear and pain.
- In *Glory*, there are many characters who oppose the creation of the first African American regiment in the Union Army. In addition, there are also strong forces of racism that complicate and oppose the main characters' journeys.

Even if you have a strong traditional antagonist, such as the power hungry Ronan in *Guardians of the Galaxy*, you need to establish many opposition characters in your set-up so that you have multiple forces to complicate the main character's journey throughout the second act.

- In *Guardians of the Galaxy*, the four Guardians are in opposition to each other throughout the second act. It isn't until the end of the second act that they let go of their antagonism and begin to pull together as a united team.

To be an opposition force, a character does not have to be bad, evil, dastardly, or dangerous. They just need to have an agenda that runs counter to the main character's agenda.

- In *On the Waterfront*, even Edie, Terry's love interest, occasionally acts as in opposition to Terry. She loves him, but she opposes his reluctance to do the right thing and testify against Johnny Friendly and the mob.

No matter which film you are writing, your main character must face opposition from all sides. There can be no safe port in the storm and you must have many different forces of opposition to make the main character's journey fraught with endless compilations and obstacles.

Stakes

At some point, all writers get the note: The stakes are not high enough. Stakes must be established in the first forty pages of the Set-Up. There are two kinds of stakes: personal stakes and plot stakes. If the main character does not have a personal stake in the story, then the screenplay will feel weak and inconsequential. You need to commit your main character to an internal story, and make sure that story involves an emotional issue. The plot stakes must also be substantial or the third act resolution will be inconsequential and anticlimactic.

Personal stakes and plot stakes must be established early, and then escalate throughout the second act. The more the main character has to lose, the higher the stakes. If the main character fails in their journey, there should be collateral damage and dire consequences to characters around them.

- In the set-up of *Erin Brockovich*, it's quickly established that Erin is at the end of her rope and her life is falling apart.

- Her personal stakes are established early: she can't get a job; she gets in a serious car accident; she doesn't have money to feed her kids; and she is about to be evicted from her home.
- In addition, Erin believes she has a lot to offer but finds herself disappearing into a cloud of doubt and despair. If she fails to find purpose and meaning in her life, she will lose not only her family, but also her sense of purpose.
- The plot stakes are established later in the Set-Up. The residents of Hinkley have been poisoned by PG&E and need serious medical care as well as compensation for their pain and suffering.
- To add to her problems, Erin has to convince her boss, Ed Masry, to take the case and fight for the people of Hinkley.

Key Relationship

Strong relationships are an essential ingredient in all great screenplays. This is the key relationship that runs throughout your entire screenplay. You can use this relationship to help examine your main character's internal story and to complicate your main character's life. The key relationship should be introduced in the Set-Up.

- In *Erin Brockovich*, the key relationship is with her boss, Ed Masry. At first their relationship is adversarial, but then evolves into mutual respect.
- In *Toy Story*, Buzz is introduced early in the screenplay, but it takes Woody and Buzz the entire screenplay to find common ground.
- In *Tootsie*, there are a number of relationships introduced in the Set-Up. Dorothy's relationship with Julie is the key relationship which builds and develops throughout the screenplay.

The basic human need for connection is at the core of all great art whether it is in the cinema, theater, painting, or music.

Supporting Characters

Introduce your cast of supporting characters during the first forty pages of the Set-Up, and then use them consistently throughout the rest of the screenplay.

Give each major supporting character a story and a strong attitude—something to play. Well-crafted supporting characters give your screenplay a sense of cohesion and continuity.

Spread character introductions out over several scenes during the Set-Up and make every introduction memorable. Give each supporting character a defining action so they will be firmly established in the reader's mind. Once established it is important to use your characters to complicate the main character's journey during the second act. At the end of the film, each major supporting character should play a role in the climax of the film.

- *Glory* has many strong supporting characters with memorable introductions. Each character is well crafted with their own personal story and defining attitude. Their relationships continue to evolve during the second act, and each character plays a role in the climax.

When writing a screenplay, think of your supporting characters as a cast of great actors who need interesting roles to play. You don't want them sitting around your office with nothing to do.

Subplots

Screenplays are multiple stories woven around a central character. Use subplots to explore different aspects of your main character's life and complicate their journey. Launch your subplots in the first forty pages of the Set-Up. Get your multiple story lines and relationships going early. Subplots can be introduced well into the second act, but generally not after the mid-point.

Action films tend to have multiple plot lines which eventually complicate the A or main plotline.

- In *Die Hard*, the main plotline is John McClane trying to stop Hans Gruber from stealing the bonds and killing the hostages. Additional subplots include McClane's rocky relationship with his wife; his wife's coworker trying to save himself at the expense of the others; McClane's relationship with Sergeant Powell; Powell's own story about shooting an innocent man; McClane trying to contact the police force; and Gruber holding McClane's wife hostage. There are other subplots including the ambitious reporter and the skeptical FBI Agent.

In independent films, subplots are often relationships.

* In *Little Miss Sunshine*, the A plotline revolves around getting Olive to the beauty contest on time, but the real stories are found in the subplots. The major subplots are: Richard and Sheryl; Richard and Frank; Richard and his literary agent; Richard and Olive; and Richard and his father; Grandpa and Olive; Grandpa and Dwayne; Frank and Dwayne; Frank and his ex-lover; Dwayne and Sheryl; and Dwayne and Olive. The subplots complicate the journey and the journey complicates the subplot relationships.

Multiple subplots are essential for a multidimensional screenplay. Branch out and tell many different stories in your screenplay. Use your supporting characters to create relationships and subplots that complicate the main character's journey.

Final Thoughts

The purpose of the Set-Up is to establish important character, relationship, plot, world, and thematic elements that you can continue to develop and complicate throughout the second act, and resolve in the third act climax. Weaknesses and flaws in the Set-Up will only be magnified as you go deeper into the screenplay. The third act is totally dependent on the first forty pages of the screenplay. The characters and problems set in motion in those first forty pages must be resolved in the third act. In essence, your screenplay can only be as strong as your set-up. Weak set-up—weak screenplay.

9

Story and Theme Pass

The Emotional Underpinning

Everything you write should reflect your theme. It's the first thing I think of, and everything plays off that.

Eric Roth, Screenwriter,
Forest Gump, The Insider, The Good Shepherd

Before beginning your Story and Theme Pass, it is essential to have a clear understanding of the word "story." There are many uses for the term "story." If someone says, "Tell me the story," the writer will invariably talk about the plot – the sequence of events. This is one common use of "story." In this book the word "story" is used to describe the emotional underpinnings of the screenplay. Basically, the story is the main character's emotional journey. A screenplay without emotion is just a long string of plot events. The audience must deeply care about whether the main character can solve their personal problems as well as solve the main plot problem. But if they don't emotionally care about the character, they will surely not care about the plot.

The purpose of the Story and Theme Pass is to solidify the emotional connections between your major characters. In the Story and Theme Pass, you will examine the emotional storylines and themes that run through your screenplay. These emotional threads must be skillfully woven together with the main character at the heart of the tapestry. Your screenplay should have many different stories being told simultaneously: the main character's story, the supporting characters' stories, and the story of each relationship. Your major characters need to have emotional lives and interactions, and those must ultimately support or hinder the main character's journey. Make sure these interactions are not just plot moments, but moments of human interactions exploring real human emotions. Do not just copy generic "movie emotions," but draw from your life experiences to bring human emotions to your characters.

Objectives of The Story and Theme Pass

- Know your story. Reduce it to one word.
- Make your story consistent throughout the screenplay.
- Make your story and theme work together and support one another.
- Use the main character's journey to build the emotional core of your screenplay.
- Use plot to pressure the main character's internal story.
- Add dimension and stakes.
- Align character, story, theme, and plot.
- Link the supporting characters' stories to the main character's emotional story.

Story and Theme Notes

Because the words "story" and "plot" are interchanged so often, it's easy for a writer to address plot when in reality they are getting "story" notes. If the notes are about making a screenplay more exciting, then that would be a plot note. But if the notes are about core emotional issues such as motivation, stakes, relationships, or rooting interest, then those would be story notes.

Story and Theme Notes

Common Note:	Potential Solutions:
I was not very involved in the screenplay.	Main Character's Story, Antagonist's Story, Multiple Stories, Lives in Crisis*, Plot and Story, Stakes*, Main Plot Problem*
I didn't really care about anyone.	Main Character's Story, Motivation*, Multiple Stories, Relationships*, Stakes*
I'm not sure what the script is about.	Theme, Story, Main Character's Story, Antagonist's Story, Story Alignment, Plot and Story
The story seemed to change half way through the screenplay.	Theme, Main Character's Story, Main Character's Want*, Main Plot Problem*, Plot and Story, Antagonist's Story, Central Dramatic Conflict*, Consistency*
I don't know what the main character wanted.	Main Character's Story, Main Character's Want*, Motivation*, Key Relationship*, Stakes*
All the characters sound the same.	Multiple Character Stories, Attitude*

*See index: concept found in other chapter.

What is Your Story About?

The story is the main character's emotional journey of self-discovery and truth, and ultimate transformation. To succeed with your rewrite you must know what your story is about. You must be able to reduce your story to a single word or phrase such as: redemption, second chance, or renewal.

- *Top Gun* is a second chance story. Maverick arrives at the Top Gun School as a second choice and is determined to prove that he should be number one. After Goose's death he has a second chance to become a team player. He has a second chance to reconnect with his girlfriend, Charlie.

Before you add complexity and layers, you must understand your story in simple terms. Once you know your story, then you want to make sure you are consistently telling that story from beginning to The End.

On a small piece of paper, write down a single word or phrase describing what your story is about. Paste that paper at the top of your computer screen. Look at it every day before you begin writing. Use your cards, or your outline, to track the main character's emotional storyline throughout your entire screenplay. Make notations of scenes and moments when the main character's personal story is examined or challenged. If you only find a few moments, you need to create new scenes and moments that support the main character's story. Use repetition and consistency to reinforce the story.

- What is your story about?
- Can you reduce your story to a single word or phrase?
- Is your story reflected in your main character's personal story?
- Do the supporting characters also reflect aspects of the story?
- Is your story repeated through relationships and scenes?
- Are you using your plot to complicate your story?

Theme

Theme is the unifying glue that binds the scenes and characters together. To know your theme is to know your movie. The main character's story must echo the theme, and theme must echo the main character's story. Your theme should be based upon a truth about life and the human condition. Theme should be something you feel strongly about and something you want the audience to consider. Your theme must be an integral part of your screenplay's fabric.

- The central theme of *Good Will Hunting* is abandonment and trust. As an orphan, Will lived in foster homes, and was abused and abandoned. Therefore, Will has serious trust issues, and does not want to make any deep attachments. The only family he trusts is Chuckie and the guys. Will has to overcome his fear of abandonment and trust issues with Sean and Skylar. In addition, the major supporting characters also have similar themes. Sean's wife died, abandoning him. Skylar's father died and abandoned her. At the end of the story, Skylar leaves Boston and abandons Will. Will is torn between leaving, and "abandoning" Chuckie, or taking a chance on fulfilling his potential and creating a new life for himself. Stories of abandonment tie the screenplay together thematically.

In this pass you want to strengthen and repeat your theme. If you find you are not using your theme effectively, look for four or five places you can restate your theme through your characters or your scenes. In addition, look for new opportunities to add thematic elements to your screenplay by creating new characters, scenes, or situations that state your theme.

- What is your theme?
- Does the main character's internal story reflect your theme?
- Do your scenes restate and reflect your theme?
- Are you using your theme consistently and repeatedly?
- Does your third act climax confirm your theme?

Plot and Story

Plot and story work together. Plot provides interesting events and situations that pressure both the overall story and the main character's individual story. Plot is the maze, the complications and obstacles the main character must navigate during their journey. Design the plot to support the central story.

Review your plot events to create situations that pressure the overall story and the main character's personal story. Identify at least five or six plot events that significantly affect the overall story or the main character's internal story. The plot should not just make things more difficult; the plot should pressure the emotional aspects of the main character's journey. If you find that you do not have enough specific plot events that tie into the story, see if you can revise them, or create new plot events that connect to the overall story or the main character's story.

- Are you using plot events to pressure the overall story and the main character's story?
- Do you have multiple plot events that elicit strong emotional responses from the main character?
- Is there a major plot event that forces the main character to face their shortcomings?

Story Alignment

The main character's story, overall story, theme, and plot all work together to tell the same story. An important part of any rewrite is to create a cohesive screenplay. If each element is not working together toward the same end, the screenplay will feel disjointed and episodic. In *On the Waterfront*, each major element is intertwined and works to support one another. There is not a wasted moment or wasted line of dialogue in the film. Budd Schulberg, the screenwriter, knew exactly what story he was writing and used every element efficiently to tell that story. The internal and the external stories fit together seamlessly to build to a suspenseful and satisfying climax.

Look at how each element in *On the Waterfront* supports one another:

- Character Story: Terry sold himself out for pennies and lives a life of regret and shame.
- Theme: Redemption.
- Overall Story: Terry falls in love with Edie and has one last opportunity for true happiness and redemption. Terry has to decide whether to choose a life filled with love and hope, or cling to the security and obligation of his corrupt life that has continually betrayed him.
- Plot: When a whistleblower is killed to keep him from testifying to the Waterfront Crime Commission, Terry must decide between following his conscience to testify, or following his sense of obligation to mob boss Johnny Friendly and the code of silence on the docks.

Review your screenplay to make sure that your story, plot, theme, and character are in alignment and supporting each other. If they are not, then revise your elements to ensure they are telling the same story.

- Is each of your major elements telling the same story?
- Does your theme resonate in each element?
- Does the plot pressure the overall story and main character's story?

Antagonist's Story

If your screenplay uses a traditional antagonist, then they must also have a story. Antagonists who are unmotivated, or evil for evil's sake, are one-dimensional and do not serve your screenplay. The antagonist must have something they desperately want to achieve and the only thing standing in their way is the main character. The antagonist should also have a personal reason for why it is important for them to achieve their goal. They do not need some deep psychological reason—but they need a reason that explains why this character would go to such great lengths to achieve their ends.

The antagonist's personal story should conflict and complicate the main character's story and goal.

- In *On the Waterfront,* Johnny Friendly was raised poor on a "watchman's pension" and fought his way to the top. He believes he has earned his right to be on top and he's not about to let anyone get in his way. Terry and Friendly have a previous relationship. Friendly was a father figure to Terry, and Terry feels beholden to Friendly. But Terry is beginning to see things differently. If he testifies he would destroy Friendly's power and influence. The more Friendly acts to protect his power, the more he pushes Terry away from him. These two stories are headed toward a head-on collision and only one can survive.

Look at the scenes between the antagonist and the main character to make sure their stories are in opposition to each other and put them into direct conflict. If not, then revise the antagonist's personal story and find something that makes it personal for him.

- Is the antagonist a three-dimensional character?
- Are the antagonist's actions motivated?

- Does the antagonist have an internal character story?
- What is the antagonist's personal stake in the outcome?
- Are the antagonist and main character stories in opposition to each other?
- Why is it personal between the antagonist and the main character?

Opposition Characters

Not all stories have an antagonist. In movies such as *Tootsie, Toy Story, Crazy Heart,* and *Little Miss Sunshine*, the main character is struggling with their character flaws—their internal issues—and there is no single antagonist confronting them. But there are supporting characters, or opposition characters, with individual wants which conflict with the main character's want. This clash of wants supplies the lion's share of the tension and conflict. In screenplays without a dedicated antagonist, the main character's internal story and character flaws determine the external conflict.

- Do you have enough opposition forces to create consistent conflict and tension?
- Are your major supporting characters in opposition to the main character's agenda?
- Are you using your main character's internal story and flaws to create conflict and tension?

Multiple Stories

A screenplay is actually many small stories told simultaneously which are linked together by the main character's story. If the main character's emotional arc is the center of the atom, then the supporting characters are electrons circling the atom. Think of your characters as having either a positive supporting charge or a negative opposing charge. But in either case, these smaller stories orbit the main character's story. These multiple stories complicate and pressure the main character's internal and external stories.

- In the film *Breaking Away*, screenwriter Steve Tesich deftly weaves multiple character stories into one tightly woven tapestry. Four friends have just graduated from high school and find themselves without jobs or a future.

What binds them together is the bleakness of their lives—misery loves company. To aggravate them further, they live just outside a college town, Bloomington, Indiana, the home of the University of Indiana, where each year a new batch of rich kids arrives to live the easy life with bright futures. Everywhere the friends turn, they are confronted by their second-class status. Each character is connected by story, theme, and plot, and they all revolve around the main character's journey of self-discovery and transformation.

Make a list of your major supporting characters and their individual stories. Each story should affect the main character's journey by supporting or opposing the main character's goal. The Story and Theme Pass is where you flesh out these multiple storylines and figure out the roles they play in your screenplay. If you do not know a character's purpose, then consider cutting that character. Trim your screenplay of any subplots and supporting characters that do not contribute to the whole. By trimming, you will focus and tighten your screenplay.

- Does each of your major supporting characters have a story?
- Does each supporting character's story connect to the overall main story and theme?
- Do your supporting characters help or hinder the main character?
- Do your supporting characters' stories affect the main character's journey?

Storylines

Trace your major storylines throughout your screenplay. They should be clearly marked on your cards or in your outline. Make sure each story stays active and relevant throughout your entire screenplay. Each story needs an arc to it. It can be a slight arc with the faintest resolution, but you want to resolve the most important storylines. In *Breaking Away*, each major supporting character has a story arc and undergoes a transformation.

As your screenplay progresses, each storyline should become more complicated, and the stakes continue to rise. Storylines complicate the main character's life and create more pressure on them. If your major storyline disappears or ends suddenly, then examine your scenes to see if you can find a place in an existing scene where you can add a beat to keep the storyline active.

The ability to be able to keep each story alive and pertinent to the main character and the plot is essential to creating a cohesive screenplay.

- Does each storyline stay alive and active?
- What are the beats of that story?
- Are you cutting between your many storylines?
- How does each storyline contribute to pressuring the main character's storyline?

Final Thoughts

Pay close attention to the emotional currents that run throughout your screenplay. Your main character's internal story must be the emotional core of your screenplay. In addition, track each emotional storyline to make sure that it is active, consistent, and complicates the main character's journey. Use your theme to unify your screenplay and tie the characters and their stories together.

Film is an emotional journey. Work to create an emotional bond between the audience and the main character. The audience must emotionally identify and empathize with the main character and want them to succeed. Be patient with the process. You are doing surgery, and a good surgeon takes their time and doesn't rush their work.

10

Structure

What Stays In, What Goes Out,
and In What Order?

I've done a lot of thinking myself about what a screenplay is, and I've come up with nothing except that it's carpentry, it's basically putting down some kind of structural form that they can then mess around with. And as long as they keep the structural form, whatever I have written is relatively valid: a scene will hold, regardless of the dialogue.

William Goldman, Screenwriter/Novelist,
Butch Cassidy and The Sundance Kid, All The President's Men

Structure is the way a writer organizes and tells their story. Where do you begin, and where do you end your story? At what point in the crisis do you pick up the thread of your story? What do you put in and what do you leave out? What do you reveal and when do you reveal it? Structure provides the framework to tell your story.

Creating a story structure is like as building a house. Before you build a house you must first design it for the people who are going to live in the house. In the end, it's not the structure that counts, it's who is going to live in the house and how the house is going to serve them that counts. In a screenplay, the structure must serve the characters in the story. Structure should be invisible and unobtrusive.

The Basic Three Act Structure

The three act structure dates back to the Greek plays, and is the basis of Western storytelling. It is a simple as: beginning, middle, and end. George M. Cohan, the fabled Broadway playwright, described the three act structure best: "Get your hero up a tree; throw rocks at him; get him down from the tree."

What follows is a generalized list not meant to be taken point by point. It is not a formula. The only rule in structure is "don't bore the audience."

FIRST ACT

- Commit your main character to an internal character story with a personal issue to address, i.e. a character flaw.
- Establish your main plot problem.
- Establish supporting characters, relationships, and subplots.
- Establish multiple opposition characters to block and resist the main character.
- Hold back revealing too much through exposition.

SECOND ACT

- Begin the second act with a surprising reveal that complicates the plot.
- Establish what is at stake—the dire consequences—should the main character fail to accomplish their goal.
- The antagonist continues to grow stronger.
- Complicate the second act with subplots and relationships. Cross cut between multiple storylines.
- Continue to weave the main character's story with the plot events. Often at this point, the main character is suffering from a crisis of confidence or they are simply overmatched.
- Structure a mid-point plot turn that significantly complicates the main character's journey.
- Reveal new information about the main character and the main plot problem in the back half of the second act.
- Use multiple opposition characters to complicate the back half of the second act.
- Continue to raise the stakes through plot events and relationships.
- Create a high point at the end of the second act.
- Isolate the main character as they drive toward the second act climax. Figuratively, the main character is on their own and only they can solve the plot problem.
- The audience should question whether the main character is up to the challenge of defeating the antagonist and resolving the main plot problem.

THIRD ACT

- The ending must be in doubt and unpredictable. There must be several potential scenarios for the third act resolution.
- Plot events continue to reveal new information and raise the stakes one last time.
- The main character must face their flaws and have an epiphany. Their growth and transformation gives them the personal strength to face an overwhelming opponent and succeed.
- Because of their new found confidence, and because they have realized a higher calling than their own selfish ambitions, the main character is able to persevere against great odds. Self-sacrifice triumphs over self-interest.
- Because of their difficult and trying experiences, the main character has grown stronger and wiser, and uses everything they have learned to achieve their goal.
- The main character lets go of their want, and embraces their need.
- There is hope for the future.

While these beats may sound like the pattern for an action movie, this is a basic structural pattern for creating plot situations where the main character must face their flaws and weaknesses. In a character driven screenplay, the action happens between the characters and their relationship complications. It is more difficult to structure a compelling plot line in a character drama, than it is in an action film. In a character film, the drama unfolds between the people—within the relationships. The drama must happen internally and externally from deep inside the characters. In an action film, you also create characters with internal stories, but you have the luxury to cut away to chase scenes and big special effect sequences to keep the plot moving forward. Character driven stories rely more upon the personal issues and the bond of the relationships. They often use the faintest plot to hold the story together, but in the end, it's the decisions the main character makes that decides the resolution of the drama.

Independent Films

In an independent film, the tests a character faces during the second act are often personal or relational rather than physical. The writer must still complicate their main character's life throughout the second act. The main character's internal story must also be put to the test and his weaknesses exposed. By the third act, those relationships come to a head and the main character has to make important decisions about themselves and the people in their life. The resolution may or may not involve plot elements and may be more personal in nature. The second act must pressure the main character.

Independent films need good storytelling and a character in crisis. But, it would be a mistake to believe that independent films do not need strong plot and structure. Films like *Crazy Heart*, *Little Miss Sunshine*, and *The Lives of Others*, have great character work in addition to tight structures with excellent plotting. If anything, independent films need the best of both worlds, and present the writer with more challenges and difficulties. There must be a strong central dramatic conflict that moves the story forward.

- In *Whiplash*, the abusive relationship between the student drummer, Andrew, and the band conductor, Terence Fletcher, is the central dramatic conflict. The screenplay is structured in such a way with just enough plot to move the story forward, but the main focus of the screenplay is their abusive relationship.

Sequencing—Dividing the Screenplay into Smaller Pieces

One of the challenges when structuring and plotting an entire screenplay is that it can feel overwhelming. You may find it easier to divide the screenplay into manageable parts. This can also be helpful in your rewrite when one section may need more work than another. Sequencing is a method whereby the screenplay is divided into eight separate units. This approach was first pioneered by filmmaker Frank Daniel and has continued to gain traction.

There are pluses and minuses to sequencing. The plus is that it is easier to work in small sections than three acts. This is especially true of the second act. The minus is becoming enamored with the "rules" of sequencing. I've seen students lose sight of what is really important in storytelling—their characters. Students often want to believe there is some secret code to success and mistakenly think structure is that key. Sequencing is one tool in a very large toolbox.

Most professional screenwriters tell their stories from an organic approach. They follow characters through their journeys and eventually end up at the climax. Often, they are reluctant to talk about their process and many cannot even explain how they write. They are natural storytellers. Great writers write because they have a story to tell and interesting characters to explore.

The structure, the number of sequences, is much less important than what happens to the main character. Understanding and using sequencing can be valuable in rewriting as it helps the writer identify areas of their screenplay that may be underperforming.

Step 1: Divide your Screenplay into Two Parts

Something significant must happen near the center of the screenplay. This mid-point plot turn may be the culmination of the main character's initial attempts to solve their problem, the introduction of new information, the result of a major reversal, or it may be a transition where the characters have grown and are ready to face a more difficult challenge.

Mid-Point Plot Turn

1st Half	2nd Half

- In *Turner and Hooch*, the first half is about establishing the relationship between the odd couple: the world's neatest man and the world's messiest dog. During the second half, they accept and grow to love each other. They are a team working together. The first half is comedic and highlights the differences between them. The second half focuses on solving the plot and working together as a team.
- The first half of *Erin Brockovich* focuses on developing Erin's world, family, and internal/external crises. The first half is character and relationship development. In the second half, Erin takes on PG&E and the story is David versus Goliath. The small legal firm takes on a huge corporate giant. The second half fulfills Erin's need to make a difference.
- In *Glory*, the first half of the screenplay focuses on the black soldiers' struggle to overcome racism in the Army and train for a battle they don't believe they will be allowed to fight. The second half takes place on

the battlefield where their suspicions are confirmed until they have an opportunity to prove their valor and courage, and gain the admiration of their fellow soldiers.

Not every movie has a mid-point plot turn. But those that do tend to have a stronger and more powerful second act. This is essential to keep your story moving forward. Events and personal stories must continue to evolve and change as the characters advance toward the end of the second act. Movies are about significant moments in people's lives. To have a successful screenplay, your character must continue to be pressured and challenged. A mid-point plot turn can energize your screenplay and make the second act fresh and invigorated.

Step 2: Divide Your Screenplay into Four Parts

Divide your screenplay into smaller sections. If you include the end of the first act and second act, you can effectively divide your screenplay into four sections. Each of these sections should culminate with a significant event such as a deepening of the external crisis, or the main character's internal crisis, or both. The fourth and final culmination is the climax and resolution of the main character's personal story.

1st Act	2nd Act—Part 1	2nd Act—Part 2	3rd Act

Now you have four distinct sections where the stakes rise considerably, and your main character's involvement in the crisis deepens. Take advantage of these structural demarcations. If you continue to ratchet up your main character's crisis as well as complicate plot events, your screenplay will evolve and intensify as your main character moves toward the third act climax. Your screenplay will move to higher ground as the main character's problems must continue to intensify. Like a shark, a screenplay must continue to move or it will die.

Step 3: Divide Your Screenplay into Eight Parts

Now, you may divide the sections into even smaller pieces—sequences. To review, the reason you continue to divide your screenplay into smaller and smaller pieces is to draw your main character deeper into the crisis and progress their personal story. From a plot and structural point of view, the deeper you go into the story, the more serious and important the plot events become.

Look at your sequences as steps. The main character is ascending a ladder until they reach the highest level of conflict and complication—the third act climax. With each step up the ladder, they are faced with significant plot challenges and problems with their relationships that continue to escalate. This is true whether you are writing an action movie or an independent film. The stakes and the consequences must continue to rise.

1	2	3	4	5	6	7	8

Sequencing is merely grouping scenes together around a question or a specific tension. A sequence can be three or four scenes that lead to an escalation. Or, a sequence can be six scenes that culminate with a step up the ladder. Sequencing is a way to break the whole into smaller workable pieces. Most professional writers do this instinctively. A character advances and retreats in bits and spurts. If there is one major takeaway, it's that your screenplay is a compellation of many smaller pieces that work together to create a whole story. The main character must continually have highs and lows—be on the roller coaster—and each sequence needs to reveal new information, or further complicate the main character's journey.

An Example of Sequencing:

What follows is a traditional story pattern and how it fits into an eight-sequence pattern. Each grouping of scenes should have cohesion and reach a mini-conclusion that advances either the main character or the plot. At the end of each sequence, the main character's internal or external story changes and progresses in some way. The main character takes a step up the ladder of conflict and complication. Each step should take them deeper into their journey and the stakes rise. To intensify your screenplay, incrementally ratchet up the stakes and deepen the main character's commitment at the end of each grouping.

Sequence One

- Establish the main character and their world.
- Establish who, what, when, and where.
- Establish the set-up through sequences 1, 2, & 3.
- Establish status quo—the world before the problem enters the character's life.
- Begin to establish a cast of supporting characters.
- Inciting incident sets in motion the main dramatic conflict.

Sequence Two

- Goal of the main character is clearly stated
- Introduce the antagonist by sequence 1 or 2.
- Continue to establish relationships.
- Establish the main story problem.
- Set up the main tension for the second act.
- Main character may think the problem can be easily solved.
- Point of attack may also be the end of act one.

Sequence Three

- Main character is locked into the story.
- It's not as bad as it looks. *I can handle this.*
- Main character makes an attempt to solve problem and fails.
- Intro subplots—work your cast of supporting characters.
- Begin to raise the stakes.
- Main character may solve an immediate problem leading to a bigger problem.

Sequence Four

- Things are getting worse—rising action.
- Main character may be in a state of denial—not facing the truth.
- Obstacles get bigger and bigger.
- Subplots begin to grow and expand the scope of the story.
- Continue to expand the main character's world and relationships.
- Antagonist has also gained power.
- Main character is beginning to realize they are unprepared for the journey before them.
- Main character and antagonist parry to test each other's strengths.
- Build toward the mid-point plot turn or first culmination.

Sequence Five

- Main character acknowledges they have a problem: *It's worse than I thought!*
- Because of the high point at the end the fourth sequence, sequence five tends to be a reflective sequence. Often an intimate relationship is explored.
- Main character has nowhere to turn for relief.
- Stakes continue to rise.
- Subplots and relationships become more complicated.

Sequence Six

- Highest obstacle leads to lowest point.
- Does the main character have what it takes to succeed?
- Have they learned enough to succeed?
- Physical plot and the inner story converge. The main character must solve one to solve the other.
- Main character makes their most ambitious attempt yet to solve the problem—and fails.
- If the main character had succeeded, the movie would be over now.
- They are not ready yet. More to learn.
- Antagonist may have anticipated the main character's move.
- Antagonist is stronger than the main character.
- Resolve the main tension of second act.
- End of this sequence is the second culmination.

Sequence Seven

- False resolution.
- Preparation for the ultimate test of character mettle and will.
- A new main tension may be established.
- Unexpected consequences—the situation becomes dire.
- Stakes are at their highest level.
- Begin to resolve important subplots.
- Sequence may end with a surprise or unexpected occurrence.

Sequence Eight

- True resolution.
- Obligatory scene is finally realized—the climax.
- Major obstacle is confronted and overcome.
- Main character succeeds by personal growth and knowledge gained.
- Antagonist has been defeated or redirected.
- Main character's story is resolved.
- Main character embraces their need.
- Major relationships are resolved.
- Subplots are resolved.
- Epilogue—allow audience to digest the ending—a sense of satisfaction.
- A hint of the character's life beyond the story.

Reverse Seven & Eight

- Sequences 7 and 8 can sometimes be reversed.
- Sometimes the climax comes in sequence 7 and sequence 8 is the epilogue—the aftermath of the story.
- Main character may grow and realize his faults in sequence 7 and solve the problem in sequence 8.
- Main character may solve the problem and realize their faults in sequence 8.

All scene groupings must serve the main character's personal story. Use sequencing to progress your story, develop your characters and their relationships, raise the stakes, and focus your screenplay on a consistent path toward the climax. Remember, if the audience doesn't care about your characters, they won't care about your structure.

Reveals

One of the fundamental functions of structure is to reveal essential character and plot information. Determining when and where to reveal that essential information is an important structural decision. Reveal too much too soon, and the audience and the reader may end up ahead of your story. Create more tension, and make the audience want to know more, by revealing as little information as possible. The seeds of a reveal must to be planted early, so that when something significant is revealed it doesn't feel like a rabbit pulled out of a hat.

- In *Gone Girl*, the writer, Gillian Flynn, constantly fools, misdirects, and toys with the audience. Flynn plants false leads and false expectations only to pull away the curtain and reveal what is really going on—at least what we believe is going on at that moment. She keeps the audience off balance and her screenplay highly unpredictable.
- *Chinatown*, written by Robert Towne, is a structural masterpiece. But Towne admits that in the fog of writing he struggled with the structure until the last draft. In early drafts, he considered revealing the incest plot before the Water Department corruption story. With 20/20 hindsight it is clear the water corruption story must come first and the incest story should remain hidden until late in the script. In *Chinatown*, the character work and plot information are revealed slowly, carefully, and artfully. Jake Gittes has to earn each bit of new information. Like Gittes, the audience is always just a step behind. In *Chinatown*, reveals are an important structural device that enhances the story and complicates the main character's journey.

Reveals energize your screenplay with new information that significantly affect the main character's emotional journey and plot events. They are reversals and major setbacks for the main character. They add urgency and raise the stakes.

Reversals

Reversals are another important structural tool. As the main character works their way through the obstacles and complications along their journey, they must have successes and setbacks. From a structural point of view, the writer must decide where to place their reversals for best effect and also to make the main character's journey more difficult. Reversals keep the second act active, progressing, and unpredictable.

- *Toy Story* uses reversals very effectively. Buzz's arrival as a new toy is a major reversal for Woody.
- Woody's mission to get Buzz back to Andy's house is one complication, obstacle, and reversal after another. At the gas station, Woody and Buzz wrestle and fall out of Andy's car—a reversal. At Pizza Planet, Woody and Buzz are captured by Sid and taken to his room filled with mutant toys.
- In a positive reversal, Woody scares Sid from blasting Buzz into a million pieces.
- During the chase to catch Andy's car, the batteries run down and strand Buzz and Woody in the middle of the road. The match to light Buzz's rocket is blown out by a passing car but Woody figures out another solution—a positive reversal.

Reversals complicate the plot and pressure the main character's story. They help create highs and lows, and keep the screenplay from becoming predictable. You can use reversals to end sequences and begin new sequences. There is also the cliffhanger effect to a reversal. This thrusts the main character into new problems as well as enhancing tension and anxiety in the audience. How will the character get out of this situation?

Time

In motion pictures, time is malleable and can be easily manipulated for dramatic effect. The use of flashbacks, and the compression or expansion of time, can have a huge impact on your structure. Time can be limited, like in *High Noon*, told in a twenty-four-hour period, or *Groundhog Day*, with a series of endlessly repeating days. Time can extend over a period of years or a character's entire lifetime as in *Forest Gump*. Time can be fleeting or feel like a punishment as in *Cast Away*. Whether your screenplay is told in a straightforward linear manner, like *Little Miss Sunshine*, or through a series of flashbacks, is a storytelling and structural decision.

Movies that take place over longer periods of time need clear markers and sign posts to help the audience understand a significant period of time has passed.

- *Little Miss Sunshine* takes place over a two-day period, and deftly breaks time into days and nights. Most of the scenes take place during the day, but there are scenes at night that mark the passage of time.
- *Forest Gump* covers a thirty-year period of time and is told as a flashback. To mark time passing, Forest goes through huge physical changes and participates in many significant historical periods as part of his unlikely journey. The scenes with Forest sitting on the bench telling strangers his life story tie the screenplay together as well as mark the passage of time.
- *Gone Girl* jumps back and forth in time. Time is marked by on-screen cards that help the audience keep track of time. The writer, Gillian Flynn, carefully controls what the audience knows and when they know it. She uses time to create mystery, suspense, and conflict. She also deftly holds back essential information and constantly misleads the audience.

Establish the rules and be consistent with the way you use time. If your story is told in a flashback, like *The Usual Suspects*, there must be a structural consistency to the way time is used to tell your story. Time should be used to heighten the suspense and increase the tension and pressure on the main character. A ticking clock is a good storytelling tool, but also a structural device. Time running out increases the pressure on the main character and also dictates the structural framework.

- In *Back to the Future*, time is running out on Marty, but he has one last chance to get back to the future. He has to be at an exact spot at the exact moment the lightening hits the clock tower. The screenplay is structured to build to this climactic moment. Time continues to be compressed until everything comes down to a few seconds.

Alternative Structure

A lot of writers like to take a nontraditional approach to structure. They like to work with time, through flashbacks, or tell separate stories simultaneously tied together by theme.

- *Citizen Kane* has a remarkable structure and uses it effectively to tell the story of one man through multiple points of view. Each character reveals another aspect of Charles Forster Kane, yet, in the end, he remains a mystery and an enigma.

- *Pulp Fiction* is basically three separate stories combined in a pulp fiction magazine format which are tied together thematically and by characters. Tarantino's inventive structure enhanced the overall effect of the drama by interweaving multiple stories and characters, and let the audience draw the threads together.
- *Memento* is told in reverse. This is a unique way to structure a screenplay. *Memento* is still a three act structure: present the problem, complicate the problem, and resolve the problem.
- Because of its unique structure, *Rashomon* is one of the most critically acclaimed films of all time. It is a "must see" for all serious writers. The story is told from multiple points of view with each point of view revealing a different perspective about a vicious crime. It is left up to the viewer to draw their own conclusion. This unique and influential structure is constantly referenced throughout the film industry.

Ultimately, the writer must determine the best way to tell *their* story. The tail should not wag the dog. The structure should not determine the story. The story and the character should determine which structure best works to tell the story. Make sure you understand the three act structure before you experiment with time. Once a writer can handle characters and plot successfully, they can begin to test other structures. Fractured narratives can be difficult to write and read. Making your screenplay structure more complicated does not always improve the screenplay.

Final Thoughts

Structure is the way you organize and tell the events of your story. Structure determines the way the main character's story unfolds throughout your entire screenplay. When does your story begin and when does it end? What do you leave in and what do you leave out? How does your structure enhance your screenplay to develop and complicate the main character's journey?

You don't get extra points for a complicated structure. Whether your story is told in linear fashion or flashback, your structure should enhance tension and conflict, and continue to complicate the main character's journey. Your structure must support your main character's transformation. Structure is not an end in itself. It is part of your tool box to support the characters and their stories. Build the right house for your characters to live in.

11

Structure Pass

Architecture and Design

The key is to find the spine, and that's not easy; you have to look and look and look, and it may take months—but once I do, I put a piece of paper on my wall with about twenty-five or thirty words that describe what the movie is about.

William Goldman, Screenwriter/Novelist,
Butch Cassidy and the Sundance Kid, All the President's Men

Economy is the essence of screenwriting. A well-structured screenplay is tight and lean with each scene building toward an intense third act climax. One of the goals of the Structure Pass is to tighten and focus your screenplay to tell your story as efficiently as possible. The elements must work together to drive the screenplay to an exciting unpredictable climax. You must find your spine and hold on to it. Anything that does not support your spine should be eliminated.

Objectives for your Structure Pass

- Tighten and focus the structure.
- Make sure you have the most effective scene order.
- Use sequences and scene groups to make your screenplay more cohesive.
- Create more highs and lows for your main character.
- Use the four major structural high points in your structure.
- Create a structural mid-point to intensify the back half of the second act.
- Build to the third act climax.

Structure Notes

Structure is the most amorphous of all the screenwriting elements. Generally, most notes will tend to come in the form of character and plot notes. Notes that complain about having difficulty following the story or being confused point toward potential structural issues. A good structure makes effective use of time, holds the reader's attention, and reveals essential story points at precisely the right moments.

Structure Notes

Common Note:	Potential Solutions:
The screenplay gets off to a slow start.	What Kind of Structure? Scene Order, Four Major High Points
I got lost.	What Kind of Structure? Scene Order, Sequences
The screenplay seems repetitious.	Internal Character Story*, Opposition Characters*, Subplot*, Relationships*, Four Major High Points, Highs and Lows, Reveals, Reversals, Misdirection
The ending felt predictable.	Scene Order, Sequences, Want*, Need*, Reveals, Reversals, Misdirection
The screenplay lagged in the middle	Conflict, Antagonist*, Opposition Characters*, Scene Order, Mid-Point Plot Turn, Highs and Lows, Reveals, Reversals, Obstacles*
The end of the second act felt flat.	Internal Character Story*, Stakes*, Time, Reveals, Reversals, Four Major High Points
The ending felt like an anticlimax.	Internal Character Story*, Want*, Need*, Stakes*, Predictable*, Third Act Climax, The Set-Up*, Time
The stakes are not high enough.	Internal Character Story*, Stakes*, Mid-Point Plot Turn, Antagonist*, Key Relationship*
The script doesn't feel like there is any urgency or tension.	Internal Character Story*, What Kind of Structure? Time, Scene Order, Sequences, Four Major High Points, Highs and Lows

*See index: concept found in other chapter.

What Kind of Structure?

Several types of structure are frequently used: the traditional three act design; a linear story in "real time"; a story told through flashbacks; a fractured narrative moving back and forth through time; or a fractured narrative from multiple points of view. Use the structure that tells your story best. Once you decide upon a type of structure, remain consistent in the way you use that structure throughout your entire screenplay. An inconsistent structure can be very confusing and can make a screenplay difficult to read.

If you are getting notes that your screenplay is not interesting enough, consider using a different structure such as telling your story through a flashback. On the other hand, if you are getting notes that your screenplay is hard to follow, then you may be using a structure that is too complicated. You are writing a screenplay to be read by readers, producers, and executives. They have to be able to follow the story.

- Are you using the right structure for your story?
- Is your structure too complicated to follow?
- Have you structured a logical progression to the story?
- Is your structure consistent throughout the entire screenplay?

Index Cards

We're Luddites, so we use index cards on corkboard. Each story line—Castle Black, say, or Arya/Hound—gets its own color. At our peak in Season 3 we were up to 13 different colors. Once we've mapped out each story line we start putting cards on the board and argue over which scenes should be in which episode and in what order.

D. B. Weiss and David Benioff, Writers/Producers,
Game of Thrones

The best way to get the big picture of your structure is to use index cards to break your screenplay into individual scenes. They help the writer get an overview of their entire story in ways that an outline cannot. If you are an outline writer, there is no reason you cannot use both an outline and cards to help examine your structure. Cards enable you to reconfigure your screenplay, and move scenes and sequences around. Since cards are easy to write, you are less invested in them and they are easy to change. You can try starting with a flashback, or cutting the entire opening, or losing a sequence to see what the cause and effect on subsequent scenes will be.

Write a card for each scene of your existing screenplay. Keep the words on your cards to a minimum. Write a headline about what happens in the scene and give a short description about the story and character points. Lay the cards across a table or tape them to a wall. Create a separate column for each sequence of your screenplay. Use the white cards for the main character and different colored cards for each supporting character. Number your cards so when you move them around, you can put them back together.

Maverick Flies Patrol	1
Establish Maverick and Goose	
They encounter a MIG	
Have an engagement—Maverick wins	
Establish Maverick as a great pilot	

Maverick Aborts His Landing	2
Cougar is in trouble	
Maverick ignores commands from the Bridge	
Establish Maverick bends rules	
Flies to Cougar	
Cougar is disoriented	
Maverick has to fly him down	

To find the spine of your screenplay, read over your cards and remove any scenes that are not essential character beats or major plot developments. Remove any scenes that do not advance the main character's story or the plot. Prune everything down to the bare spine. You should be left with just the major character and plot beats. The remaining cards are the spine of your screenplay.

- Do you have a big picture view of your structure?
- Have your pared away all the excess to reveal your spine?

- Where are the weaknesses to your spine and how can you strengthen them?
- If you move scenes and sequences, how does that affect your narrative?
- What if you told your story as a flashback?

Experiment With Scene Order

Once a writer settles on their initial structure, there is a tendency to stick with that structure. A first draft structure can often be too linear and can benefit from experimenting with scene order as well as some judicious cutting. It is good to step back to see if there is a better way to structure the story. This is where the card method is helpful because you can move scenes and try out different structures. You can always put the cards back together.

Play with your scenes and sequence order. Spend a day moving scenes and sequences around and see how they work. Be experimental, and a bit playful. Take the wildest idea you can think of and then try it. Start your story in motion. Explain later. Take the mid-point and move it to the opening. Start with the ending, and tell your story as a flashback. Play with where you introduce important information. Add reversals. Cut anything that isn't your story. Pull out tangents and scenes that are not essential to your story. Don't be precious with your scenes. You may have spent a lot of time writing them, but that doesn't mean you have to use them. Once you settle on the changes, renumber your cards.

- Can you start your screenplay in motion?
- What if you cut the opening scenes and started later in your screenplay?
- How late can you start your screenplay?
- What if you started your screenplay at the mid-point?
- What if you told your story as a flashback?

Pace Your Highs and Lows

Structure is the frame that holds your screenplay together. When designing your frame, one of the goals is to create a structure which deepens and intensifies the main character's journey through timely use of complications and obstacles. The main character must have ups and downs—the roller-coaster effect. Where you position each high and low, affects your overall structure.

If your notes suggest the second act is slow or runs out of stream, then you may not have enough structural highs and lows. Go through your screenplay scene by scene and track whether the scene is positive, negative, or neutral. Write down what the character gains and what the character loses. If you have too many positives, then you need more negatives and vice versa. If you have too many neutral scenes, then you need to convert them to positive or negative scenes.

Spread the obstacles and challenges your main character faces across your entire screenplay. Consider whether your major structural movements are spaced effectively so there is ever-increasing conflict and crisis. If your dramatic highs and lows are clumped together, then consider spreading them out for greater effect.

- Does the main character have substantial highs and lows?
- Do you have a balance of positive and negative scenes?
- Is the main character riding an emotional roller coaster?

Four Major High Points—Three Act Design

If you are getting notes that not enough is happening in your screenplay, it feels repetitious, or the stakes are not high enough, these can be due to a lack of major high points that significantly affect the main character and the plot. There are four major high points usually found in strong screenplays. Where these high points are placed has a significant effect on your structure, which in turn affects the plot. Often, the four major high points are reveals and/or reversals.

1st High Point—The End of The First Act—The Point of No Return

If your screenplay starts slowly, you may not have a strong end to the first act. Structurally, this must be a high point as well as a point of no return. The movement into the second act must be dramatic and establish the main plot problem.

- In *Back to the Future*, Marty escapes into the past and crashes head-on into a barn. His time machine is damaged and he is trapped in the past.

Many times, first acts suffer from a soft opening with unnecessary exposition and too many characters being introduced at one time. You may be well served to tighten your structure, cut your opening scenes, and begin your screenplay a few scenes later. Judicious editing can pick up the pace of your first act. There are no rules about how long a first act must be; the first act can be as long or as short as necessary. It has to quickly capture the reader's attention by thrusting the main character into a situation from which there is no return. What if you removed your first act entirely, and started your screenplay in motion with the main character scrambling from page one? Be open to all options.

- Is your first act endpoint dramatic?
- Does the first act endpoint thrust the main character into a crisis?
- Does the first act endpoint set up the main plot problem?

2nd High Point—Mid-Point Plot Turn

If your second act is flat or repetitious, look for a substantial event near the mid-point of your screenplay. Structurally, a mid-point plot turn significantly increases the personal stakes for the main character and also raises the level of conflict and complication.

- In *Top Gun*, the death of Goose is a significant mid-point plot turn that changes everything that follows. The loss of Goose affects the main character as well as all the supporting characters. It also raises the stakes as well as changes the tone from semi-comedic to dramatic. If we remove Goose's death, the second act would lack tension, urgency, stakes, and drama. The mid-point plot turn caught the audience off guard and energized the back half of the second act.

Often, a mid-point plot turn signals significant change for the main character. The first half of the screenplay focuses on character development, while the second half focuses on plot events that complicate the character's story.

- In *Erin Brockovich*, the first half is about Erin finding her voice and being taken seriously; the second half is about Erin proving she is capable fighting for the rights of the citizens of Hinkley. The first half of *Erin Brockovich* is character development, and the second half focuses on solving the main plot problem.

This should not be just another plot event, but a significant event that emotionally or physically affects the main character or a key relationship. The mid-point plot turn is often a major reveal or a reversal that significantly affects everything that follows.

- Do you have a substantial emotional or plot complication, reveal, or reversal near the middle of your screenplay?
- Does the mid-point plot turn have a significant affect on the characters and scenes that follow?
- Does this event increase the conflict and tension in the second act?

3rd High Point—End of The Second Act—Doubt

If your screenplay seems flat or anticlimactic, then the end of your second act may not be significant enough. Review your structure to make sure all your characters, relationships, and subplots converge at the end of the second act.

- At the end of the second act in *Good Will Hunting*, Skylar has left Will, and Will seems to be letting the opportunity to use his gifts slip away. Will has some serious decisions to make.

The end of the second act should be the most complicated part of your screenplay where the greatest pressure is brought to bear on the main character. Often, the end of the second act has a low point where the main character doubts their abilities to solve their personal problems and the main plot problem.

- In *Glory*, at the end of the second act, the men of the 54th Regiment are at a low point because they know they will face certain death in the morning in the battle to take Fort Wagner. But the low point transforms into a high point when they express their devotion to each other. They had been rootless abused slaves but now have found a family and a cause worth dying for.

The end of the second act needs both a high point and a low point. A high point because all the elements of the screenplay—character, plot, emotion, relationships—must converge to a single moment where the main character must make a decision and steel themselves to face the challenge before them. A low point because this is where the main character must also have their greatest moment of doubt.

- Does your structure drive toward the end of the second act?
- At the end of the second act is your main character in doubt about their ability to solve the main crisis?
- At the end of the second act are the main character's personal stakes at their highest point?

4th High Point—Third Act—Climax

If your climax doesn't feel significant or consequential, then you have not laid in the groundwork in your set-up for your third act climax. Structure your character development and plot events so that they build toward this moment. In addition, without significant personal stakes, the ending will feel perfunctory and lack substantial consequences or emotional involvement.

- In *Little Miss Sunshine*, Richard has an epiphany, realizes his daughter is about to be humiliated, and jumps on stage and dances with her as a show of love and support. This single action brings the entire family together.

When creating the third act climax, aspiring writers often focus too much on the plot consequences and not enough on the main character's personal consequences.

- Is your third act climax the highest point in your screenplay?
- Have you established and complicated the characters, relationships, plot, and subplots throughout your first and second act to resolve in your third act?
- Are the main character's personal stakes clear and significant?
- Will there be dire consequences to the main character and major supporting characters if the main character fails?
- Have you constructed your narrative so the ending is in doubt and unpredictable?

Sequences and Scene Groupings

The order of your sequences and scene groupings determines your structure. If your second act is repetitive or there isn't enough conflict, then review each sequence to see if your sequences have new tensions and new problems to solve. Make a list of each of your sequences and scene groupings. Write down the tension of each sequence. Each sequence should be like a building block that takes the story up a level.

- What is the tension of each sequence?
- What is the major problem the main character is facing in each sequence?
- How does each sequence advance the main character's story?
- How does each sequence advance the plot?
- What happens if you move sequences around?

Reveals

Where and when you reveal important character and plot information is a function of your structure. Aspiring writers often make the mistake of revealing too much information too early—usually in the first act, and sometimes all in one big scene. Revealing too much, too soon, can have a negative effect on your entire structure. Hold back important information so you can reveal it at strategic points throughout the second act.

If not enough is happening in your screenplay, look at your structure. See if you can move significant reveals later in your screenplay. See if you can mislead the audience when and where you reveal information. You may need to add more character secrets and plot reveals. You want to hold your reveals like trump cards and use them strategically and sparingly. To learn more about reveals, see Part Two, Chapter 16: "Complications, Obstacles, Reveals, and Reversals."

- Are you revealing too much information too soon?
- Can you spread out information across your second act?
- Do you have enough reveals or do you need to create more secrets?
- Does each reveal intensify the main character's journey?

Misdirection

Chinatown is a great example of using structure to mislead an audience. Screenwriter Robert Towne misleads the audience into believing there is only one crime happening when actually there are several crimes being committed. Towne uses structure to hold back information, and only releases snips of "the crime" which is then misinterpreted by the main character and the audience. He could very well let the audience in on all the crimes, but he holds back and uses misdirection to create suspense, tension, and conflict. *Chinatown* is a great example of how structure can help make your screenplay unpredictable by being very selective about what, where, and when you reveal information to the audience.

If your screenplay is predictable or the second act is repetitive, then review your structure to see where you can misdirect the audience with essential information. Limiting what the audience sees, and when they see it, can lead to false conclusions and surprises.

- Are you misleading the audience to create more mystery and tension?
- Can you adjust your scene placement so the audience draws false conclusions?

Reversals

Reversals play an important role in determining structure. Reversals are major setbacks and failures. Your screenplay must have several significant reversals for structure, plot, and character development reasons. When and where you place each reversal has a significant effect on the main character and the scenes that follow. Reversals change the plot, as well as emotionally challenge the main character. Audiences judge the character of the main character by their ability to pick themselves up and come back stronger.

Make a list of each reversal you have in your screenplay. If you only have one or two reversals, then you need to add more. If they are too close together, you need to spread them out evenly. If you do not have enough reversals, write "reversal" on index cards and place the cards where you think you need them. Identify places in your structure that need significant changes in the main character's journey and the plot. To learn more about reversals, see Part Two, Chapter 16: "Complications, Obstacles, Reveals, and Reversals."

- Do you have at least four or five major reversals in your screenplay?
- What is the emotional effect of each reversal on the main character?
- What is the narrative effect of each reversal on the plot?
- Are your four major high points a reveal and/or a reversal?

Time

Time is structure. The time frame in which your screenplay takes place must be carefully structured. Movies are about limited short periods of time, and generally, the more immediate the better. During the back half of the second act, and in the third act, time must be compressed and shortened until the main character sometimes has seconds to make a decision and react.

If your screenplay seems to lack urgency, review the way you are structuring time. You may use the device of a "ticking clock." Look for strategic places to increase tension and a sense of urgency. Make sure you are using your structure to focus and compress time during the back half of the second act and throughout the third act.

- How are you using time to structure your screenplay?
- Have you established a ticking clock to add a sense of urgency?
- Do you have signposts to help the audience know how much time has passed?
- Are you tightening time in the second and third acts?

Final Thoughts

Structure is the way you tell your story—the way you order events. Where does it start? What happens in the middle? Where does it end? Structure is as much about what you choose to put in as what you choose to leave out. Structure must be designed to tell your main character's story by creating significant emotional highs and lows, and meaningful plot events that challenge the main character every step of the way. Structure should never determine character or story. Structure serves character and story. Structure provides form and shape to reveal story. Structure helps you tell one character's story and follow their difficult and challenging journey of self-discovery.

Be playful and bold when revising your structure. Scene placement affects all aspects of your story. Making changes and moving scenes around can have a profound effect on your entire screenplay. It is important to hold back information and develop a little mystery or intrigue to keep the audience guessing. Make them want to know more, and misdirect them. Choose what the audience sees and when they see it. Use your structure to keep your screenplay unpredictable and the ending an unexpected surprise. Structure for intensity—structure for storytelling.

12

Plot

How Will This Turn Out?

I think it's always a struggle to make sure your characters are engaging and have some basis in humanity so that people care about them. [But] at the same time, you need a plot that's interesting. You can't just have interesting characters, you have to have a plot that supports your characters. So I think the struggle is creating a plot that is worthy of your characters and characters that are worthy of your plot.

Kimberly Simi, Screenwriter,
Casanova

There is no "one size fits all" when it comes to story plotting. Big action films need one kind of plot—big and brassy—while small independent films require another kind of plot—more subtle and character oriented. But in all cases, the plot is the engine that drives the screenplay and tests the main character's mettle. Plot is the labyrinth—the maze—the main character must navigate to prove their worth and earn the ending. Plot must entertain and provide big screen moments that surprise and delight the audience. Plot creates curiosity. How will this turn out? Character creates emotional involvement and anxiety. The audience cares how this turns out.

A good plot tells an intriguing story about a person in a life-altering crisis. Plot informs the *actions* a character takes to either resolve, or escape the crisis. Plot is *what happens* to that character on their journey to achieve their goal. To have a good plot, there must be someone or something very powerful stopping the character from achieving their goal. This collision between what the character wants, and the resistance they meet in trying to achieve it, is the plot. Each plot must be specific and tailored to the main character's story, so that if you were to change the main character, you would need to revise the plot.

The audience will cry for a character, but won't cry over a plot unless that plot revolves around a character they deeply care about. You can't develop an effective plot unless you clearly understand what the main character wants and why it is important to them. And you can't have an effective story unless the character has flaws the audience empathizes with. Character creates plot and plot reveals character.

Character in Crisis

Movies are about lives in crisis. No crisis—no movie. The main character must be in an external and internal crisis. The external crisis is the plot problem the main character must ultimately resolve in the third act. To solve their crisis, the main character must take direct action. The main character's *action* to solve the external crisis is the plot. For there to be a plot, there must be conflict and resistance. The main character wants something and someone stands in their way. Along the way, they face obstacles, setbacks, near misses, and physical or psychological challenges that test their mettle. The writer creates a series of obstacles, roadblocks, and challenges in the form of plot events.

The main character is an imperfect person, deeply flawed and in denial about their flaws. Their flaws have caused them serious problems throughout all areas of their life, especially in their relationships. Now, faced with a significant external crisis, the main character's flaws are suddenly magnified and rise to the surface where they seriously complicate the main character's ability to resolve the main plot problem. Unless the main character can open their eyes, and accept the truth about their flaws and transform, they will be unable to resolve their external crisis and the main plot problem.

The external crisis is easy to write. A character fights through obstacles and defeats the antagonist to save the day. The internal character crisis is much trickier. A character fights through personal obstacles and must face their flaws have an epiphany, and transform in order to defeat the antagonist. Weaving the external and internal crises together takes practice and skill.

Formulas vs. Patterns

Writers are always looking for a magic formula on how to plot a screenplay. However, there are no formulas that yield quality screenplays. The only formula

I know is: Boy meets girl—boy loses girl—boy gets girl. That's a formula and it is not very helpful. There are no shortcuts to creating an original plot. Story and plot patterns are the basis of Western literature and these patterns are repeated again and again. Western Civilization storytelling is heavily based on Greek mythology and plays, and Bible stories. Both Greek Mythology and the Bible use parables with underlying ethical and moral lessons.

At the center of all great myths is a strong central character in a personal crisis, as well as a life-altering external crisis, which leads to eventual insight and transformation. Myths and Bible stories continue to assert a strong influence in the kind of stories we tell today. For instance, all road movies are in one way or another, a version of Homer's "The Odyssey." Redemption stories mirror the parables about redemption in the Bible. The ancient Greek plays revolve around fatally flawed characters who suffer from hubris or arrogance. The key is to use patterns as a template, but not as a formula.

In Joseph Campbell's seminal work, *The Hero with a Thousand Faces*, he analyzed classical mythological structure, story patterns, and transformation. Films such as *Star Wars*, *Jaws*, and the *Guardians of the Galaxy* closely follow classical mythological story structure. Christopher Vogler's, *The Writer's Journey: Mythic Structure for Storytellers & Screenwriters*, is based on Campbell's work and is a valuable resource for further understanding mythic story structure and patterns. Story patterns help to create a framework for the writer to explore characters and their relationships.

Main Plot Problem

For a successful plot, there needs to be a main plot problem that causes catastrophic problems for the main character and/or a host of supporting characters. The problem may be a devastating alien invasion as in *Edge of Tomorrow*, or a cancer diagnosis as in *50/50*. In both films, there is a significant problem in need of a solution or there will be catastrophic consequences for the main character. The main plot problem must be difficult, if not nearly impossible, to solve.

At the beginning of the second act, when the main character is initially confronted with the main plot problem, they do not have the emotional or physical skills necessary to solve the problem. Throughout the course of the second act, the main character must go through a series of trials and tribulations where they gain the necessary skills to resolve the main plot problem. In action films, during the climax the main character may be weaker than their opponent, but they make up for their weakness by being clever. In independent films, the main character has to face personal issues or relationship problems before they can undergo a significant personal transformation which then enables them to resolve the main plot problem.

The main plot problem represents the overarching problem of your screenplay that must be resolved, but at its core, the movie is not about the main plot problem.

- In *Groundhog Day*, Phil Connors is trapped in a repeated day. The main plot problem is that Connors must figure out how to escape his repeated day. The movie is really about Connors' personal journey from being a selfish narcissist to a person who learns the value of putting the welfare of others before his own needs. The main plot problem creates scenes and situations that challenge and pressure the main character's flaws which ultimately lead to Connor's personal transformation.

It is virtually impossible to plot a screenplay without a main plot problem. Before you begin writing, you must know what dragons your main character must slay.

Main Character's Want

Your main character must have something they desperately want. The main character's active pursuit of their want is the key to creating a strong workable central plot. The plot is about how the main character tries to obtain their want, what happens to them along the way, and the personal insight they gain from their challenging experiences. The goal must be clear and specific, as well as difficult to achieve, if not nearly impossible. You cannot plot unless you understand *what* is driving your character in every scene throughout the screenplay—and *why* it is essential for them to achieve their goal.

- What is motivating the main character?
- What are the dire consequences if they fail?
- Who else will be negatively affected if the main character fails to reach their goal?
- Goal equals plot.

Conflict, Resistance, and Opposition

The plot runs on conflict, resistance, and opposition. The main character faces an uphill battle throughout the second act until they reach the climax in the third act. Conflict is the lifeblood of drama and comedy, and is created by physical and emotional resistance to the main character achieving their goal. Someone, or something, must stand in the main character's way. The main character must face relentless opposition each step of the way.

The drive and momentum of the plot is directly proportional to the strength and power of the antagonist, or the main opposition force. Weak opposition, weak plot. If you are writing a Hollywood film, then your antagonist will supply most of the conflict and resistance in your screenplay. The conflict between the main character and the antagonist is based upon their opposing agendas. Both characters desperately want something, but only one of them can get what they want. In addition to the central conflict, there needs to be sustained conflict and resistance in the subplots and relationships. Everywhere the main character turns, they must face more conflict. Even the best friend should be a source of tension and resistance. Your plot, then, is based on multiple sources of conflict and tension. You are plotting not just one story; you are plotting multiple stories which run simultaneously. In a cohesive screenplay, what happens in one story affects the others.

Independent films often use dysfunctional relationships and the main character's personal issues to create many sources of conflict and tension. But independent films also need a central plot to drive the story. All stories need a strong opposition force and/or opposition characters that block, resist, oppose, or hinder the main character from reaching their goal. Opposition characters do not have to be "bad," but need to have their own agenda which conflicts with the main character's agenda. There can be no safe port in the storm, and everywhere the main character turns, they encounter resistance and obstacles.

Plot Driven Screenplays

The plot driven screenplay is where the action and the events are more important than the characters. A generic character is dropped into a crisis and explosions ensue. The main character does not have an inner struggle, or at best, just a thin thread of a personal story. Films, like *Transformers*, the Bourne series, and the Bond series, are examples of well-plotted movies with a universal main character. Their intent is to take the audience on a ride. If you are a plot wiz, then maybe plot is your ticket to the big game. You will need to spend a great deal of your time creating unexpected twists and turns, and big set pieces. But even the biggest action film is more interesting if there is a character story in the middle of all that mayhem. There are plot driven action films with strong characters that are successful.

- *The Matrix delivers* on action and set-pieces as well as characters with stories. The plot is about enslaved humans that take on the Matrix to liberate mankind. The story is about a rag tag group of rebels and one man in particular growing and accepting his role as the leader the rebellion. Neo, Morpheus, Trinity, Tank, and Agent Smith are all memorable big screen characters with individual stories.
- Other action films with good character work include *Guardians of the Galaxy, Collateral, In the Line of Fire, Iron Man,* and the X-Men Series.

If you want to write action, you must create interesting and unique set pieces, but you also need to create empathic characters that leap off the page. Hollywood readers get thousands of scripts filled with special effects but thin on character development. In this genre, set pieces are important, but the ability to write great character in the middle of a huge action film is a rare talent that stands out from the pile.

Action Plots—The Antagonist's Plan

When writing an action movie, one thing you learn quickly is that you must know the antagonist's plan before you can plot your movie. It may sound counterintuitive, but you are actually writing the antagonist's movie from the protagonist's point of view. If you are writing an X-Men film, you must know Magneto's plan before you can begin to construct a plot. While Cyclops, Storm, and Wolverine are interesting characters with internal stories, the plot is actually determined by the antagonist, Magneto. He has a plan that the X-men must discover and then defeat. Most action films are "stop the plot" movies.

- Figure out the antagonist's plan.
- What is the antagonist's goal and what will be the consequences if they accomplish their plan?
- As the writer, once you know the antagonist's plan, you must obscure it.

- Employ subterfuge and misdirection with your plotting.
- Make the audience think the antagonist's plan is one thing, when really it is another.
- Have the main character begin to piece together the antagonist's actual plan.
- The ending is a race against time.

Character Driven Screenplays

Character driven screenplays depend upon multidimensional characters with genuine relatable flaws. The main question of the screenplay is whether the main character and their significant relationships will survive their personal crisis. In independent films, there needs to be a significant plot problem which must also be resolved, but the outcome depends upon the main character facing their personal failings. Plot is secondary to character, but plot plays an important role in revealing and forcing the main character to confront their demons. The plot is about the main character's arc as well as the arcs of their significant relationships.

To write a character driven screenplay, the screenwriter must be an astute student of human nature; be willing to look deep within themselves; understand the struggle to connect through relationships; be able to see their own flaws and weaknesses, and write about them. Independent films often do not have a strong central antagonist driving the plot. Independent films focus on relationships. The main character is going through a life-altering crisis that affects each area of their life. Usually the main character's relationships are in transition and taking the force of the punishment.

- In *Crazy Heart* there are no classical antagonists. Bad Blake is his own worst enemy.
- In *50/50* the main plot problem is that the main character, Adam, is diagnosed with cancer. An illness is not an antagonist, but an illness is a very strong opposition force and works as the agent of change that forces Adam to take stock of his life. Adam is surrounded by opposition characters that react in different ways to his cancer.
- In *Sideways*, the plot places Miles Raymond into situations where he is forced to see the barren landscape of his life, and each time, instead of seizing the day, Miles blames himself and escapes deeper into a wine haze. After he meets his happily remarried ex-wife, Miles hits bottom and is finally able to hear an offer of true friendship and understanding.

In addition to entertaining the audience, the main purpose of the independent film plot is to pressure the main character's flaws and force an epiphany.

Subplots and Multiple Storylines

There are basically two types of subplots: event subplots which are offshoots of the main plot, and relationship subplots. Your screenplay should not be comprised of just one plotline, but told through multiple subplots, all running concurrent with the main plot. Crosscutting between the main plot and the subplots is an excellent way to keep the overall plot fresh and complicated. *On The Waterfront* has many event and relationship subplots that run throughout the screenplay.

On The Waterfront

The Central Plot

A witness for a crime commission investigating corruption at the waterfront is killed, and the man who unwittingly lured the witness to his death is being pressured to testify to the commission. He is also being pressured and threatened by the mob not to testify.

Relationship Subplots

1. Terry and Edie—love interest
2. Terry and Charlie—brothers
3. Terry and Johnny Friendly—symbolic father/son relationship
4. Terry and the Priest—moral conscience
5. Terry and the Dockworkers—colleagues
6. Terry and Jimmy from the Golden Warriors—mentor relationship
7. Charlie and Johnny Friendly—employee/boss relationship
8. Edie and the Priest—student/teacher relationship

Event Subplots

1. Edie wants to find out who killed her brother.
2. The Crime Commission is investigating crime on the waterfront.
3. Johnny Friendly is under suspicion by the Crime Commission.
4. K. O. Dugan talks to the Crime Commission.

5. Terry is pressured to testify to the Crime Commission.
6. Friendly pressures Terry not to testify.
7. Friendly has Charlie killed.
8. Terry goes after Friendly for killing his brother.

Subplots can run the entire length of the screenplay or be short parallel stories that run just a few scenes. Subplots play an important role in giving the screenwriter more than one plot to develop. This is particularly useful during the second act.

Reverse Engineering

A good way to build a strong plot is to start with the ending. You really can't tell a story unless you know where it is heading. Once you know your main character's personal story, you should have an idea of their character arc. You may not know what the scenes are yet, but you should know what you want the main character to have learned by the end. At the beginning, the character can't do "this," but at the end, they can do "that."

Once you know the ending, you can establish it in your set-up, and plot the second act to reach it. You will discover important things about your character along the way, and your plot will take some surprise turns, but you will know where you are heading and can drive to the ending.

Obstacles

Your second act must have significant plot obstacles for the main character to overcome. Obstacles can be physical challenges, or a dangerous character that stands in the main character's way. Obstacles also pressure the main character's internal story. Mine your world for obstacles. To learn more about obstacles, see Part Two, Chapter 16: "Complications, Obstacles, Reveals, and Reversals."

Reveals

Another constant challenge of plotting is to keep the plot fresh and changing. The second act is particularly difficult to plot. One way to keep the plot active and evolving is by strategically revealing new information throughout the second act. To learn more about reveals, see Part Two, Chapter 16: "Complications, Obstacles, Reveals, and Reversals."

Reversals

Reversals energize the plot. Just when things seem to be going well for the main character, they suddenly suffer an unexpected setback or reversal. Reversals are important plotting tools. To learn more about reversals, see Part Two, Chapter 16: "Complications, Obstacles, Reveals, and Reversals."

Cause and Effect Plotting

Cause and effect plotting occurs when the events of one scene affects another scene, which in turn affects other scenes. Your character's actions and behavior must have significant consequences and those consequences should reverberate in later scenes. This is how a character's actions and behavior creates plot.

Below is an example of cause and effect plotting from *Top Gun*. Maverick's poor decision in one scene affects five scenes that follow.

1. In an aerial dogfighting exercise, Maverick breaks the rules of engagement, chases Top Gun instructor, Jester, below the "hard deck" and records a "kill."
2. Because he beat Jester, Maverick celebrates his victory and buzzes the tower without permission.
3. In the locker room, Iceman confronts Maverick and tells him he's dangerous.
4. Commanding Officer Viper issues a warning to Maverick for breaking the rules of engagement.
5. Viper and Jester discuss Maverick's fitness to be a fighter pilot.
6. Goose admonishes Maverick not to mess up this opportunity. Maverick admits the flyby wasn't a good idea and pledges to do better.

Use cause and effect to link your main characters' actions and behaviors across your entire screenplay. Linking and connecting your scenes creates a sense of cohesion and ties your characters together.

Great Scenes and Set Pieces

First and foremost, you are an entertainer. Movies must be exciting. Whether you are writing a big Hollywood action film or a small independent film, the audience wants to disappear into the film for a few hours. If it's a big Hollywood film, they want great action and huge set pieces. They want the spectacular and the unusual. If you are writing for the big screen, then write big. Create memorable big movie moments with great visual effects and a twisting plotline. If you are writing an independent film, the audience wants to look deeply into a character's soul and explore a truth about human existence. They want insight and perspective. They want characters in the middle of life-changing crises. No halfway measures.

- Be bold. Nothing kills a screenplay quicker than the writer playing it too safe.
- Push your characters and your plot to extremes.
- Think of the worst thing that can happen to your character and then do it to them many times over.

This is not an intellectual exercise. You are writing a movie, and movies are played on big screens in front of paying audiences. Give them their money's worth. They want high drama and a tale well told. They want lives in crisis and dysfunctional relationships. And they want an unpredictable plot with surprises along the way.

- Think visually.
- Create pictures and big movie moments.
- You aren't writing a screenplay—you are writing a movie.

Essential Three Act Questions

Before writing a screenplay, I ask myself a host of questions. This is an important process where I try to flush out the characters, plot, structure, and theme by continually asking: "Why?" In fact, you could say, that writing a screenplay is really asking question after question until you have no more questions. Over time I've put together a list of questions that every writer must know before they begin a first draft, or a rewrite. You will find these questions in Part Four: "Essential Three Act Questions."

These questions can help you frame your idea and develop your plot. If there are questions you cannot answer, dig deeper. Learn everything you can about your characters and their stories—*what* they want and *why* they want it. As you go through these questions, you will discover a world of things about your characters. A big part of rewriting is making decisions, and then testing them out. No matter how much you plan, rewriting is very much a process of trial and error. Not every idea will pan out, but the discoveries outweigh the failures. To succeed, you have to fail occasionally.

Final Thoughts

Your plot is the story of one person's journey. Someone or something more powerful than the main character must be standing in their way. The main character must be put through an emotional and physical obstacle course which tests their mettle. Multiple storylines complicate and intensify the main character's crises and dilemmas. The main character's problems must get worse before they get better. High points and low points in your plot, as well as significant reversals, will keep the plot unpredictable. The plot should be relentless and intensify throughout the second act until it reaches its high point at the third act climax. The ending must always be in doubt, and the main character must earn the ending.

Make the audience care about the main character and then put the character through hell. Don't let up. Pile it on. Let your characters guide your plot and let your plot challenge your characters. Keep the audience in suspense and wondering how it will all turn out. Plot is curiosity and character is emotion. Combine the two and you will have a powerful combination which makes for a great screenplay.

13

Plot Pass

Cause and Effect

Plot is people. Human emotions and desires founded on the realities of life, working at cross purposes, getting hotter and fiercer as they strike against each other until finally there's an explosion—that's plot.

Leigh Brackett, Screenwriter/Novelist,
Star Wars Episode V—The Empire Strikes Back, The Big Sleep, Rio Bravo

Plot is often mistaken as something separate and distinct from the other elements of the screenplay. It is looked upon as a series of exciting scenes and set pieces— explosions and car chases. In reality, plot facilitates important screenwriting elements such as character development, relationships, and theme. In addition to being exciting and unpredictable, plot must pressure the main character's emotional issues and put them through a series of tests to see if they are worthy of the ending. Each plot should be specific to the main character. Change the main character and you should have to change the plot.

Many aspiring writers put way too much emphasis on plot at the expense of character development. Even when addressing plot issues, the writer should always be asking: How do these changes affect the main character? If you put aside all the chases, gun fights, and explosions, your story ultimately must be about one character's journey through a life-altering crisis.

Objectives for Your Plot Pass

- Create strong "character centric" plot events.
- Link and connect plot and character.
- Use the main character's want to create plot events.

- Strengthen and focus the main plot problem.
- Use the antagonist's plan to develop the plot.
- Intensify the central dramatic conflict.
- Create plot questions the main character must answer.
- Raise the emotional stakes.
- Use a ticking clock to add more urgency to the plot.
- Make the screenplay believable and unpredictable.

Plot Notes

Plot notes are easy to give, and therefore, tend to be the most plentiful notes you may receive. Unfortunately, most reader's solutions to plot issues are usually to add more plot. Rarely will you get the suggestion to use your character's flaws or complicate their relationships to develop the plot. But if the audience deeply cares about the main character, then each plot event will be that much more heightened and significant. Plot is not just about what happens, but who it happens to.

Plot Notes

Common Note:	Potential Solutions:
The plot is too episodic.	Internal Character Story*, Cause and Effect, Plot And Character, Main Plot Problem, Central Dramatic Conflict, Antagonist, Plot Questions
The main character isn't that interesting.	Internal Character Story*, Plot and Character, Want*, Need*, Active vs. Passive, Antagonist, Stakes, Predictable
The main character is too passive.	Internal Character Story*, Active vs. Passive, Cause and Effect, Main Plot Problem, Central Dramatic Conflict, Antagonist
I didn't believe the main character would do that.	Internal Character Story*, Want*, Need*, Predictable
There isn't enough conflict.	Conflict, Main Plot Problem, Central Dramatic Conflict, Active vs. Passive, Antagonist, Opposition Characters, Stakes, Subplots Are Plot
There is not enough at stake.	Internal Character Story*, Key Relationship*, Cause and Effect, Want*, Stakes, Predictable, Ticking Clock

(Continued)

Plot Notes (Continued)

Common Note:	Potential Solutions:
The screenplay seems repetitious.	Cause and Effect, Plot Questions, Stakes, Ticking Clock, Reveals*, Reversals*, Combine Scenes, Four Major High Points*, Undeveloped Gems
The screenplay is not exciting enough.	Conflict, Central Dramatic Conflict, Antagonist, Opposition Characters, Plot Questions, Reveals*, Reversals*, Stakes, Ticking Clock, Structure*, Four Major High Points*, Underdeveloped Gems
The story felt predictable.	Predictable, Active vs. Passive, Want*, Need*, Central Dramatic Conflict, Antagonist, Reversals*, Plot Questions

*See index: concept found in other chapter.

Index Cards

Index cards are invaluable when working on plot. With cards, you can quickly move scenes around and try new ideas. One of the most important games to play when working on plot is: What if? What if I moved this here? What if I cut this scene? What if I combined these two scenes? What if I moved this sequence to the opening? Be playful and try out new ideas throughout your rewrite. With cards, you can experiment without having to spend a great deal of time and energy writing an outline. You can also easily make notes on your cards as you work to link and connect your characters, relationships, and plot developments. Index cards are also an easy way to track changes across your entire screenplay.

When it's time to write, I put a card in front of me and I'm off. I keep the detail on my cards sparse so I can discover the scene as I write it. I understand the big points of the scene, but I don't have to worry about "what happens next?" because I know what happens next. I leave the details to discover during the writing. The scene can come alive, and when it's going well, the scene writes itself.

Conflict

Plot is conflict. The more conflict in your screenplay, the more opportunities to develop the plot. Conflict must come from all areas of your screenplay, and not just through the antagonist or the A plotline. The main character should find conflict in their relationships, subplots, and the central plot. No matter where they turn, they should face some degree of conflict in their life. One of the skills writers need to master is how to modulate the levels of conflict throughout their screenplays. If the conflict is at the same level throughout, the screenplay will become monotonous.

Think of your screenplay as a ladder and each step up the ladder intensifies the conflict, crisis, compilations, and obstacles facing your main character. The first few steps up the ladder are relatively easy, but the higher your character climbs, the more harrowing and dangerous the challenges they face. These can be physical, emotional, or psychological challenges. Your plot and structure should walk the main character up the ladder scene by scene in ever-increasing jeopardy and conflict until they reach the top—at the third act climax.

- In *Erin Brockovich*, Erin faces conflicts from her boss, coworkers, boyfriend, children, finances, the skeptical citizens of Hinkley, and the PG&E attorneys— from everywhere.

Assess conflict in your screenplay. Make a list of the sources of conflict in your screenplay. The list should include the central A plot, subplots, and major relationships. Next, review each scene and note the level and source of the conflict in each scene. As you do your review, look for opportunities to increase the conflict as well as develop more conflict from multiple sources. If you hit a patch of scenes with little or no conflict, then you need to add conflict to those scenes, or create new scenes. Cut stalled scenes that do not advance the plot or the main character's story to help move your plot forward more quickly. Remember, put the main character in the center of the conflict so that the plot and character support each other.

- Do you have enough conflict in your screenplay?
- Is the main character facing conflict in all aspects of their life?
- Is your main character at the center of the conflict?
- Is the main character climbing the ladder of conflict and complications?
- Do you have stretches of scenes without any significant conflict?

Plot and Character

Plot and Character have a hand-in-glove relationship. Character creates plot and plot reveals character. Character creates plot because the main character's flaws must be challenged by specific plot events tailored to pressure the flaws. Plot reveals character because specific plot events force the character to act in ways that reveal their flaws.

If your main character is flat or uninteresting, you may not have enough tailored plot events that directly pressure the main character's story. Go through your list of scenes and note which plot events directly pressure the main character's story. You do not need to have every plot event pressure the main character's story, but you do need a substantial number of tailored scenes, especially at critical points in the screenplay, such as the Four Major High Points. If you do not have them, then convert some of the plot scenes to character/plot scenes. Look for ways to link and connect the plot with the main character's story.

- Does your plot continually test the main character's mettle?
- Does your plot attack the main character's emotional flaws?
- Does your plot force the main character to learn from their mistakes and become smarter and stronger?
- Can you convert plot scenes into character/plot scenes?

Give the audience an exciting scene, but also write it in such a way that the plot event pressures the main character's emotional flaws. The challenge is to find the right balance between the need to advance the plot and entertain the audience while at the same time reveal and complicate the character.

Plot Questions

The plot must create questions in the audience's mind. What's going to happen next? How will they get out of this situation? Will she learn that he is lying to her? The answer to each question has to be unpredictable so that the audience isn't able to get ahead of the story. Many questions remain unanswered until the third act climax.

- In *Back to the Future* there are a lot of questions that need to be answered. Will Marty return to the future? Will Marty's true identity be discovered? Will Doc Brown believe Marty? Will Marty be able to unite his mother and father? Will Marty be able to get enough energy to power his car to get back to the future?

If there is not enough conflict in your screenplay, your plot may not be asking enough questions. Make a list of all the questions you are asking throughout your screenplay. If you only have a few questions, then create cliffhangers to your scenes and leave problems unresolved until later scenes. Review your subplot conflicts and complications with supporting characters and their relationships. Establish several balls in the air for the main character to juggle throughout the second act.

- What are the major questions of your screenplay?
- When you answer one question do you create another question?
- Are you using questions to create plot beats?

Cause and Effect

Plot is cumulative and builds upon itself. Each scene must be connected and linked, not a series of isolated or random events. There must be a cause and effect relationship between your scenes. What happens in one scene must effect following scenes. A good plot revolves around a character going through a life-altering crisis. Because of this crisis the main character makes decisions and takes actions—sometimes good, sometimes bad—which in turn affect other characters and later scenes.

South Park creators, Matt Parker and Trey Stone, have isolated two words that can help link and connect your scenes: "but" and "therefore." You can test whether your scenes are connected by inserting one of these two words after each scene.

- This happens, but then that happens
- But this happens, therefore that happens.

Each example shows a cause and effect relationship between two scenes. Scenes are a series of chain reactions, and each scene has consequences. Something happens and the character reacts physically or emotionally. The main character travels down a road of connected scenes that leads to the third act climax.

If your screenplay is too episodic, or your plot is repetitious, you need to work on linking your main character's actions to the plot and the major supporting characters. Go through your scenes and use the "but" and "therefore" test to see if you are connecting your scenes. Random scenes with random events can lead to a disconnected screenplay.

- Are you using cause and effect plotting?
- Does your screenplay pass the "but" and "therefore" test?
- Do the main character's actions affect the plot?
- Does the plot affect the main character?

Linking the main character's actions with individual plot events is essential to creating a cohesive screenplay. The main character's actions should also affect the major supporting characters and subplots.

Main Character's Want

The main character's pursuit of their want is one of the main sources of plot. Your main character must have something they are desperately trying to achieve or accomplish. The pursuit of their want must put them into direct conflict with characters who are pursuing their wants. This clash of agendas creates plot events where characters battle over their competing agendas. These battles can be physical, emotional, or psychological.

- In *Top Gun*, Maverick pursues his want to be "the best of the best." Maverick's relentless pursuit of his want puts him into direct conflict with his main adversary, Iceman, as well as his Commanding Officer, his fellow pilots, and Navy regulations..

If there isn't enough conflict in your screenplay, review your main character's want to effectively strengthen their want to create plot events. The main character's want must put them into direct conflict with the antagonist as well as other supporting characters.

- What is the main character's want?
- Is the main character's pursuit of their want consistent and relentless?
- Does the main character's want directly conflict with the antagonist's want?
- Does the main character's want also conflict with supporting characters' wants?
- Are you using the clash of agendas to create plot events?

Main Plot Problem

The main plot problem is the engine that drives the screenplay and allows the writer to explore character and relationship along the way. Once established, the main plot problem must become more complicated and difficult to solve throughout the second act. Solving the main plot problem pits the main character against the antagonist. Failing to solve the main plot problem must have dire consequences for the main character.

- In *Winter's Bone*, the main plot problem is that Ree's father jumped bail. Unless Ree can find him, the sheriff will foreclose on the family home and throw them into the street. Because Ree's father was a cook for a meth syndicate, the syndicate sees Ree's search for her father as a threat to their organization. The problem becomes further complicated when it appears her father was murdered, but without proof of his death, the sheriff will still evict Ree's family. To solve the main plot problem, Ree must find her father's body to prove he is dead.

Make a list of scenes where the main character tries to resolve the main plot problem. If you only have a few, then you need to create more scenes that address solving the main plot problem. If your second act is slow, or the screenplay loses focus, make the plot problem difficult if not impossible to solve. The solution to the main plot problem must become harder and harder until the final climax.

- Is the main plot problem difficult, if not impossible, to solve?
- In each step of the way, does the main character face new difficulties and complications in solving the main plot problem?
- Does trying to solve the main plot problem throw the main character into direct conflict with the antagonist?
- What are the dire consequences if the main character fails to solve the main plot problem?

Active vs. Passive

To have a vibrant plot, the main character cannot be passive and let the action come to them. While they may be initially reluctant to take up the challenge, the main character must force the action—sooner rather than later. The central plot grows out of the main character's efforts to pursue their want and solve the main plot problem. Whether they are the reluctant hero, or the knight in shining armor, they must be active, and the action must revolve around them. In independent films, the main character may be reluctant, but events and relationships force them to act.

- In *Erin Brockovich*, Erin is actively trying to find a job; pursuing work at the law firm; pursuing information about the case; and confronting the PG&E attorneys.

If your main character is not active, convert them to an active character, and make them force the action. Turning your main character into an active character can have a profound effect on your entire screenplay. This is no small task since changing a main character from passive to active requires substantially revising them, their scenes, and virtually the entire plot. But the results will be worth the time and effort.

- Is your main character active and forcing the action?
- Is your main character pursuing their want?
- By trying to solve the main plot problem, is your main character generating plot?

Central Dramatic Conflict

At the core of your screenplay there must be two strong characters or ideas that are diametrically opposed to each other. The conflict between these two characters, or ideas, must be intense and unrelenting. The main character's pursuit of their want puts them into direct conflict with the antagonist's want. The struggle between these two forces is the central dramatic conflict. It must be at the core of your screenplay and generate your major plot events. It is like a whirlpool that sucks the supporting characters into a maelstrom.

- In action films, the central dramatic conflict can be as simple as the X-Men series where the X-men oppose Magneto.
- In independent films, the central dramatic conflict can be more complex like in *Crazy Heart* where Bad Blake's central dramatic conflict is a struggle between his desire for love and connection, and his relentless alcohol addiction.

If your central dramatic conflict is between two competing ideas, each should be equally strong. The outcome of the battle must be in doubt.

- Do you have two strong characters or ideas with diametrically opposed wants locked in a battle for supremacy?
- Are you using your central dramatic conflict to create conflict and tension?
- Are you using your central dramatic conflict to create major plot events?
- Is the struggle between the two opposition characters or ideas consistent and unrelenting, and resolved in the third act?

Antagonist—The Action Film

In action films, the antagonist is usually the "instigator" of the plot—not the main character. The antagonist has a plan which is hidden from the main character. If the conflict or plot seems to run out of steam, then make your antagonist determined with a clear plan. Use the antagonist's plan to generate your plot and scenes. Do not reveal the plan too early. Use misdirection to fool the main character, as well as the audience.

- Is the antagonist stronger than the main character?
- In addition to the physical battles, are there emotion battles?
- Is the antagonist using misdirection and subterfuge to obscure their real plan?
- Is the main character scrambling to figure out the antagonist's plan?

Opposition Characters—The Independent Film

If you are rewriting an independent film, have your main character struggle with a significant internal crisis that you use to construct the plot and create scenes. Examine whether your supporting characters are also in opposition to the main character's agenda, and if you are using their clashes to create conflict and tension. List each major supporting character and how they are in opposition to the main character. Then, add scenes where they clash with the main character. Chart how much opposition is generated from these various conflicts. No screenplay suffers from too much conflict and tension.

- Is the conflict in your screenplay coming from multiple sources?

- Is the main character surrounded by opposition characters with their own agendas?
- Are you using your major relationships to create plot complications and obstacles for the main character?

Subplots are Plot

To keep your screenplay interesting, add multiple stories—multiple subplots—that run throughout your screenplay. Subplots are great tools to keep your plot complicated and moving forward. Have a central A plotline, as well as multiple B, C, D, and E subplots that further complicate your second act. Advance and intercut between plotlines to keep your screenplay progressing. Each subplot should create problems for the main character and the major supporting characters.

If the back half of your second act is repetitious or flat, you probably do not have enough subplots to keep the plot moving and complications rising. Review your subplots and cut between them throughout the second act. Create new subplots to complicate the second act, and make sure you weave them throughout your screenplay.

- Does your screenplay have multiple storylines and subplots?
- Are you cutting between multiple storylines to complicate your plot to keep it moving forward?
- Are your subplots woven into the fabric of the screenplay?

Stakes

When trying to address notes about raising the stakes, it is a common mistake to add more plot or make the explosions bigger. To raise the stakes, the main character has to have something important they will lose. To raise stakes even further, there must be someone important to the main character who will also suffer dire consequences if the main character fails.

- In *Die Hard*, thieves posing as terrorists hold the employees of the Nakatomi Corporation hostage. The overall stakes are that all the hostages could be killed. But what raises the stakes to the next level is that McClane's wife,

Holly, is one of the hostages. The audience's emotional stake is that the terrorist will discover Holly's true identity and use her against McClane, and eventually kill her. Remove Holly and the stakes would evaporate.

If there is not enough at stake in your screenplay, list which characters are at risk and what will happen to them should the main character fail. If only the main character is at risk, then you need to create scenes and events that put another major character in jeopardy.

- What big picture stake is at risk if the main character fails in their journey?
- What does the main character have to lose?
- Who does the main character have to lose?

Ticking Clock

Movies need to be immediate, and time should be compressed and running out for the main character. A ticking clock pressures the characters, adds suspense, intensifies the plot, and raises the stakes. A ticking clock also heightens the audience's anxiety and raises their concern for the main character. The main character must be under intense pressure, and the pressure must increase the closer they get to the end of the third act. The main character must fight against time and perform their tasks under time pressure. For the main character, time should always be running out.

- In *High Noon*, the ticking clock is built into the fabric of the story and all its characters. There isn't a single scene where time does not play a central role in the drama. Years ago, the town sheriff sent a gunslinger to prison, now the gunslinger is getting out of jail and has vowed revenge. He is arriving on the twelve o'clock train. Racing against time, the sheriff desperately tries to put together a posse to defend the town. The citizens of the town fold under the pressure and desert the sheriff. As minutes tick away, the sheriff becomes more desperate and isolated. The stakes continue to rise as the clock marches toward high noon and the train arrives.

Ticking clocks also add tension to individual scenes.

- In *Broadcast News*, the national news show is already on air while a new producer is trying to finish a final edit on a story. The pressure mounts as the deadline approaches to air the story. With seconds to spare, the tape is raced across the office to the control booth and just makes it on air.

Make a list of the ticking clocks in your screenplay—in individual scenes, sequences, and in the final third act climax. Look for places to add ticking clocks. Time running out will help your plot feel urgent and suspenseful. A ticking clock is an important plot device and something that can have an enormous affect on your screenplay.

- Do you have any ticking clocks in your screenplay?
- Have you established the main ticking clock early in your screenplay?
- Are you using "time running out" to pressure your main character and heighten the tension in your plot?

Combining Scenes

A relatively easy way to tighten a plot is to combine scenes and beats to move your narrative forward quicker. You don't need an entire scene to reveal information. Be experimental with your index cards and see if combining scenes speeds up the plot. Be careful of going to the other extreme and cramming too much information into a scene. You need far less exposition than you think. Cutting exposition always helps plot. Find ways to pick up the pace of your narrative and make your screenplay more intense.

- Can you combine scenes to tighten your screenplay?
- Do you have exposition scenes that can be combined with another scene?

Mine Your Screenplay for Undeveloped Gems

If the second act is repetitious, then add more subplots to complicate it. Before you create new subplots, mine your screenplay for existing characters, relationships, and subplots that can be developed further. If you look closely, you probably have a relationship that can be expanded, or a character that can play a bigger role. By expanding one or two opposition characters, you can add significant tension and conflict throughout the second act. Remember, opposition characters do not have to be bad—they just need to oppose the main character's want.

- Do you have supporting characters that can play a bigger role, and create more tension and conflict in your screenplay?
- Do you have a subplot or relationships that you can further develop?
- Can you enlarge a subplot to complicate the second act?

Predictable

A predictable screenplay is a dead screenplay. A good plot must be several steps ahead of the audience at all times. The audience is constantly trying to figure out where the plot is heading and how the movie will end. If they are able to predict the screenplay, they will quickly become bored. Like a magician, the skilled screenwriter misdirects audience expectations, then surprises them with an unexpected solution. The plot must be unpredictable and the resolution must be unexpected, yet believable and satisfying.

If the plot is predictable, it may be too familiar and generic. Use plot reversals and setbacks early in your screenplay to establish that anything can happen. Use misdirection to fool the audience and keep them on their toes. Reveal information as late as possible. Keep your ending in doubt with several possible end scenarios.

- Is your plot generic and familiar?
- Are you keeping the audience guessing?
- Are you holding back revealing secrets and lies?
- Is the outcome of the screenplay in doubt?
- Are there several possible end scenarios?
- Does the main character chase their want but get their need instead?

Final Thoughts

As you consider your plot revisions, increase the emotional stakes for your main character by tying the main character's flaws to specific plot events. Turn plot beats into character/plot beats. Plot events must have personal consequences. By linking plot events to the main character's story, your screenplay will be more cohesive and focused. Use plot as a series of tests for the main character.

The harder the test—the more interesting the contest—the more deserving the victory.

A good plot is unexpected. It cannot travel the familiar and predictable. It must have highs and lows, unexpected surprises, and challenge the main character each step of the way. Events by themselves are only mildly entertaining. Unless there is a character the audience deeply cares about, the plot will just be a series of events. The challenge is to strike the right balance between character and plot.

14

Feedback on Your Interim Draft

Checking-In

*Writing really is a process of discovery. The biggest enemy is being satisfied.
When I think, "Oh, this is so great. They can't change a word. They've got
to film it exactly like this," that's when I know I'm not pushing hard enough.
That's when you have to be most suspicious.*

William Broyles, Jr., Screenwriter,
Flags of Our Fathers, Cast Away, Apollo 13

Once you have completed several passes and your screenplay is taking shape, it
may be helpful to get feedback from a trusted source to make sure you are on
track. If you are off on a tangent or not addressing your character, theme, and
plot notes effectively, it's better to step back and do another pass on these areas
before you move forward. For this to be effective, you must have significantly
reworked your screenplay so there is new work to review.

Beware that you are opening yourself up to notes, and notes are always
unpredictable. You could receive notes that might feel like a setback and
undermine your confidence. If you feel confident and are writing with
momentum, then you may not want notes at this stage in your rewrite. If you are
on a roll, you might want to keep rolling. But at some point before you send out
your draft, you *do* need to get feedback. It's up to you to determine the best time
during your rewrite to have your screenplay read.

Pick One Trusted Reader

Rewriting is like being in the middle of a dense fog. You think you know where
you are headed, but it's easy to veer off course. If you have lingering questions,
then the key is to give your current draft to someone you trust, someone you
know, and someone who has been reliable in the past. Rather than open yourself

up to another full set of notes, pick one trusted person to read your interim draft. This must be a person you respect, and who has given you notes previously, so you know what to expect.

For your initial set of notes, you wanted hard notes, but for an interim draft, you need smart notes. Be careful about giving this draft to your writers group. A writers group can open the door to a flood of notes. Absolutely do not give this pass to "Mister I-Am-Critical-of-Everything." In your vulnerable state of mind, you want to explicitly trust the person giving you notes. The last thing you need now is to lose confidence. You're looking for that one person who gets your idea, understands this is a work in progress, and can give you constructive notes.

Set the Ground Rules

You *do* need to give the reader clear instructions on the areas they should cover. Remind the reader this is a work in progress and there are a lot of things you are planning to fix in future passes. You might even point out a few of these future fixes. This will help the reader ignore glaring problems if they know you are planning to address them in the future. Make sure the reader is aware you are not looking for a complete set of notes.

Keep the Conversation Short and Focused

When you were getting first draft notes, I strongly recommended you just listen and not explain your screenplay. Either it worked or it didn't, and you can't convince people otherwise. At this stage in your rewrite, it is important that you lead the discussion and ask pointed questions about the areas of concern. If the discussion goes in another direction, refocus the discussion. "That's something I'm planning to work on in the next pass, but I want to continue with your thoughts about the structure."

Keep the session short, about thirty minutes. The longer it runs, the deeper the notes will go, and the session could turn counterproductive. On the other hand, if the discussion continues to be valuable, let it run longer. Cut off the discussion once you have gotten what you need. Do not solicit deeper notes unless the reader is insightful and helps to *solve* problems. It can be tremendously helpful to have a sounding board to bounce ideas against. Verbalizing problems can lead to quicker solutions. Remember to record all your note sessions. You want to be part of the discussion and not just a note taker. Later, review your note sessions.

Ask Pointed Questions

Always start with the positive: "What did you like?" Do not ask leading questions such as: "I changed my main character to ABC. Did it work for you?" Instead, better to ask open-ended questions.

- Where did you feel the character was strongest?
- What was the weakest aspect of the character?
- How could I strengthen the character?

Try not to phrase the question in a judgmental way: "Did the plot read better for you?" Instead, you might ask:

- What are your thoughts about the plot?
- What areas worked for you?
- Where were you bored?

Invite them to give you a critique on the plot. Ask them to identify where you have done good work. If the reader likes something, pursue why they like it and how you might build similar scenes and moments. This should be more a creative discussion than a note session. You can open up your process. This is the first of several passes where you deepen the characters and their stories with each successive pass.

Once you are in discussion and have a sense of how the reader is responding, you can explain what you were trying to accomplish. "I was trying to do XYZ, but maybe I should be doing DEF. What are your thoughts about that?" It is okay to discuss your work in progress as long as you are open to hearing the reader's ideas at this stage. Again, this should be a person you respect who understands screenplays and stories. Do not argue if the reader misses something. You must assume it wasn't there and you need to do more work.

Early Notes from the Studio

If you are involved with a studio or a producer, *never* let them look at an interim draft. Even if they say they understand it's a work in progress—they don't.

An incomplete draft could make them lose confidence. While a fellow writer understands the writing process, studio execs and producers who do not write, nor fully understand the writing process, will think this is your finished draft. The first impression is the last impression.

If you are working with a director, and you have confidence in them, you may show them some scenes to get their feedback. Good confident directors can be a terrific creative partner and help you continue to focus your rewrite. But anything you show a director must be committed and specific. I worked with a director who wanted pages virtually every day, and I ended up chasing my tail. That kind of micromanagement does not yield a better screenplay.

Everyone wants the draft "yesterday," so being fast is almost as important as being good. Don't hand in junk—they will know it is junk—but you can learn to write faster by making better character and story decisions earlier in the process. The more you work through these multiple passes, the better you will be at making the right decisions first.

Final Thoughts

The only reason to get interim feedback on your work in progress is to make sure you are on the right track and to give you a bit of guidance along the way. Better to catch flaws now than to continue to build on a weak foundation. You should also be adjusting your game plan as you move through your passes. Hopefully, you have discovered and developed new ideas and directions, and adjusted your game plan accordingly.

Take satisfaction in the areas where you are succeeding, and apply yourself to the areas that need more work. Continue to deepen and add dimension with each new pass. Do not be discouraged by any feedback. What you are trying to do is enormously difficult. Use critiques to grow. Writers that refuse to give up, and push themselves to go deeper, will grow and succeed in the end. You are in the early stages of your marathon so it is important to continue to pace yourself for the long haul. Be in the moment.

Part Two

Layering and Details

15

Opposition Characters

Sources of Conflict and Tension

I always look for amazing characters who I find are fascinating, charming, flawed, romantic and in trouble. These are the key elements.

David O. Russell, Writer/Director,
Three Kings, Silver Linings Playbook, American Hustle

Every character in your screenplay is a potential source of conflict and tension for the main character. The main character must be under constant stress and pressure, and a great deal of that pressure comes from characters and relationships that are closest to them. No matter where they turn, the main character must face resistance each step of the way. Resistance breeds conflict, and conflict is the lifeblood of good storytelling.

While most aspiring writers understand the role of the antagonist, often they do not grasp that the main character must be surrounded by conflict, tension, and resistance. The antagonist cannot supply all the conflict in a screenplay. There needs to be multiple sources of conflict and tension in all aspects of the main character's life. These sources of conflict must be of varying degrees. From minor misunderstandings to outright confrontations, each element of conflict intensifies the main character's struggle.

No Safe Port in the Storm

The main character is in the midst of a life-altering crisis. Their life is a shambles, their relationships are under stress, and their future is unclear. They have personal issues they don't want to face, and if they do not succeed in achieving their goal, their life will be an utter failure. To make matters worse, at every step along the way, they are faced with resistance and conflict. Their closest friends are critical of them, their goal is seemingly unattainable, and they are facing a crisis of confidence. On top of all this, they are facing opposition from their lover, their best friend, their parents, their coworkers, a megalomaniac, the Russian Army, and they have to climb the Swiss Alps in the dead of winter . . . . The list is endless.

The main character must have no place to turn for relief from their problems. Each aspect of the main character's life should be causing them some degree of difficulty. The main character's journey should be fraught with endless complications and obstacles. Their relationships should be troublesome and their personal story should be in turmoil. In other words, the main character must be challenged to solve one problem after another. Relief can only come once the main character faces their personal issues and resolves the main plot problem.

Opposition Characters

Every major character in your screenplay must offer some degree of opposition to the main character's want. Their opposition can be subtle or can be fierce. In addition to resisting the main character's want, opposition characters must also pressure the main character's story. The main character's failure to face their personal issues complicates their relationships and thereby continues to increase the pressure.

- In *The Imitation Game*, Alan Turing faces strong opposition from every direction. From his supervisor, his teammates, his girlfriend, and a police detective, Turing faces constant resistance and conflict. He also struggles with tremendous inner turmoil trying to reconcile his sexuality with society's judgmental rules.
- In *Little Miss Sunshine*, virtually every character in the van is in opposition to one another. The degree of opposition is different with each relationship. Richard is in conflict with his wife, Sheryl; his brother-in-law, Frank; his son, Dwayne; and his father. In addition, he's also fighting with his book agent. Dwayne has stopped talking and can't wait to escape the family. Frank tried to commit suicide and is on suicide watch. Grandpa is doing heroin and pushing Richard to be a better father.

- In *Guardians of the Galaxy*, the Guardians, bickering adversaries, establish an uneasy truce to get the orb and sell it for billions. Each character has a different motivation to get the orb. They are at each other's throats until they let go of their differences and join forces. The fun of the movie is the tension and animosity between the characters.

Opposition characters do not have to be the "bad guys." An opposition character can be the best friend or a lover. They need to have their own agenda which puts them into conflict with the main character's agenda. Each major character in your screenplay must have a personal history, and bring their baggage and scars to their relationships.

Main Opposition Character—The Antagonist

The antagonist is the main character's adversary, and in a Hollywood film, usually supplies the majority of the conflict and tension in the screenplay. A common mistake is to make the antagonist a one-dimensional cardboard character that is "evil for evil's sake." The same care and attention that goes into creating a multidimensional main character must also go into developing the antagonist. Both characters need internal stories, but the antagonist does not have an epiphany and transform. They do not learn from their mistakes.

- Strong antagonists live by their own set of rules.
- They have no ethical or moral concerns or constraints.
- They don't see themselves as evil or criminal.
- They see themselves as opportunists.
- The antagonist's actions must be motivated.
- There must be a personal reason for their actions beyond simple greed or power.

The main character's journey can only be as difficult as the antagonist's fierce determination to achieve their agenda and keep the main character from achieving their goals. This battle of wills feeds the central plot and is the main source of conflict and tension throughout the screenplay.

- In *In the Line of Fire*, Mitch Leary, was fired by the CIA and feels betrayed and unappreciated by the government. He is going to show them how good an agent he was by daring the CIA to catch him before he kills the president.

He believes he's better than the rest of the agents, and enjoys tormenting Secret Service Agent Frank Horrigan by playing cat and mouse with him.

- In *One Flew Over the Cuckoo's Nest*, Nurse Ratchet controls her ward with an iron hand. McMurphy is a threat to her control and power. After McMurphy appears to get the upper hand, Nurse Ratchet uses her authority to neutralize McMurphy once and for all.

The best battles are personal battles where there is more on the line than just achieving agendas. The more you personalize the antagonist's motivation, the stronger the character, and the more intense the battle between the antagonist and the main character. It really does have to be personal this time.

Not Every Film Has An Antagonist

Independent films tend to be more character driven and often do not have a traditional central antagonist. In character driven films, instead of plot complications, the stories are about characters needing to look deep inside themselves to face truths they have been avoiding their entire lives. The conflict and tension comes out of characters with complex personal issues and dysfunctional relationships. It is essential that the major characters have personal stories and crises which further complicate their messy relationships. The subtlety and nuances between the characters and their relationships is usually being explored. Therefore, in place of the traditional antagonist, independent films need strong opposition characters.

- In the film *50/50*, Adam is battling cancer, but in addition, his girlfriend, Rachael, is cheating on him; his overbearing mother is smothering him; his best friend, Kyle, seems to be totally oblivious that Adam is possibly dying of cancer; and his therapist, Katherine, is inexperienced and ineffective. Everywhere Adam turns he is met with opposition, tension, and resistance. While they may love him, each character has their own agenda which in turn adds to Adam's confusion.

Opposition characters do not have to be against the main character. Since everyone, including the main character, is pursuing their own self-interests, this naturally puts the characters into conflict. In addition, the opposition character's relationships are also under stress and falling apart. In independent films, the plot conflict may not be the major issue to resolve. The plot problem often acts as a device to pressure the characters and force them to face their issues once and for all.

Measure Your Conflict

On a ten-point scale, go through your screenplay and give a numeral value to the conflict in each scene. In addition, note the source of the conflict and tension in each scene. Note whether the conflict comes from the plot, the main character's personal story, opposition characters, or the antagonist. Be even more specific and list which type of characters are supplying the conflict. Are they the love interest, close friend, supervisor, authority figure, adversary, or antagonist?

Look for multiple sources and different degrees of conflict throughout your screenplay. You should see peaks and valleys, and the numbers should fluctuate. The numbers should be higher the closer you get to the end of the second act, until they reach their peak during the third act climax.

If the numbers are low, then you clearly need to add more conflict. If your numbers are all the same, then create more ups and downs. Modulation and variety help the rhythm and tempo of your screenplay. If your conflict is only coming from one main source such as the antagonist, then you need to spread out the conflict and tension in your screenplay across more characters and relationships.

Final Thoughts

The main character is in the midst of a life-altering crisis, and everywhere they turn they are faced with more conflict, tension, and resistance. They are surrounded by friends, family, and adversaries with their own competing agendas that make the main character's life more difficult. By creating opposition characters, you greatly increase the number of conflicts in your screenplay and produce a much stronger second act. There can be no safe port in the storm for the main character until they face their personal issues and resolve the main plot problem.

Complications, Obstacles, Reveals, and Reversals

Complicate, Complicate, Complicate

As a writer, before I create anything I often think, "What are the obstacles?"
Cameron Crowe, Writer/Director,
Jerry McGuire, Almost Famous

Complications, obstacles, reveals, and reversals are some of the most important tools in the screenwriter's tool box. Together, they make the main character's life more difficult and the plot infinitely more interesting. They make the movie unpredictable and keep the audience on their toes. Used separately or combined, they enhance any scene or sequence.

The closer the main character gets to the end of the second act, the more intense their journey must become. But the writer must complicate and reveal more than just the plot. The writer must complicate the main character's internal story as well as their major relationships. Complications, obstacles, reveals, and reversals help make the main character's journey difficult, if not impossible.

Complications

Complications are small problems that make life more complex and difficult for the main character. They can also be small hindrances that keep the main character from achieving their goal in a scene. They need to be solved in the moment. These little problems make each scene more interesting and more real. They also create suspense, tension, and anxiety. Add a "ticking clock" to a series of complications, and you heighten the tension exponentially.

- In *Mission Impossible*, Agent Ethan Hunt must drop from the ceiling into a secure vault. If Hunt had a fake ID card and passed each level of security without any problem, this would be a boring scene. Instead, he has to crawl through a vent, drop from the ceiling, hang suspended over the floor, and outwit multiple laser detectors, until, ironically, a single drop of sweat almost undoes the entire operation. One complication after another.

In addition to scene and plot complications, there are also relationship complications.

- In *The King's Speech*, Lionel Logue is a speech therapist, but when his patient is the King of England, and both men are stubborn and headstrong, their relationship becomes complicated.
- In *Erin Brockovich*, Erin's relentless search for evidence against PG&E for polluting groundwater complicates her relationship with her boyfriend. Ultimately, she must choose between her career and her relationship.

Complications make scenes infinitely more interesting and the character's life more difficult. The key to creating effective physical complications is to make them small, but difficult to solve. They also show that the main character is not a super human and everything does not go right for them all the time. Emotional complications also make the main character's life more difficult and complicate their internal story.

Obstacles

An obstacle is a formidable challenge the main character must overcome. Where complications are small problems, obstacles are figurative mountains which block the main character's path. Obstacles work in opposition to the main character's journey. The road must have many significant obstacles to test the main character's mettle, and pressure their personal story. An obstacle must plant doubt in the audience's mind as to whether it can be overcome. Obstacles also present opportunities for the main character to show off their capacity to problem-solve. The main character may not be stronger than his opponent, but they must be more clever. The audience values brains over brawn.

A screenplay can have an infinite number of small complications, but a limited number of large obstacles. Each obstacle should be significant and difficult to solve, and have an effect on the main character and their story. Obstacles can take many scenes or an entire sequence to overcome. Like complications, obstacles can by physical or psychological, or sometimes both.

One Flew Over The Cuckoo's Nest has many obstacles that challenge McMurphy.

1. Nurse Ratchet is a formidable opponent. She is an obstacle to McMurphy running the show and having a good time. McMurphy must find a way to either neutralize Nurse Ratchet or go around her.
2. The locked windows and doors, as well as the barbed wire surrounding the asylum, are obstacles to McMurphy's escape. He must find a way to escape his new prison.
3. The law which puts McMurphy's future entirely in the hands of the doctors and nurses who run the institution is an obstacle to his freedom. McMurphy must find a way to convince them that he is a changed man.
4. McMurphy's defiance of authority is a personal obstacle. To overcome this, McMurphy would need to change and become subservient to authority— which he refuses to do, and therefore he suffers the consequences.

Reveals

A reveal is when significant new information about a character or the plot is presented to the audience through dialogue or visual imagery. The reveal may be important information about the main character's emotional state of mind, their secrets or lies, or new plot information. Well-placed reveals are important tools which energize the second act and further complicate a screenplay. They must be strategically placed and used sparingly to avoid the feeling of melodrama.

- Reveals energize a screenplay because each new bit of information changes everything that follows. One of the most surprising reveals of all time is in *Star Wars: Episode V—The Empire Strikes Back* when Darth Vader reveals to Luke Skywalker that he is his father. That one statement changed everything for Luke as well as for the audience.
- There are emotional reveals, such as in *Good Will Hunting*, when Will reveals that he was the victim of extreme physical abuse. It helps the audience understand Will's self-destructive behavior.
- Another important reveal in *Good Will Hunting* is when Sean, Will's therapist, reveals that his wife died recently. Will uses that information

about Sean's vulnerability to attack Sean emotionally. This reveal adds depth to the character as well as a source of conflict between them.

- Reveals also create suspense. In thrillers and slasher films, the audience often knows more than the character, which creates tension and suspense. In *Psycho*, the audience knows that Norman Bates' mother is a vicious murderer and lives in the upstairs bedroom. When detective Arbogast sneaks into the Bates' house, and starts up the steps calling for Mrs. Bates, the audience fears for the detective's life.

- In addition to plot reveals, there are also character and relationship reveals. In the iconic taxi scene from *On the Waterfront*, Terry Malloy reveals the depth of his inner despair about his wasted opportunity to have a shot at the title, and have dignity and respect. This is a startling reveal and helps to clarify a lot about Terry's personal story. Terry suddenly becomes a deeper, sympathetic character.

Reveals bring new knowledge and understanding to your screenplay. Reveals add new layers and dimensions to your characters and their stories. Character reveals add depth to your characters and deepen the emotional stakes. Plot reveals create new complications and obstacles. Be strategic about where you place your reveals. Fight the tendency to reveal too much in the opening of your screenplay. Hold back some essential information to reveal along the way so that each reveal has a significant effect on your screenplay. Each reveal adds energy to your screenplay and raises the stakes.

Reversals

A reversal is an unexpected setback or defeat for the main character—a change of fortune. Not only does the main character lose ground, but also they find themselves in a deeper hole than where they started. One step forward, two steps back. The main character is now faced with an even more formidable challenge. These can be physical reversals and/or emotional reversals. Significant reversals also pressure the main character's personal story.

Reversals raise the stakes significantly to prove the main character's mettle. The way a character handles a reversal says a lot about them. The main character has lost ground and must fight harder to achieve their goal. There are also positive reversals, when the main character overcomes adversity and effects a positive change. Reversals keep the screenplay unpredictable and signal anything can happen. Use reversals throughout the second act to keep the narrative active and unpredictable.

- In *Toy Story*, Woody suffers a reversal of fortune when Buzz arrives and takes his spot on Andy's bed. Woody goes from being number one, to just another toy. Woody later suffers another more serious reversal when the toys turn against him and accuse him of intentionally knocking Buzz out the window.
- In *Little Miss Sunshine*, Richard suffers a reversal when no one is interested in publishing his book. Dwayne suffers a reversal when he learns he is color blind and can't realize his dream to fly for the Air Force.
- A character can also face relationship reversals. In *Crazy Heart*, Bad Blake suffers a relationship reversal when his girlfriend abruptly ends their relationship after Blake loses her son in a crowded bar. This is a devastating emotional loss for Blake, but also the pivotal event that forces him to seek help for his addiction.

A good plot should never be a straight line, but should resemble an obstacle course or a maze with all kinds of difficulties and setbacks. The harder it is for the main character to reach their destination, the more interesting the screenplay, and the more the audience roots for them to succeed. Through the main character's struggles and attempts to persevere, the audience gains respect for them and believes they have earned the ending.

Opening Sequence of Raiders of the Lost Ark

Raiders of the Lost Ark uses reversals as a plot technique. Many times Indy seems to have the upper hand only to suffer a setback when his nemesis, Belloq, turns the tables on him. The opening sequence of *Raiders* has a several quick reversals.

1. Indy finds the cave entrance to the hidden treasure only to have one of his expedition partners, Barranca, turn traitor and pull a gun on him. *Reversal.*
2. Indy cracks his bullwhip and pulls the gun from Barranca's hand. *Reversal.*
3. Indy enters the cave and finds the golden idol on a pedestal. Carefully, he switches the idol with a bag of sand. But the bag of sand is not heavy enough and the tomb begins to shut down. *Reversal.*

4. As the tomb is shutting down, Indy's guide, Satipo uses a bullwhip to swing over the pit. Satipo lands on the other side with the bullwhip in his hand. He gets Indy to throw him golden idol, but Satipo refuses to throw him the whip, leaving Indy stranded on the other side of the pit. *Reversal*.
5. Indy jumps across the pit and rolls under the descending slab just in time. He finds Satipo impaled on spikes, eyes wide in surprise. Indy grabs the idol. *Reversal*.
6. Indy escapes the giant rolling stone ball and lands at the feet of his nemesis, Belloq. He takes the idol from Indy. *Reversal*.
7. Before Belloq's Indians can kill Indy, he escapes into the jungle and eventually onto a waiting amphibious plane that quickly takes off. *Reversal*.

These are short reversals that work as scene complications. Plot reversals are larger problems that have significant impact on the main character's personal story. The bigger the reversal—the bigger the impact on the main character.

Final Sequence of Toy Story

The climactic sequence to the first *Toy Story* is a brilliant example of how to effectively combine complications, obstacles, and reversals to heighten tension, conflict, and suspense. To set the scene: With the help of the Lost Toys, Woody turns the tables on Sid and scares him away. Woody and Buzz rush to the fence and see Andy's family packing a minivan to move to their new house.

TOY STORY FINAL SEQUENCE

1. Woody and Buzz run to look through the fence. The family minivan's motor starts. Woody presses through the openings between the fence, but Buzz gets stuck because of the rocket attached to his back. *Complication*.
2. Woody hops on the back of the minivan and grabs hold of the rear windshield wiper. He looks back to see Buzz stuck in the fence. Buzz tells Woody to leave him and he'll catch up. *Complication*.
3. Woody jumps off the minivan to help Buzz. *Complication*.
4. Woody frees Buzz from the fence, but before they can reach the minivan, it disappears up the street. *Reversal*.

5. In the street, the family's moving van barrels toward Woody and Buzz. They roll between the wheels. *Complication.*

6. Woody and Buzz chase after the moving van. *Complication.*

7. Sid's dog, Scud, sees Woody and Buzz in the street and takes off after them, growling. *Obstacle.*

8. Buzz catches up to the moving van, grabs a long strap hanging from the back, and climbs onto the truck bed. *Complication.*

9. Woody misses the strap, but then grabs on. *Complication.*

10. Scud grabs Woody's foot and tries to rip him off the strap. *Complication.*

11. Buzz leaps on the vicious dog to help rescue Woody. (Sacrifice and friendship is the theme of this sequence.) *Complication.*

12. Buzz flaps the dog's eyelids and the dog releases Woody. *Complication.*

13. Woody hangs on the strap and Buzz is left behind in the dog's mouth. *Reversal.*

14. Woody climbs up the strap, unhooks the latch, but can't open the moving van's door. *Complication.*

15. Red light. The moving van stops. Momentum opens the rear door, sending Woody into the air hanging from the strap. *Complication.*

16. Scud viciously shakes Buzz and flips him under a parked car. *Reversal.*

17. Woody drops into the back of the moving van, frantically searches the boxes, finds the electric car, and pushes it out of the truck. Based on Woody's previous behavior, the Toys misinterpret Woody's actions and believe Woody is throwing another toy away. *Complication.*

18. From the back of the moving van, Woody uses remote control to steer the electric car to Buzz. Buzz jumps on the car and Woody drives it back toward the moving van. Scud gives chase. *Complication.*

19. Green light. The moving van takes off again. *Complication.*

20. The Toys rush Woody. *Complication.*

21. Scud is close to catching Buzz. *Complication.*

22. The Muscle Man spins Woody above his head which causes the electric car with Buzz to spin in circles on the street eluding Scud. *Complication.*

23. Buzz hangs on as the electric car races toward a busy intersection. *Complication.*

24. In the intersection, Buzz slides under several cars narrowly avoiding disaster. A car swerves to avoid hitting Scud, but hits another car causing a five car smashup. Scud is boxed-in by the accident. Buzz narrowly escapes. *Reversal.*

25. The Toys throw Woody off the back of the moving van. It disappears into the distance. *Reversal.*

26. Woody rolls out of the way as a car horn blares. He narrowly misses being flattened. *Complication.*

27. Woody and Buzz reunite and chase the moving van in the electric car. Woody almost hits a car but quickly steers under it. Woody shifts the electric car into turbo. *Complication.*

28. Bo Peep uses the binoculars to see Woody has rescued Buzz and is trying to catch up to the moving van. The Toys realize their mistake and now try to help them. *Reveal and reversal.*

29. Muscle Man lowers the ramp so Woody can drive the electric can onto the moving van. The metal ramp flips over and almost smashes Woody and Buzz. They swerve barely maintaining control. *Complication.*

30. Slink jumps down so they can grab his tail. *Complication.*

31. At the moment Woody and Slink join hand and paw, the electric car's battery starts to run down and lose speed. *Complication.*

32. Slink's coiled body stretches out. Woody and Buzz fishtail behind the moving van, narrowly missing parked cars. *Complication.*

33. Slink cannot hold on and lets go. *Complication.*

34. Woody and Buzz are once again separated from the Toys and the moving van. The batteries run out and the electric car comes to a stop. So close, yet so far. *Reversal.*

35. Buzz realizes he has the rocket on his back and Woody has the match. *Reversal.*

36. Just as Woody lights the match to light the rocket, a car zooms by and extinguishes the match. *Reversal.*

37. Woody and Buzz hang their heads. Buzz's helmet focuses the sun on Woody's hand and burns him. Woody grabs Buzz's helmet and lights the fuse. *Reversal.*

38. The electric car takes off at a high rate of speed past cars in the center of the road. *Complication.*

39. As they get closer to the moving van, the electric car leaves the ground and flies. Buzz holds tight to Woody and Woody holds onto the car. Forces pull them apart. *Complication.*

40. Woody lets go of the car and it sails into the back of the moving van. With the rocket propelling them, Woody and Buzz head up into the sky. *Complication.*

41. Woody and Buzz go straight up, higher and higher. The rocket is about to blow up. *Complication.*
42. Buzz pushes a button on his space suit and disconnects from the rocket which blows up seconds later. Woody and Buzz fall straight down. *Reversal and complication.*
43. Holding Woody, Buzz pulls up just before they hit the ground. *Complication.*
44. Buzz misses the open back door to the moving van and flies past. *Complication.*
45. Buzz aims for family minivan's sunroof and lands in Andy's toy box. Andy is surprised to see Woody and Buzz. All is well. *Reversal.*

In this climactic sequence, plot and character combine seamlessly for an emotionally fulfilling conclusion to the film. It takes a lot of work and ingenuity, but Woody and Buzz earn their place beside Andy. This sequence uses complications, obstacles, and reversals brilliantly to create an exciting climax to the film, and also completes Buzz and Woody's personal stories to take their relationship to a new level. If Buzz and Woody had not learned from their early mistakes to grow emotionally and respect each other, they never would have gotten back to Andy. Their own personal growth enables them to sacrifice for each other and work as a team.

The Back Half of the Second Act
Where Screenplays Go to Die

The back half of the second act is the place where most screenplays run out of steam. It is also where you can ratchet up complications, obstacles, reveals, and reversals. Complicate each character's story and relationships, as well as the overall plotline. The closer the main character gets to the end of the second act, the more things must get worse and more complex.

Your main character is like a sword fighter fending off multiple assailants. The attacks should be a mix of personal, emotional, and physical challenges. Some of these challenges are large obstacles and others may be a series of small complications. The main character must suffer reversals which test their mettle and force them to earn the ending. No matter where they turn, the main character is under siege in another aspect of their life.

If the back half of your second act is flat, the problem can be found in your set-up. Who and what you establish in the Set-Up is who and what you will complicate in the back half of the second act. Failure to set up your characters, their relationships, and multiple plot problems will not give you enough material to complicate the second act.

Final Thoughts

It is easy to dismiss complications, obstacles, reveals, and reversals as mere plot tricks. Nothing could be further from the truth. These are essential storytelling tools that make any story more exciting and unpredictable. Complications, obstacles, reveals, and reversals intensify the main character's problems physically and emotionally. The main character's journey should go from bad to worse to a nightmare.

Everything is execution and these tools are no exception. If reveals and reversals are well motivated and come out of the main character's story or the dramatic situation, they will feel organic and holistic to the plot. If they are summarily imposed upon the main character out of nowhere, they will feel like plot tricks.

Practice using these tools and they will soon become second nature to you. You will quickly find you cannot tell a story without them, and your screenplays will become infinitely more interesting because of them.

Complications, Obstacles, Reveals, and Reversals Pass

Making Life Much More Difficult

You know, everybody writes differently. But for me I have to stick—really closely, like it's a life raft—to intention and obstacles. Just the basics of somebody wants something, something is standing in their way of getting it. Make sure you have that cemented in place.

Aaron Sorkin, Screenwriter/Playwright,
A Few Good Men, West Wing, The Social Network

Your main character must face a number of physical, psychological, and emotional challenges. The audience must continually ask: Is the main character up to the challenge? Your main character's path to the third act confrontation and climax must be fraught with problems, setbacks, hurdles, and roadblocks. Creating these challenges for your main character requires: complications, obstacles, reveals, and reversals. These four screenwriting elements must pressure the main character's story.

As you progress with your rewrite, look for ways to tighten and unify your screenplay. In this chapter, you will focus on creating more tension, suspense, conflict, and movie moments. Heightening conflict and tension improves any screenplay.

Objectives for Your Complications, Obstacles, Reveals, and Reversals Pass

- Increase the tension and conflict in your scenes and screenplay.
- Hold back information to create more character mystery and suspense.
- Make the main character's journey more difficult and complicated.

- Add more peaks and valleys for your main character to traverse.
- Energize the second act.
- Make your screenplay less predictable and repetitious.
- Make your screenplay more exciting to read.

Obstacles and Complications Notes

No one is going to give you notes that say you should add more complications and obstacles. Complication and obstacle notes come in the form of plot and character notes. Make the characters and plot more interesting by making their lives and relationships more complicated. To solve these notes, look at your individual scenes and sequences. See how you can increase the degree of difficulty of each problem, as well as add new complications and obstacles.

Complications, Obstacles, Reveals, and Reversals Notes

The Note:	Potential Solutions:
The screenplay is slow.	Central Dramatic Conflict*, Complications, Obstacles, Reveals, Reversals, Antagonist*, Four Major High Points*, Subplots, Plot*
The story seems repetitious.	Complications, Obstacles, Reveals, Reversals, Want*, Antagonist*, Opposition Characters*, Relationships*, Four Major High Points
The main character seems to solve things too easily.	Complications, Obstacles, Reveals, Reversals, Antagonist*, Opposition Characters*
The main character doesn't have enough challenges. It's way too easy.	Complications, Obstacles, Reveals, Reversals, Central Dramatic Conflict*, Antagonist*, Opposition Characters*, Relationships*
The stakes are not high enough.	Internal Character Story*, Obstacles, Reveals, Reversals, Stakes*, Key Relationship*, Want*
The scenes are flat.	Conflict*, Tension*, Attitude*, Complications, Reveals, Reversals, Relationships*, Opposition Characters*
The ending doesn't seem big enough.	Internal Character Story*, Character Arc, Want*, Need*, Complications, Obstacles, Key Relationship*, Stakes*, Antagonist*, Opposition Characters*, Set Pieces*, Four Major High Points

*See index: concept found in other chapter.

Scene Complications—One Thing After Another

Scene complications are small problems that make the main character's journey more difficult and stressful. Complications create tension and immediate problems for the main character to solve. There can be physical complications, relationship complications, and time complications. Scenes can have a single complication or a series of complications that leads to an unexpected result. The more complicated the task, the more interesting it is for the audience.

- In the opening minutes of *Toy Story*, when one of the green army rangers is accidentally stepped on, there is a series of complications as his fellow rangers try to retrieve the wounded soldier. They have to go through an elaborate routine to escape detection from the humans and save their comrade. If they could save the wounded soldier easily, there would be no scene. All the small problems they have to solve heighten the tension and the audience's concern for the fallen ranger.

If your scenes are flat, look for places to increase the tension and conflict by adding complications. Complications make scenes inherently more interesting and tense. Go through your draft scene by scene and make a list of your scene complications. Review the tension of each scene and look for places to add one or two compilations to make your scene more interesting.

- Are you using complications effectively in your scenes to create tension?
- Can you find other places in your scenes to add more small complications?

Relationship Complications—It's Going To Be Complicated

In your rewrite, you can address many of your conflict and tension notes by making your main character's major relationships more complicated. Complications are not only small little problems to solve; they also set up character and relationship issues.

- In *Good Will Hunting*, Will has low self-esteem so he lies to Skylar to make her believe he is a student at Harvard when in reality he's a janitor at Harvard. Will's lie seriously complicates their relationship. To keep up the pretense, Will has to continue lying to Skylar. The lie adds dynamic tension to their relationship and leads to additional complications which eventually undercut their relationship.

Examine your major relationships for ways to complicate each relationship. Secrets, lies, betrayals, or duplicity can be used to significantly complicate a major relationship. Remember, relationships going bad are infinitely more interesting than happy supporting relationships.

- Are you using complications to make your relationships more interesting?
- Do your relationship complications challenge the main character?
- Do your relationship complications reveal something important about the main character?

Obstacles—And Now They Face An Even Bigger Hurdle

Obstacles are figurative mountains the main character must conquer. Obstacles can be physical or emotional. Unlike complications, obstacles can take many scenes, or an entire sequence, to resolve. Obstacles keep the second act active and force the main character to confront new challenges. The closer the main character comes to the end of their journey, the greater the obstacles.

- In *Die Hard*, McClane is faced with the obstacle of hiding out on an upper floor with no weapons and two of the Gruber's henchmen on their way to kill him. He has to find a way to neutralize the threat, and save his wife and other hostages.

If you are getting notes that there isn't enough conflict or that your screenplay seems repetitive, then create several significant obstacles to challenge your main character. Aim for three or four major obstacles in your screenplay as well as several minor obstacles. As you get near the end of the second act, the obstacles must become larger and more formidable. Make sure your obstacles test the main character's flaws.

- Do you have three or four significant obstacles in your screenplay?
- Are your obstacles difficult to resolve?
- Do your obstacles take several scenes to resolve?
- Are your obstacles spread throughout the screenplay?

- Do your obstacles challenge and test the main character's story?
- Do your obstacles get bigger and more difficult as the screenplay progresses toward the end of the second act?

Reveals—New Information Creates Energy

A screenplay must build momentum to become more exciting and complicated as it moves through the second act toward the final climax. To keep your screenplay active and interesting, new information must be revealed throughout your screenplay—not just in the opening. This new information may be secrets, lies, motivations, alliances, or betrayals. Reveals change the status quo and create new tensions and conflicts. They also change the nature of relationships, which in turn changes the conflict between the characters. Reveals can also raise the stakes.

- There are reveals when a character bears their soul. In *Erin Brockovich*, she reveals that she was once a beauty queen and believed that she could make a difference and change the world. Now she finds herself a failure and a fool for believing her silly dreams.
- There are plot reveals where new information radically affects the main character. In *One Flew Over the Cuckoo's Nest*, McMurphy is shocked to learn that his release from the asylum is controlled by his nemesis, Nurse Ratchet. This reveal is a major setback for McMurphy and significantly raises the stakes. This is an example of a reveal and a reversal.

For notes that your screenplay is predictable, or that there is not enough conflict, review how and where you are using reveals. You should have several significant reveals in your screenplay. See if you can hold back important information to a more strategic time in the screenplay. If you do not have enough reveals, then try to add them to key places such as the end of the first act, the mid-point, and the end of the second act. You may need to add more secrets and lies, alliances and betrayals, to your characters and plot.

- What is the least information the audience needs to know to follow the story?
- Do you have significant reveals throughout your second act?
- Do you have enough surprises in your screenplay?
- Is your antagonist holding a few trump cards to play later on?
- Are you tracking your changes?

Your antagonist should also have significant reveals. Good antagonists do not show all their cards at the outset of the story. Remember, if you add a reveal you will need to adjust the characters, relationships, scenes, structure, and plot that follow. Always track your changes—link and connect.

Reversals—Just When It Was Going So Well

Reversals are not plot tricks or gimmicks but essential tools of good storytelling. To work effectively, reversals must pressure the main character's internal story. It is not only the surprise of the reversal that is important, but also the way the character emotionally reacts to each reversal that counts. Your main character should be on a physical as well as emotional roller-coaster ride—one step forward, two steps back. Adversity strengthens the main character and makes the case for character growth and change in the third act.

- In the opening of *Top Gun*, fighter pilot Cougar has a crisis of confidence and Maverick ends up taking Cougar's seat at the Navy Fighter Weapons School—a reversal of fortune. At Top Gun, Maverick wins his first engagement, but he also breaks a rule of engagement by going below the hard deck. His victory quickly turns into a loss—another reversal. When Goose dies, Maverick suffers a serious emotional reversal which severely shakes his confidence. Each reversal tests Maverick's resolve.

If your plot is repetitious or predictable, then look to add several well-placed reversals that work as setbacks for your main character. These reversals make your screenplay exciting and unpredictable. Make sure you have emotional reversals that test the main character's personal story as well as plot reversals that physically set them back. The aftereffects of a reversal will reverberate throughout the screenplay and be felt for many scenes that follow. This is cause and effect plotting.

- Do you have significant reversals in your screenplay?
- Do you have physical and emotional reversals?
- Do the reversals make your main character's life more difficult?
- Do the reversals affect other major characters and scenes?
- Ultimately, do the reversals make the main character stronger?

Final Thoughts

When possible, tie each obstacle or reversal to the main character's story. Challenge the main character's physical and emotional capacity, and probe their weaknesses. Reveals, reversals, complications, and obstacles are the cornerstones of good storytelling. You can't really tell a story without them. Learn how to use these elements effectively and eventually they will become second nature.

Reveals, reversals, complications, and obstacles make your screenplay infinitely more interesting. They address notes concerning conflict, tension, excitement, and stakes. They create ups and downs, and make the screenplay less predictable. When used effectively, these important screenwriting tools energize your screenplay and keep the plot fresh and unfolding.

Relationships

The Ties that Bind

The difference between books and movies is that books are about what happens within people, and movies are about what happens between people.
Ron Bass, Screenwriter,
Rain Man, Snow Falling On Cedars

One of the most important, yet often overlooked elements in screenwriting is relationships. Relationships contribute to all aspects of screenwriting including character, plot, theme, conflict, obstacles, and reversals. Just as we are defined by the people we associate with, so your characters are defined by the people they surround themselves with in your screenplay. The company a character keeps has great influence over them. In addition, the way a character acts in a relationship also defines them dramatically. There are positive supporting relationships, and negative dysfunctional relationships.

It is not enough to just create characters and put them in a scene together. Each character must have a clear story, and the writer must determine the nature and dynamic of each relationship. Not only does the main character have an arc, but each of the main character's major relationships needs an arc as well.

Making A Connection

Your main character should be struggling to make a connection. Maybe there are scars from their past that preclude them from forgiving and trusting again—Rick and Elsa in *Casablanca*; or maybe they are more in love than the person they are pursuing—Tom and Summer in *500 Days of Summer*; or maybe they are good friends who can't see the handwriting on the wall—Harry and Sally in *When Harry Met Sally*; or maybe the connection is strange and unwanted—Clarice and Hannibal Lecter in *The Silence of the Lambs*.

In a world of over seven billion people, it's amazing how hard it is to have a meaningful lasting relationship. Most relationships are short lived, and even when long term, they are fraught with problems. Our worst flaws are magnified in our relationships. We fall in love, fall out of love, lie, cheat, and betray each other. Connecting is one life's great challenges and most of us are pretty bad at it. Your screen characters should be pretty bad at it too. The main character's desperate attempt to make a meaningful connection is the basis of many, if not most, motion pictures. The plot carries the action, but the main character's attempt to make a connection, to find that one person who "gets them," is the emotional core of a screenplay.

- What human connection is your main character trying to make?
- Are they reaching out to the right person?
- If they are with the wrong person, will they be able to connect with the right person?
- What is keeping them from making the right connection?
- What do they learn over the course of their journey that helps them finally realize the importance of the connection?

Character Stories Contribute to Relationships

Strong relationships come down to character. For a relationship to work, each character in the relationship needs to have a story, agenda, and attitude. If a character has no story, then it is difficult, if not impossible, to create an authentic relationship. Since each character's internal story motivates their actions, characters without stories are one-dimensional and their relationships will be contrived.

You must be writing about people and not creating expositional devices to push the plot forward. Everyone in your screenplay should want something. Some are actively pursuing their agenda, while others are abject failures, feeling sorry for themselves. Who and what they are is up to you, but commit each character to a story or they will be cardboard characters. You cannot base a relationship on a cardboard character.

As an exercise, go through your major characters and answer these simple questions.

- What do they want?
- What is their personal agenda?

- What is their attitude?
- What is their flaw?
- What do they fear?
- What is their character arc?

Relationships are complex and that's what makes them interesting. Relationships help the main character or destroy them. It's the mix that is interesting. Relationships also pressure the main character and force them to live outside their comfort zone. They complicate the main character's life and make their journey much more difficult.

The Ties That Bind

To write an effective relationship, you have to understand the bond that ties the two characters together. The bond can be family, friends, marriage, work, or a common enemy. The list is endless. In some relationships bonds are built, while in others, bonds are destroyed. But the nature of each relationship is undergoing dramatic change. Often the ties that bind a relationship are for all the wrong reasons, and the relationship is doomed to fail. Bonds get pressured, broken, and reformed over the course of a movie.

Each character has a specific role they play in each relationship. They enter into the relationship with expectations such as friendship, protection, love, sex, or security.

Relationships are not all equal, and often, there is a dominant member of the relationship—a character who drives the relationship. In a father-son relationship, they both have different expectations about what they bring to the relationship as well as what they expect from it. In the best of worlds, the father is a protector, nurturer, and teacher to his son. He expects his son to listen to him and learn from him. He sees his son as vulnerable and must protect him from the dangers of the world. The son looks up to the father for safety and guidance. He understands he is vulnerable and knows there is much to learn. But what if the father is an alcoholic and the son rebels against his father's drunken rages? Or, if the son hangs out with the bad kids and gets into drugs? Or, if the father is ill, cannot care for his family and has lost his self-respect? While the bond of family remains the same, what each character expects and contributes to the relationship will change, and the scenes that portray that relationship will also be markedly different.

Good Will Hunting has several relationships that pull Will in different directions.

- Will is torn between his loyalty to Chuckie, who is like a brother to him, and pursuing his intellectual potential. He knows he can't have both. Will suffered from abuse and abandonment, and he needs stability and connection. Their bond is based on family and mutual respect.
- Will and Sean, the psychiatrist, are like father and son. At first Will is suspicious of Sean, but later embraces him as a mentor and guide. Sean initially sees Will as another patient, but begins to see greatness in him, and becomes a friend and father figure to Will. As their bond grows stronger, Sean becomes the father Will never had.
- Skylar is attracted to Will for both his intellect and his charm. Will sees Skylar as above his station in life, and deceives her by pretending to be a Harvard student. Their relationship is based on deceit and lies, and Will struggles to feel he is worthy of Skylar's love. Their bond is broken when Skylar learns that Will has been lying to her. Will sets out after her to create a new bond.
- Will's relationship with Lambeau, the physicist, is a teacher-student relationship that later reverses when Will becomes the teacher and Lambeau, his student.

As Will goes through his personal struggle, his relationships bear the brunt of his emotional problems and each relationship undergoes a transformation. In the end, Will's changes affect the other major characters' lives. Understanding the nature of each bond, and each character's role in the relationship is essential in creating strong screen relationships.

Dysfunctional Relationships

Is there any other kind of relationship than dysfunctional?
                                        Tim Burton, Writer/Director,
                              Beetlejuice, Edward Scissorhands, Ed Wood

The best movie relationships are dysfunctional. Functional relationships are not very interesting. Movies are not about happy people. Movies are about lives in crisis and people who are knee-deep in mess. The more messed up the characters, the more messed up the relationships, and the more material the writer has to work with. The main character should have the messiest life of all because they are in the middle of a life-altering crisis. Their crisis must affect each of their relationships in negative ways. The main character plays out their personal crisis through their relationships. The only way for the audience to understand the main character's issues is by the interactions of their relationships. Characters take out their problems on the characters closest to them. There is a reason for the saying: "You always hurt the ones you love." The main character is under stress and therefore each of their major relationships must also be under stress.

Characters are either trying to make their dysfunctional relationships work or struggling to get out of them. The audience wants to see the main character in a healthy relationship so when they are stuck in a dysfunctional relationship, it creates tension and anxiety in the audience. Audiences like messy characters and messy relationships because they are more interesting to watch. Actors like messy characters and messy relationships because they are more challenging to play. Writers like messy characters and messy relationships because they are easier to write.

Key Relationship

The key relationship is a powerful emotional force in a screenplay. It is usually the one relationship that is more important, and plays a bigger role, than all other relationships. The key relationship is also the one important connection the main character is struggling to make. The main character pursues the key relationship, or struggles to realize its importance throughout the screenplay. It isn't until the main character has faced their personal issues that they are able to finally complete the connection.

The key relationship also plays an essential role in revealing the main character's personal story and flaws. Good key relationships are tumultuous. They should have ups and downs, highs and lows. They should be on the verge of falling apart, and coming back together. In addition, the key relationship is the prime motivator that eventually forces the main character to grow and transform. They come to the realization that the key relationship is the most important thing in their life and if they lose it, they will lose a "once in a lifetime" opportunity for happiness and connection. This is Terry and Edie in *On the Waterfront*, Michael and Julie in *Tootsie*, and Sam and Annie in *Sleepless in Seattle*. The key relationship is often the love interest but it can also be important relationships such as Will and Sean in *Good Will Hunting*, Thelma and Louise in *Thelma and Louise*, and Turner and Hooch in *Turner & Hooch*.

Dynamic Relationships

Major relationships in a screenplay should not be static, but dynamic, and in constant flux. There should be no "neutral" relationships; each must exert pressure on the main character's story. They should be active molecules orbiting around the chaos of the main character's life.

Tootsie is an interesting film to study for character, relationship, and subplot because the plot is advanced through relationship complications and not through plot twists and turns. There is a plot, but the plot is driven by the relationships. Each character has a clear want that motivates their actions. In addition, each relationship has a progression and an arc.

TOOTSIE

Michael (Teacher) and Sandy (Student)
> *Nature of the Relationship:* Michael is Sandy's acting teacher.
> *Michael to Sandy:* Michael sees Sandy as a student and friend.
> *Sandy to Michael:* Sandy sees Michael as a teacher and a lover.
> *Want:* Michael does not want to hurt Sandy.
> *Want:* Sandy wants Michael to be her boyfriend.
> *Progression of Relationship:* teacher>lovers>estranged>unresolved
> *Goes from:* honest to dishonest

Michael (Dorothy) and Julie (Actor)
> *Nature of the Relationship:* Dorothy and Julie work together.
> *Dorothy to Julie:* Michael wants to seduce Julie.
> *Julie to Dorothy:* Julie sees Dorothy as a role model to help her get out of negative relationships and build her self-esteem.
> *Want:* Initially Michael wants to sleep with Julie. Then, he falls in love with Julie and wants her to love him in return.
> *Want:* Julie wants to be more like Dorothy, to be confident and make better choices.
> *Progression of Relationship:* colleagues>friends>confidants>estranged> new hope
> *Goes from:* dishonest to honest

Michael (Dorothy) and Ron (Director)

> *Nature of the Relationship:* Ron is Dorothy's director.
>
> *Dorothy to Ron:* Dorothy challenges Ron's authority on set and with Julie.
>
> *Ron to Dorothy:* Ron is the boss on the set.
>
> *Want:* Michael wants to be respected as an actor.
>
> *Want:* Ron wants Dorothy to follow his directions—be a submissive woman.
>
> *Progression of Relationship:* employer/employee>confrontational>power struggle>truce
>
> *Goes from:* combatants to uneasy truce

Michael (Roommate) and Jeff (Roommate)

> *Nature of the Relationship:* roommates and starving artists.
>
> *Michael to Jeff:* Michael sees Jeff as a talented writer, roommate, and friend.
>
> *Jeff to Michael:* Jeff sees Michael as a desperate actor who has crossed the line.
>
> *Want:* Michael wants to produce Jeff's play.
>
> *Want:* Jeff wants their shared apartment to return to normal.
>
> *Progression of Relationship:* friends>estranged
>
> *Goes from:* friends to estranged friends.

Michael (Dorothy) and Les (Julie's Father)

> *Nature of the Relationship:* Les is Julie's father. He finds Dorothy attractive.
>
> *Dorothy to Les:* Michael sees Les as a problem.
>
> *Les to Dorothy:* Les sees Dorothy as an answer to his loneliness— a potential wife.
>
> *Want:* Michael wants Les to go away.
>
> *Want:* Les wants to marry Dorothy.
>
> *Progression of Relationship:* acquaintances>pursuit>estranged> reconciliation
>
> *Goes from:* courtship to friends

Michael (Dorothy) and Van Horn (The Actor)

> *Nature of Relationship:* Fellow actors.
>
> *Dorothy to Van Horn:* Michael sees Horn as a potential rapist.
>
> *Van Horn to Dorothy:* Van Horn sees Dorothy as a conquest.
>
> *Want:* Michael wants Van Horn to leave him alone sexually.
>
> *Want:* Van Horn wants to sleep with Dorothy to validate his manhood.
>
> *Progression of Relationship:* colleagues>sexually dangerous
>
> *Goes from:* does not change.

What makes these relationships work so well is that each character has their own story and wants something different from either Michael or Dorothy.

Each character actively pursues something they want from Michael which in turn creates more tension and complications in the relationship. Complicated relationships create endless situations and scenes. These are the kind of dynamic relationships you want to create in your screenplay. As an exercise, break down your current relationships according to the paradigm used above.

Sounding Board Character

The sounding board character has been discussed previously but it bears reviewing again. It is impossible for the audience to read the main character's mind to know what they are thinking. So, it is helpful for the main character, and the writer, to have a sounding board character in the screenplay, a confidant, someone to talk to about their hopes, dreams, and fears. Usually, this is a best friend the main character trusts and has known for a long time. For intimate moments to be believable, they must be motivated by the main character's emotional state. These moments happen when the main character is at an emotional low point and most vulnerable.

Another advantage of the best friend is that they can call the main character on their bad behavior and force them to face the truth about themselves. Often the main character is in denial about what the best friend is telling them. But the best friend helps cue the audience, and the reader, into an important piece of information about the main character's story.

- In *Stand By Me*, Chris Chambers admits to his best friend Gordie, that he stole the milk money, but gave it back, and no one believed him. Chris feels trapped by his family's low station in town. The audience gets a glimpse into the deep sense of betrayal that haunts Chris.
- In *Toy Story*, Buzz is Woody's adversary, but in a low moment, Woody admits he is jealous of Buzz. Woody's honesty helps clear the air between Woody and Buzz and begins the next chapter in their relationship.
- In *Tootsie*, Jeff is the voice of reason and calls Michael out on his poor treatment of Sandy.

It is always better to dramatize—to show rather than tell—but there are times when it is helpful for the main character to verbally express their innermost thoughts to their best friend. These are poignant cathartic moments for the main character and signal a significant emotional growth.

Relationships Add Complication and Tension

Relationships are entanglements and entanglements complicate the main character's life. However, many aspiring writers believe the best way to complicate a story is to add more plot. The best way to complicate a story is to create relationship entanglements at the same time the plot becomes more involved so the relationships add fuel to the fire.

In *Little Miss Sunshine*, the relationships between each of the six characters in the van are fraught with complications and tension. Getting to the beauty pageant is a goal, and the van breaking down is an obstacle, but the story is between the characters and their dysfunctional relationships.

- Richard's relationship with his wife, Sheryl, is on life support. Their marriage is in tatters and they are at each other's throats.
- Richard is saddled with his brother-in-law Frank, and their long history of strongly disagreeing with each other.
- Richard and his father do not communicate well and have years of baggage between them.
- Richard is estranged from his son, Dwayne.
- Richard treats his seven year old daughter, Olive, like one of his "Refuse to Lose" students rather than as his child. He fills her head with fear instead of being a father, and supporting her dreams.

Personal stories complicate relationships with the main character. Not only does the main character have to deal with plot obstacles, they must manage their problematic relationships. No matter which way they turn, they face another complication.

The Triangle

Relationships can be further complicated by bringing in a third character to create a triangle relationship. Triangle relationships are complications commonly known as "Love Triangles" where two characters compete for the affections of the same character. But there are other triangles such as in *On the Waterfront* where Edie and Charlie vie for Terry's soul. By putting the main character squarely in the middle of a difficult dilemma, triangles create suspense and tension.

- In *The Apartment*, C.C. Baxter has a crush on the elevator operator, Miss Kubelik. Little does Baxter know that Kubelik is carrying on a secret affair with her boss, Mr. Sheldrake. Sheldrake is also Baxter's boss and because he is married, Sheldrake uses Baxter's apartment to carry on with Kubelik. When Sheldrake breaks up with Kubelik, she tries to kill herself, and Baxter is left to care for her in his apartment. Baxter is pressured to keep Sheldrake's infidelity a secret. Kubelik is blind to Baxter's devotion, and Baxter, ever the gentleman, keeps his affections under wraps. Two broken hearts and one scoundrel make for a great triangle and a lot of complications.
- In *Casablanca*, Ilsa is torn between her love for Rick and her admiration for Victor Laszlo and his efforts against the Nazis. The unexpected ending to this triangle is that both Rick and Ilsa sacrifice their love for the good of the world.
- In *Broadcast News*, news producer Jane Craig is torn between her intellect and her passion. She is best friends and intellectual equals with news reporter Aaron Altman, who is passionately in love with her. But Jane is physically attracted to an up-and-coming handsome news anchor, Tom Grunick. Grunick is an intellectual lightweight and repudiates everything Jane stands for in the news world. No matter which choice, Jane loses something—her best friend or her self-respect.

Triangles magnify and complicate each character's problems. They make a love story more interesting, and further complicate the main character's internal story. Triangles do not have to be cheesy or cliché. It's a matter of who the characters are and how the writer chooses to develop the triangle. The key is to find a little twist on the classic triangle to make it feel fresh. A character in a dilemma is always the best part of a triangle.

Negative Relationships

Relationships are based on unique bonds that tie two characters together. Sometimes the bonds are supportive; sometimes the bonds are negative. A negative relationship creates strong tension and suspense, and the audience wants the main character to end the relationship. *On the Waterfront* has strong positive and negative relationships. Terry's dilemma is deciding which relationships he will choose.

- Brothers Terry and Charlie's relationship is negative. When Terry was a young prizefighter, his older brother, Charlie, betrayed him by making him throw a fight for a mob bet. Charlie tries to assuage his guilt and by giving Terry small meaningless jobs. Terry deeply resents his older brother and blames him for ruining his life. These two brothers harbor deep resentments toward each other but neither one wants to let go of the other. The thin bonds of family barely hold them together.
- Waterfront mob boss, Johnny Friendly, is also a negative relationship for Terry. Terry was an orphan, and when Terry was a kid, Johnny acted like a father and took him to the ball games. He feels he owes Friendly his loyalty. In reality, Johnny sees Terry as a "has been" and treats him more like a pet than a son. Ultimately, he orders Charlie to kill Terry.
- To counter Terry's negative relationships, screenwriter Bud Schulberg balances his screenplay with positive relationships. Edie sees Terry as misguided and wants to save him like one of the stray cats she brings home. Terry sees Edie as angelic, and a way to start over and begin a new life.
- Initially, Father Barry sees Terry as a hoodlum and Terry sees the Father as a hypocrite. But as the story unfolds Terry and Father Barry's initial antagonism and suspicion turns into respect.

Terry's four major relationships evolve and change as the screenplay develops. Part of Terry's character arc is coming to terms with his own flaws, and seeing the truth about the people around him who have been using him and keeping him down.

Relationships and the Second Act

Progressing and intensifying the second act of your screenplay can be challenging. Yet, the back half of the second act should be the most exciting and complicated part of your screenplay. This is why you should consider breaking the second act into four major sections. The main character's relationships play an important role in keeping the second act interesting and in advancing and complicating the plot. In some cases, the relationships are the plot.

In addition to the A storyline—the main plotline—it is also helpful to have B, C, D, and E subplots and relationships develop during the second act. Multiple relationships allow the writer to intercut between the A story and the B, C, D, and E stories. They help relieve the burden of the A storyline to carry all the conflict and action. They allow you to spread out the conflict and complications across your screenplay. Relationships also raise the stakes. If the main character fails to resolve the main plot problem, someone important to the main character, such as the key relationship, is also at risk.

Final Thoughts

Strong characters create strong relationships. If a character is flat and one-dimensional, their relationships will also be flat and one-dimensional. Just as the main character must have a character arc, so should your major relationships also have an arc. As the writer, you must know what each character expects from their relationships. Sometimes the expectations are met and it's a positive relationship, and other times the relationship is a failure.

Your screenplay's relationships must pressure and reveal the main character's personal story. Each relationship should offer the audience a small bit of information so they can piece together a whole picture of the main character. Through the main character's relationships, the audience learns everything they need to know about the main character—their hopes, dreams, fears, and aspirations. Strong relationships create a strong main character.

Relationship Pass

Interconnecting

Two people connecting, trying to be intimate, is as complicated an idea as there is.

Spike Jonze, Writer/Director,
Being John Malkovich, Her

All great screenwriters write compelling relationships. Mastering the art of writing and rewriting complex relationships is essential to your development and success as a screenwriter. As you move further into your revision, a primary goal is to layer and deepen your major relationships. Bring the major and minor characters into alignment so they either work together or at cross purposes. You must have a myriad of relationships—some supporting, some in opposition, some disintegrating, and some coming together. Your major relationships must be in flux and have relationship arcs. By creating vibrant energetic relationships, you will add significant depth and dimension to your screenplay.

Objectives For Your Relationship Pass

- Strengthen the ties that bind the characters.
- To ensure each major relationship has a specific tension.
- Each relationship must be either positive or negative.
- Your key relationship must be central to the main character's story.
- Your supporting characters are unique with strong attitudes.
- Your supporting characters add tension and complications to your scenes.
- Create or strengthen the best friend character.
- Create an emotional bond between the main character and the antagonist.
- Make sure your major relationships have arcs.
- Use your major relationships to raise the stakes.

Relationship Notes

Relationships are the most frequently overlooked area in terms of notes. Most relationship notes usually revolve around the love interest. Relationship notes tend to come in the form of general overall conflict notes or plot notes. Relationships add conflict and tension. Many general notes are best resolved by strengthening the relationships

Relationship Notes

The Note:	Potential Solutions:
The main character is vague.	Internal Character Story*, Want*, Key Relationship, Sounding Board Character, Opposition Characters*
There isn't enough conflict.	Relationships Thrive On Tension, Relationships and Plot, Relationships Need An Arc, Opposition Characters*
The main character seems isolated.	Key Relationship, Sounding Board Character, Relationships and Plot, Opposition Characters*
The relationships all feel the same.	Key Relationship, Attitude*, Opposition Characters*, Relationships Need An Arc
There isn't enough going on in the screenplay.	Key Relationship, Relationships Thrive On Tension, Relationships and Plot, Opposition Characters*
The scenes are flat. There isn't enough tension.	Ties That Bind, Relationships Thrive On Tension, Opposition Characters*
I don't feel a connection between the characters.	Ties That Bind, Key Relationship, Sounding Board Character, Relationships Raise Stakes
I don't understand why they are together.	Internal Character Story*, Ties That Bind, Key Relationship, Relationships Raise Stakes
The battle between the main character and the antagonist is familiar and predictable.	Antagonist, Ties that Bind, Relationships Need An Arc, Relationships Raise Stakes, Central Dramatic Conflict*

*See index: concept found in other chapter.

Relationships

In movies, the audience hungers for the screen characters to make connections. The main character is in the midst of a life crisis, and to top it off, their relationships are dysfunctional and falling apart. Each major relationship must pressure the main character's story. Just as the main character's life is in flux, so should their relationships also be turbulent. The link between the audience and on-screen relationships is very powerful. Use this deep emotional connection in your relationships to move your audience.

- In *Cast Away*, Chuck Nolen is marooned on a deserted island. He so desperately craves a connection with another human being that he creates a relationship with a volleyball he names Wilson. Remarkably, when Wilson is lost at sea, the audience mourns the loss of the volleyball.

List how each major relationship affects the main character in a positive or negative way. There should be no neutral relationships. If you connect your relationships to the main character's journey, your screenplay will become tighter and more cohesive.

- Are you using your relationships to pressure the main character?
- Are the main character's relationships making life more difficult?
- Are you linking your major relationships to the main character's story?

Ties That Bind

Each major relationship needs a bond, an emotional connection, which ties the relationship together. If there is no emotional connection, there is no relationship. A vague bond is like a vague character—uncommitted and one-dimensional. In order for screen relationships to be dramatic and dynamic, the emotional bond must be under pressure. When the ties that bind a relationship are for the wrong reasons, the relationship is doomed to fail.

- In *Crazy Heart*, Bad Blake is like a drowning man clinging to his girlfriend, Jean, as a lifeline. Jean needs Blake as a lover and a father figure to her young son. Blake's drinking undercuts their relationship and eventually destroys their bond beyond repair.

In this pass, each of your relationships needs an emotional bond that ties them together. It is not enough to just force two characters into a relationship. They must need each other in some way—constructive or destructive—but the audience must understand why they are together. In addition, each character must be in a personal crisis which is also affecting the relationship.

- Does each of your major relationships have an emotional bond that ties them together?
- What does each character emotionally need from the relationship?
- What is holding the relationship together?
- What is tearing the relationship apart?
- Is each bond under pressure?
- Are you using your character's flaws to pressure the relationship?
- Are you using external plot complications to pressure the relationship?

Relationships Thrive On Tension

Your screenplay must be in a constant state of change. Your major relationships need tension, problems, or wedges between the characters. Since most relationships are played out over the course of just five or six scenes, each scene must focus on the issues between the characters and not just the plot.

- In *The Guardians of the Galaxy*, the main tension and conflict in the screenplay is between the characters and their relationships, not the antagonist.

For constant conflict in your relationships, increase the tension in your scenes as well as in your overall screenplay. Whether your scenes are written in text or subtext, scenes should be primarily about the problems between the characters. Turn plot beats into character/relationship/plot beats.

- Does each major relationship have a specific tension?
- Do your relationships contribute to the overall tension of your screenplay?
- Are you using each character's personal story, goals, and agenda to add tension to the relationship?
- Are you using your relationships to further complicate the overall screenplay?
- Are you using your plot complications to pressure the relationships?

Key Relationship

All films need a key relationship. The key relationship is the central relationship of the screenplay. It is often also the central dramatic conflict. The key relationship can be a love story, a bromance, a relationship between family members, or even a relationship between the main character and the antagonist. The key relationship must be involved in the main character's emotional life as well as the plotline. The key relationship is essential to create a strong emotional attachment with the audience.

- In *Erin Brockovich*, the key relationship is between Erin and her boss, Ed Masry; in *Stand By Me*, between friends Gordie and Chris; in *X-Men: First Class*, between Professor X and Magneto.

If you do not have a key relationship, then you will need to create one. Look at the best friend, love interest, mentor, even the antagonist, to develop as a key relationship. The key relationship must be under stress and on the brink of disintegrating. If it's a positive relationship, the audience must fear that it will fall apart, and if it's a negative relationship, the audience will hope that the main character will end it before it's too late.

- What are the bonds that tie the key relationship together?
- Does each character in the key relationship have a personal story?
- Does each character in the key relationship have a clear goal and agenda?
- What is the problem that threatens to tear the key relationship apart?
- How does the key relationship pressure the main character's personal story?
- What role does the key relationship play in the plot?
- How does the key relationship change over the course of the screenplay?
- What is the arc of your key relationship?
- Will the character in the key relationship suffer dire consequences if the main character fails to resolve the main plot problem?
- How does each final resolution affect the key relationship?

Sounding Board Character

If you have a sounding board character or a confidant, like a best friend, utilize that character to its full extent. A sounding board character allows the main character to explicitly state what they are thinking, without it feeling forced or contrived. The confidant should also challenge the main character and hold them accountable. Their relationship, like all strong relationships, should have an arc with peaks and valleys. It must be a dynamic changing relationship.

- In *The Big Lebowski*, the Dude and Walter are best friends but also continually clash with each other. They are like an old bickering married couple, but the Dude uses Walter as a confidant and a sounding board. The best friend can also provide comic relief.

If it's unclear what the main character wants, or what is motivating them, consider adding a sounding board character. Establish their relationship early in your screenplay. They should have a clear agenda, a want, and a distinct attitude. They should not be passive or just a listening ear. If it's a best friend, there is always some degree of tension between them. Remember, the main character is going through a major life crisis and everyone around them should be impacted— especially the best friend.

- Does the confidant help the main character verbalize their hopes, dreams, and fears?
- Does the best friend hold the main character accountable for their bad behavior?
- What is the tension in their relationship?
- What is the arc of their relationship?

Antagonist

The antagonist must be one of the major relationships in your screenplay. Three-dimensional characters are more interesting than cardboard villains. Find a way to make the battle between them personal and not just a quest for power and money. Give them a past to make the present more personal.

- In *The Incredibles*, Buddy was Bob Parr's number one fan, but Bob sees Buddy as a crank and an annoyance. The tables turn when the number one fan turns into Bob's number one enemy. Buddy is not just some one-dimensional raving lunatic who wants to take over the world. Buddy is like a jilted lover, and wants revenge and respect. Their history makes their antagonistic relationship fresh and personal.

Since many independent films do not have a traditional antagonist, the key relationship is often the central source of conflict and tension throughout the screenplay. In independent films, the key relationship is more dynamic with a strong arc. In addition, there must be strong multiple dysfunctional relationships in an independent film to help carry the conflict and tension throughout the screenplay.

If your screenplay lacks conflict, examine your antagonist's relationship with the main character. Look for ways to make the relationship personal. If they do not know each other before the screenplay begins, make sure there is something that ties them together other than just who wins in the end. In addition to any physical battle, use their connection to build an emotional battle between them. The more personal the conflict—the higher the stakes.

- Is the antagonist a three-dimensional character with a personal story and a clear agenda?
- Does the main character and the antagonist have a past together?
- Is there an emotional connection between the main character and the antagonist?
- What is the arc of their relationship?

Relationships Arcs

In addition to the main character's arc, each major relationship needs an arc. Each major relationship should be a separate story with a beginning, middle, and end. Establish the nature of the relationship in the first act; stress and pressure the relationship in the second act, and then resolve the relationship in the third act.

- In *Good Will Hunting*, Will and Sean's relationship is fraught with conflict and tension. It goes through a series of highs and lows, has a dynamic active arc, and is never static. Their arc goes from mistrust and confrontation to trust and respect. Their relationship also mirrors the theme.

List and trace the arc of your major relationships. Each relationship should have a beginning, middle, and an end. Your major relationships must be dynamic with peaks and valleys.

- Do your major relationships have a beginning, middle, and end?

- What is the arc of your major relationships?
- What do the characters learn from each other?

Relationships Are Plot

By creating multiple relationships, you expand the number of plotlines in your screenplay. You are not just telling one story—you are telling multiple stories that weave around the A plotline. Each relationship is a subplot which further complicates the A plot, and, the A plot also complicates the relationships. Relationships help relieve the burden on the A plot to carry the screenplay. Cut away to a subplot to keep things interesting and progressing. As you cut back and forth think: "Meanwhile. . . ."

If you do not have enough conflict or your plot is repetitious, you need to add more conflict and tension to your relationships. Focus on how each relationship makes the main character's life more difficult and how the relationships also affect the main plot.

- Does the plot pressure the relationships?
- Do the relationships affect the plot?
- Are you using multiple relationships to complicate the plot?
- Are you cutting away to different subplots to help relieve the A Plot?

Relationships Raise Stakes

"The stakes are not high enough" is one of the most consistent notes for writers. By creating dynamic relationships, with strong ties that bind, you increase the audience's emotional identification with the characters thereby increasing the stakes. Personal stakes are always more effective than plot stakes. You raise the stakes by creating characters the audience cares about and who will suffer dire consequences should the main character fail to resolve the third act crisis.

- In *Die Hard*, should John McClane fail to defeat Hans Gruber, his wife, Holly, will die along with the other hostages.

Increase the stakes by focusing on developing strong emotional connections between your characters. Someone important to the main character, such as the key relationship, will suffer dire consequences should the main character fail. In addition, see what other characters you can put in harm's way. The audience will care about these other characters if they are important to the main character and the audience understands the nature of their relationships.

- What major character will suffer dire consequences if the main character fails?
- Which supporting character will also suffer dire consequences if the main character fails?

Use Index Cards to Track the Arc

Index cards are helpful to track the arc of a relationship throughout your screenplay. By assigning different colored cards to each major relationship, you can see at a glance whether there are sufficient story and character beats that keep the relationship active and progressing. In addition, if one color of your relationship cards is bunched together, that is a strong indication that you need to spread the relationship across your screenplay.

Break out the cards that make up the major beats of each relationship to see how they progress. It can also be helpful to copy the scenes of each relationship from your screenplay and put them into a separate document. Then read the scenes back to back to get a sense of whether the relationship is progressing. If you are repeating the same beats, revise the relationship so that each scene progresses their story.

On each card, record the emotional ups and downs of the relationship. Make sure each relationship has peaks, valleys, and an arc. If a relationship is static, then create new scenes or beats to make the relationship more dynamic and complicated. Work new cards into your existing structure.

- Are your relationships clumped together or are they spread across your entire screenplay?
- Does each major relationship progress and become more complicated?
- Is there an arc to each major relationship?

Final Thoughts

Relationships help broaden and expand your main character's story and world. They are dynamic and complicated. Dysfunctional is more interesting than functional. Populate your screenplay with strong supporting characters that bring different agendas and voices to your screenplay. Each major relationship should pressure the main character's story.

Relationships reveal character, and add conflict and tension to your screenplay. Relationships relieve the pressure on the A plotline to carry the entire movie. You are telling the story about the main character's pursuit of their goal, and you are also telling the story of their many relationships. Eventually, you will come to a place where you will wonder how you ever wrote a screenplay that was not based on relationships.

20

Scene Pass

Link and Connect

Where you enter and where you exit a scene have everything to do with what just happened and with what's coming next. I am always looking for what connects one scene to the next.

William Goldman, Screenwriter/Novelist,
Butch Cassidy and the Sundance Kid, Misery, Marathon Man

Everyone talks about the "screenplay," but a screenplay is really just a collection of individual scenes strung together into a narrative. Scenes are a writer's stock in trade. Your screenplay can only be as good as each and every scene. If your scenes are not dramatic, your screenplay will lack excitement. Each scene is a piece of the puzzle that eventually reveals a complete picture. If important pieces of the puzzle are missing, your picture will be incomplete. This pass will focus on improving the dramatic or comedic nature of each scene, and making each scene contribute to the whole.

In the Scene Pass, each scene must reveal something important about the main character and/or advance the plot. Each scene builds upon the previous scene pressuring, complicating, or challenging the major characters. Your scenes must be dynamic, unpredictable, and filled with tension and conflict. Scenes should not wander, but move the story forward with a consistent rhythm and pace. In addition, there needs to be an economy to your scenes. Tell your story succinctly and efficiently, and create a sense of narrative momentum.

Objectives for Your Scene Pass

- Use your scenes to tell the main character's story.
- Shape your scenes to emotionally affect the characters.

- Keep the characters consistent scene by scene.
- Review the intent and purpose of each scene.
- Each scene must contribute to the whole.
- Link and connect your scenes across your entire screenplay.
- Create dynamic scenes with rising and falling action.
- Use conflict, tension, and suspense to intensify your scenes.
- Use unique locations to create a strong sense of place in your scenes.
- Tighten and trim excess dialogue and description.

Scene Notes

Since a screenplay is a series of scenes, each note, in some way, refers to your scenes. If you have a plot note, it's a scene note; if you have a character note, it's a scene note. To fix any one scene note, you may also have to make adjustments to several scenes. As you go deeper into your revision, link and connect your changes across your entire screenplay.

Scene Notes

The Note:	Potential Solutions:
The screenplay is flat.	Internal Character Story, Scene Point, Scene Tension, Suspense, Scene Structure and Dynamics, Emotional Roller Coaster, Locations
Nothing seemed to happen.	Internal Character Story, Subplots*, Relationships*, Scene Point, Tension, Emotional Roller Coaster, Opposition Characters*
There is not enough conflict in your screenplay.	Tension, Emotional Roller Coaster, Scene Structure and Dynamics, Central Dramatic Conflict*, Opposition Characters*, Relationships*
The script was confusing.	Internal Character Story, Want*, Theme*, Scene Point, Cause and Effect, Structure*, Plot*
The characters all sounded the same.	Internal Character Story, Attitude*, Relationships*, Character Consistency, Scene Structure and Dynamics, Tension, Emotional Roller Coaster
The scenes just weren't exciting.	Active vs. Passive*, Scene Point, Scene Structure and Dynamics, Emotional Roller Coaster, Tension, Show Don't Tell, Variety of Scenes, Scene Length, Locations, Staging

(Continued)

Scene Notes (Continued)

The Note:	Potential Solutions:
The script felt long.	Scene Length, Scene Structure and Dynamics, Emotional Roller Coaster, Show Don't Tell, Variety of Scenes, Tighten Text
The dialogue is flat.	Internal Character Story, Want*, Attitude*, Tension Scene Point, Emotional Roller Coaster, Show Don't Tell, Opposition Characters*

*See index: concept found in other chapter.

Scene Point

Aspiring writers commonly try to accomplish too much with each scene and end up muddling the intent of the scene. It is far better to focus on one intention rather than to stuff everything in one long scene. Each scene must have a specific intent and reason for being. This specific intention is called the "Scene Point." You should be able to state each scene point clearly. "The point of this scene is . . . ." Is the point of the scene to reveal a character beat, or to complicate the plot, or to reveal new information? There may be several beats a scene will cover, but overall, there should be one main scene point.

List each of your scenes and the scene point for each scene. If a scene is trying to accomplish too many separate things, you may want to break the scene into two scenes and give each scene a specific intent.

- Is each of your scenes focused with a specific scene point?
- Does each scene contribute to the whole?
- What important information concerning character and/or plot is revealed in each scene?

If a scene lacks a clear intent, figure out what you were trying to accomplish and rewrite it. Consider whether you need the scene at all. It may be best to cut the scene. Each scene must pull its weight and contribute to the whole. Don't fall in love with your scenes. Either they contribute, or they are expendable.

Scene Structure and Dynamics

Just as a screenplay must have rising and falling action, so must your scenes also have rising and falling action. Scenes start on one level and finish at a different level. Start low, finish high, or vice versa. The characters should progress emotionally within your scenes. Each scene must affect them, or there will be nothing at stake for them.

Basic scene structure is: set the scene, present the problem or tension, complicate the problem, escalate the tension, and then have a partial resolution or no resolution at all. Scenes usually do not resolve the problem. Instead, each scene complicates the problem, which becomes a bigger problem, which in turn complicates the next scene. Scenes must make the character's lives more complicated, and raise the overall tension and conflict in your screenplay. Resolving one problem immediately creates a new problem. All scenes need tension. Let tension and conflict in your scenes lapse, and your screenplay is dead.

The structure of each scene—where it begins and where it ends—keeps each scene fresh and interesting. Vary your entrances and exits so all your scenes do not feel the same. Start your scenes as late as possible, and exit as early as possible. Start mid-scene with the characters active and doing something. Do not begin your scenes at the beginning.

If your screenplay is flat, review your scene structure for sufficient rising and falling emotional action. Trim dead spots in the middle of scenes. Dead spots are excess lines that do not serve a purpose other than slowing down or killing a scene. Enter your scenes as late as possible and in motion.

- Does each scene have tension and conflict?
- Do your scenes have rising and falling emotional action?
- Is there emotional movement within your scenes?
- Do your scenes complicate your character's lives?
- Are you entering your scenes late and exiting early?

Internal Character Story

The main character's internal story unfolds one scene at a time. Each scene must affect the main character's story either directly or tangentially. There must be a clear consistent story thread that weaves through your scenes, from the beginning to The End.

In each scene, the main character pushes against a wave of conflict and resistance either through plot, relationships, subplots, complications, or through obstacles. Conflict comes from all directions, and is relentless and unforgiving.

Err on the side of more pressure, more tension, and more conflict. Failure to pressure your main character in every scene causes your screenplay to lack significant conflict and tension.

Track your main character's internal story scene by scene. A beat here and there, adds up to a consistent story. It doesn't take a lot. Connect the main character's personal story with their relationships and subplots. Ultimately, you are writing a story about one person's journey.

- Are you using your scenes to pressure the main character's story?
- Are your scenes filled with betrayals, secrets, lies, and reversals?
- Does the main character's story link scene by scene throughout your screenplay?

Character Consistency

Inconsistent characters sharply undercut a screenplay. An established character must be the same in every scene until a major event changes them. If a character is loud, they cannot suddenly become quiet, or if a character is pessimistic, they cannot suddenly become optimistic—unless they are *motivated* to change. Change must be earned or forced upon a character.

Be consistent scene after scene with each character's personal story, philosophy, worldview, attitude, dialogue, and action. Step into your character's mind to understand the way they see the world, as well as the unique way they act and react to that world. Committing your characters to a specific attitude helps separate them and keep their voices consistent.

If all your characters sound the same, review their introductory scenes and how they are established. Create a list of major characters, including supporting characters, and their attitudes, goals, internal stories, and personal issues. Review how each character behaves in each scene. Are they consistent in how they speak and act? If not, revise their behavior to be consistent.

- Is your main character consistent scene after scene?
- Are your supporting characters consistent in each scene?
- Do your supporting characters project a consistent attitude?
- Is character change motivated by a major event?

Emotional Roller Coaster

Scenes must emotionally affect the main character. In addition to the ups and downs of the plot, your characters must ride an emotional roller coaster of highs and lows in your scenes. Use your scenes to explore a character's emotional extremes. Emotions are windows into the soul and the audience learns a great deal about a character by the way the character acts emotionally.

When the main character lacks significant emotional ups and downs, you run the risk of writing a monotonous one-dimensional character. Some characters, like Will in *Good Will Hunting*, are very expressive and let their emotions fly, while other characters, like Terry in *On the Waterfront*, carefully guard their emotions. Remember, you are writing about messy people with messy lives. They don't think—they react emotionally.

If not enough happens in your screenplay, or the second act is flat, look to add emotional movement within your scenes. Each character must have a unique emotional pattern. Then your screenplay is populated with a wide range of characters with distinct emotional patterns.

- Is your main character riding an emotional roller coaster?
- Are your characters going through emotional ups and downs?
- Do your characters have consistent emotional patterns?

Tension

To hold the audience's attention, there must be tension and conflict in the scene. Conflict is a direct confrontation between opposing characters. Tension, on the other hand, is a more subtle form of conflict—almost subtextual. Tension is the anticipation of direct conflict. Tension is like a tightly wound spring; just one more turn and the spring will snap. The more tension you create in your scenes—the threat of the spring snapping—the more conflict.

There are many different kinds of tension: physical, emotional, psychological, and/or sexual tension. Tension can be subtextual and unspoken; it can be inferred or suggested. Tension in a relationship adds tension in a scene.

- In the opening scene of *Inglorious Basterds,* Quentin Tarantino creates remarkable tension as Nazi Colonel Landa interrogates a French farmer about the location of a Jewish family while the family lies hidden inches beneath Landa's feet. Tarantino lets the tension and suspense build until the tension explodes into violence.

In your scene pass, make sure each scene has specific tension. Use more than one type of tension. Mix it up by using sexual, physical, and/or emotional tension. Just like people, characters have secrets, lies, betrayals, infidelity, resentments, jealous, envy, and hate. Review your relationships for tension in each one. In addition, vary the degree of tension—some more intense, some less—so the tensions do not feel the same. Heighten each character's want to ensure there is a clash of agendas to add a layer of tension.

- Are you using sexual, physical, psychological, or emotional tension in your scenes?
- Are there subtextual unspoken tensions between your characters?
- Is the source of the tension between your characters clear?
- Is the tension based on each character's agenda?

Suspense

Director Alfred Hitchcock described an important distinction between surprise and suspense. Surprise is two people sitting at a table when suddenly the table explodes. The explosion creates a momentary fifteen-second reaction in the audience. But if you have two people sitting at a table and reveal a bomb under the table, you create suspense—fifteen minutes of suspense. The audience knows the bomb will explode, but they don't know when. They fear for the people at the table and desperately want them to leave.

Suspense is an important tool of great scene writing. Suspense is created when the audience fears and anticipates something bad is going to happen to a character. How will this turn out? The audience is in a state of suspension awaiting the outcome of the situation. Suspense is also created when the audience knows something the character does not know, such as, there is a stranger in a house hiding behind a door. Suspense is used a lot in thriller and horror movies.

If your screenplay is not exciting enough, look for places to add suspense to your scenes. Go through your screenplay and identify suspenseful moments. Too much exposition undercuts suspense. Cut the verbal explanation and show the drama. Reveal just enough information to create concern for the main character's welfare. Also, letting the audience in on a secret or a lie can create suspense. The audience knows more than the main character, and fears for their physical and/or emotional safety.

- Do you have suspenseful moments in your screenplay?
- Are your scenes too expository?
- Does the audience know things the main character doesn't know yet?

Show Don't Tell

The audience should never see the screenwriter's hand at work; they should simply react to the ups and downs, crises and conflicts that plague the main character. The art to writing great scenes is to keep the intent of the scene hidden from the audience. The audience must be caught up in the journey, unsure how it will end, and fearful that it will not end well for the main character, but hoping they can figure it all out before it's too late.

The more you *show* and the less you *tell* the audience, the more successful your scenes. If you're showing a person with a substance abuse problem, the audience does not need to be told the character has a problem.

- In *Flight*, Captain Whip Whitaker has an abuse problem. The audience sees the emotional cost of his addiction to everyone around him.

Reveal problems and consequences through dramatic action, not through dialogue. Use dialogue to punctuate the problem.

Review your scenes to see if you are showing, not telling. If you are telling, create behaviors and actions that reveal the character's emotional issues. Show the consequences and emotional effects the main character's bad behavior has on characters close to them, especially the key relationship.

- Are you showing or telling?
- Are you revealing a character's personal issues through behavior?
- Does a character's bad behavior affect characters close to them?

Cause and Effect

One of the primary goals of every rewrite is to tighten and focus a screenplay. To create a tight cohesive screenplay it is essential that scenes are linked together, and there is a cause and effect correlation between them. Significant events or important character developments must have emotional and plot consequences in the scenes that follow. Like a stone thrown into a still pond, a significant event in one scene should create ripple effects across your screenplay. Significant events often change characters, relationships, and plotlines. Actions *must* have consequences.

Review your most significant character and plot scenes for moments that affect characters, relationships, and plotlines in other scenes. Use cause and effect to link and connect your dramatic elements. Use your cards or your outline to track the emotional consequences of a character's behavior through their relationships and subplots. The more you can connect your characters and scenes, the tighter your screenplay will be.

- Are there cause and effect actions and reactions between your characters and scenes?
- Does a character's behavior in one scene cause a reaction in a subsequent scene?
- Does a character's behavior and action create a ripple effect across your screenplay?

Scene Length—Rhythm & Pace

Your screenplay must have a distinct rhythm and pace. This includes varying scene lengths so your scenes do not all read the same. There are no rules—a scene can be as short or as long as you think necessary. Few writers are skilled enough to hold the audience's interest more than four pages. It's easy to write a long scene—it's hard to write a good long scene. If you are going to write a long scene, each line needs to hold the audience's attention, and there needs to be strong tension to pull the audience through the scene. If you are writing shorter scenes and then suddenly drop in a ten page scene, it can disrupt the rhythm and pace of your entire screenplay—unless the longer scene is motivated and necessary.

If your screenplay is repetitious, review your scenes and justify the longer scenes. Look to trim your scenes of excess verbiage. You might like the way a line reads, but do you need it? Kill your babies and make your scenes tight. Make sure you also vary your scene lengths for variety.

- Does your screenplay have a consistent rhythm and tempo?
- Are you varying your scene lengths?

- Are most of your scenes between a half page and four pages?
- Is there a specific reason or motivation for a longer scene?

Variety of Scenes

Vary the type of scenes in your screenplay. Beware of writing the same scene again and again. You should have many different kinds of scenes including introductory scenes, character development scenes, plot complication scenes, argument scenes, seduction scenes, negotiation scenes, preparation scenes, reversal scenes, scenes of reflection, confessional scenes, accusatory scenes, action scenes, love scenes, and set pieces. The list is endless. If you are getting notes that your screenplay is flat or uninteresting, this could be due to a lack of variety in the scenes.

- Do you have enough variety to your scenes?
- Are you structuring your scenes differently to keep them fresh and unpredictable?

Locations—Time & Place

Writers often overlook the importance of setting their scenes in interesting locations that provide unique ways to stage their scenes to make them original. By setting the ending of *Terminator* in a steel mill, Writer/Director James Cameron creates a memorable visual set piece with cinematic props. *Winter's Bone* is set in the backwoods of the Ozarks and uses rural locations to create a specific tone and atmosphere for the film.

Locations can also be used to reveal character. Where a character lives, hangs out, or works reveals a lot about that character.

- In *On the Waterfront*, Terry Malloy hangs out on the rough docks and cheap bars of the waterfront, but he takes refuge on the roof of his building where he raises carrier pigeons. The rooftop is the only location that doesn't feel claustrophobic and dismal. It is also a place of refuge and reveals Terry's gentler side. It's a great location, but it's an even better character reveal.

Review your locations to ensure you are setting your scenes in interesting places. Locations should also reveal something about the characters. Fully utilize locations in your staging and use unique props to give the scene a sense of place.

Original research is a good way to find interesting locations. You want to take the audience to a place they haven't been before. Even if it's a familiar place, find something unique about the location to make the story feel insightful and different.

- Are you setting your scenes in unique and interesting locations?
- Do your locations give your screenplay a unique sense of time and place?
- Are you using your locations to reveal character?
- Are you using props specific to the location?

Staging

Staging is how and when you move your characters throughout a scene. All movement must be motivated. Characters must move for a reason. Good staging also reveals character and relationship. The way people move, their closeness or distance, communicates a lot of subtextual cues to the audience. Characters moving closer suggest intimacy or attraction; characters avoiding each other suggest distance or mistrust. You should also use your staging to help create a bit of tension in the scene.

A word of caution: do not over describe the staging in your scenes, or break up your dialogue flow with minute staging directions. Strike a balance. Stage the general movement of the scene but not the minute details.

You can improve your scenes by having two actions in a scene. First, start your scene already in motion. Give one of the characters an action like rushing because they are late for a meeting. Then bring in the second character with another agenda. Your first character is active on a task while the second character pushes their agenda.

Avoid talking heads by staging your scenes in interesting ways. If you have too many talking heads, look for ways to create simple actions to make your scenes more interesting. Your characters need to talk, they just don't need to sit and talk. Make use of your locations to help stage your scenes. Moving and talking through a unique location is much more visually interesting than a sit-and-talk scene.

- Are you starting scenes already in motion?
- Do you have a lot of talking head scenes or are your characters moving and interacting?

- Are you using staging to help reveal character and relationship?
- Are you utilizing your locations in your staging?

Tighten Text

Want to improve your scenes quickly? Trim all the excess fat. You need less text description than you think you do. Too much description slows down the read. The truth is a reader will probably skip most of the text and just read the dialogue. Nobody has time to read every word on the page. If you want to be a writer, write a novel; if you want to be a screenwriter, tell a story. Use text to establish tone and atmosphere, but don't become the set decorator and describe every lamp and chair in the room. Cut the descriptions to the bone.

- Are your script pages filled with detailed descriptions?
- Have you made your screenplay skim proof by trimming excess description?

Final Thoughts

Great scenes come out of tension and conflict, competing intentions and agendas. Push your characters to their emotional extremes and put them in uncomfortable situations. Make their lives miserable. The audience wants to see how they cope under extreme adversity. Unless your scenes are dynamic and tension filled, your screenplay will be flat and uneventful. The bigger the emotional roller-coaster ride, the better the read. Tell the main character's story scene by scene from the beginning to The End. Give each relationship a specific tension you can exploit to create tension and conflict in your scenes.

All of your scenes need to contribute to the whole. Screenplays are read one scene at a time, and they need to work dramatically scene by scene. Use the elements of character, relationships, and subplot to keep your scenes progressing. Scenes should not relieve pressure, but should be used to increase pressure on all the characters until the third act climax. The bigger the emotional roller-coaster ride, the better the read.

21

Dialogue Pass

Rhythm and Flow

A good film script should be able to do completely without dialogue.
David Mamet, Writer/Director,
Glengarry Glen Ross, The Verdict, The Untouchables

Some writers have a natural ear for dialogue and it comes easy to them. Others struggle with dialogue and it sounds wooden, or the characters all sound the same. Writing effective dialogue is something that can be learned, and all dialogue can be improved with judicious editing. Most aspiring writers put too much emphasis on their dialogue and their screenplays are too talky. It's "motion" pictures. The less said is usually better. Since dialogue comes out of character, you have to know your characters well before they can begin to speak in unique voices. But letting your characters talk is a great way to discover who your characters are. To do that, you need to be willing to listen to what they have to say.

Objectives for Your Dialogue Pass

- Improve the quality of the dialogue.
- Make each character's voice specific.
- Make the dialogue effective and efficient.
- Tighten and streamline the dialogue.
- Make the dialogue more conversational.
- Improve the rhythm and flow of the dialogue.
- Increase the use of subtext.
- Effectively use confessional dialogue to reveal character.
- Effectively use accusatory dialogue to reveal character.

Dialogue Notes

Most readers will give few notes about the dialogue. Dialogue plays an important role in the development of characters, relationships, plot, and scenes. Notes about the screenplay being slow, or that the scenes are unexciting, suggest problems with the dialogue. Vague characters or unmotivated characters also suggest the dialogue may be lacking specificity.

Dialogue Notes

The Note:	Potential Solutions:
All the characters sound the same.	Dialogue Reflects Character, Unique Character Voices, Attitude
The dialogue is wooden.	Dialogue Reflects Character, Unique Character Voices, Actions Speak Louder Than Words, Dialogue Is Emotion, Subtext, Conversational Dialogue
Dialogue is too wordy.	Dialogue Is Emotion, Less Is More, Subtext, Exposition, Conversational Dialogue
The dialogue doesn't feel real.	Dialogue Reflects Character, Dialogue Is Emotion, Less Is More, Subtext, Conversational Dialogue
The scenes are long.	Less Is More, Dialogue Is Emotion, Exposition, Stage Directions, Conversational Dialogue
A lot of talk about the plot.	Dialogue Reflects Character, Unique Character Voices, Actions Speak Louder Than Words, Less Is More, Exposition
I'm not sure what the main character wants.	Internal Character Story*, Want*, Dialogue Reflects Character, Dialogue Is Emotion, Confessional Scenes, Accusatory Dialogue
I'm not sure what this is about.	Theme, Internal Character Story*, Dialogue Reflects Character, Confessional Scenes, Accusatory Dialogue

*See index: concept found in other chapter.

Listen to Write Good Dialogue

Matt Weiner, the creator of *Mad Men*, says he honed his dialogue skills by overhearing conversations and noting *how* people talk and *what* they talk about. People inadvertently reveal their hopes, dreams, fears, insecurities, prejudices, and biases when they talk. Listen for content, rhythm, and syntax.

Dialogue sounds different when read aloud. Read your screenplay aloud to get a feeling of how good dialogue flows. Get some friends, or even better, actors to do a reading. Listening to your entire screenplay being read is an eye-opening experience. One of the first lessons is: everything plays better, quicker and shorter. Those extra lines really slow down a scene. You realize you need a lot less than you think you do. Also, record dialogue from a movie on your smart phone and play it in your car.

Dialogue Reflects Character

Just as a character's actions reflect their internal story, so should their dialogue. Most characters speak without thinking and reveal things about themselves unwittingly. Characters also reveal a great deal about themselves by what they talk about—in other words, their dialogue reflects what is going on inside their mind.

- Terry Malloy, in *On the Waterfront*, is a man of few words. Terry's dialogue is an external projection of his internal story. He's a washed-up boxer, a defeated man. His dialogue reflects his deep sense of shame and cynicism. It also reflects his lower-class upbringing and the hard world he lives in.

Your characters should talk about how they see the world and how they think the world is treating them. Their world view and personal philosophies should be reflected in their dialogue. Your characters should be talking about their dysfunctional relationships, the people in their lives, the hurts, the disappointments, their hopes, dreams, and fears. Characters should barely talk about plot.

- Do your characters reveal themselves by what they talk about?
- Do you use worldview and personal philosophies to reveal character?
- Do you use a character's hopes, dreams, and fears to reveal character?
- Does your dialogue revolve around relationship issues?

Unique Character Voices

A character's voice must reflect their internal story and their external attitude. A character's attitude must remain consistent unless it is changed by events in the story. A character that acts superior can get knocked down and become humble, but the change must be motivated. A character can have many different masks to wear in public or in private. But any shifting attitudes must be motivated throughout your screenplay. In *Little Miss Sunshine*, each character has a distinct voice which comes from their internal story, attitude, and worldview.

- Richard, the Dad: The Optimist. Richard's dialogue changes as events change. At first, his dialogue is optimistic, but sarcastic, as if he has all the answers. When his world comes crashing down, his dialogue changes to be defeated and insecure. At the end when Olive is under attack, his dialogue becomes stronger and reflects his newfound values.
- Sheryl, the Mom: The Realist. Fed up and at the end of her rope, Sheryl is worn out by failed dreams and mounting bills. Her dialogue reveals her exasperation with her husband and his money-draining schemes. Her dialogue is frantic with Richard, but understanding with her family.
- Grandpa Edwin: The Wise Old Man. He realizes he's at the end of his life and can say anything he wants. His dialogue reflects his "don't give a damn" attitude. He speaks the truth and doesn't worry about how it is received. He is protective of Olive and his dialogue with her is supportive and nurturing.
- Dwayne, the Son: The Existentialist. Since Dwayne doesn't speak, his first line of dialogue is written on a note card. "I hate everyone." Dwayne is frustrated and stuck with his dysfunctional family. His lack of dialogue speaks volumes.
- Olive, the Daughter: The Innocent. Her dialogue reflects her innocence. She sees the world through a child's eyes.
- Frank, the Brother-in-Law: Depressed. Frank is defeated—the spurned lover. His pessimism contrasts Richard's relentless optimism. At first his dialogue reflects his depression. But he becomes revitalized and sees his role on the trip as a counterpoint to Richard's know-it-all attitude.

Assign each character an external attitude to project in each scene. Once you establish a character's attitude, make sure it is consistent in dialogue and behavior throughout your screenplay. If your characters do not have a story, an attitude, or a life philosophy—they will not have a voice.

- Does each character have a specific voice?
- Is their voice the product of their internal story, attitude, and philosophy?
- Is each character's attitude and voice consistent throughout the screenplay?

Actions Speak Louder Than Words

How a character behaves leaves a deeper impression on the audience than what a character says through dialogue. When the lauded nineteenth-century novelist, Henry James, was unable to make a literary convention, they asked him to send a speech to be read. When the speech arrived, it had only one word: "Dramatize."

- In *The King's Speech*, Prince Albert has a serious stutter. When asked by his speech therapist, Lionel Logue, if he knows why he stutters, the Prince is unable to answer the question, and dismisses Logue and his techniques. In the next scene, the Prince's father, the King of England, eloquently reads a speech to the nation as the Prince stands uncomfortably beside him. After the speech ends, the King pressures the Prince to practice reading it. When the Prince begins to stutter, the King becomes exasperated and shouts at him to annunciate properly. Even if the Prince does not make the connection, the audience can see exactly why he stutters. Show, don't tell.

Look for ways to convert dialogue into action. Instead of having the character talk about their problems, dramatize them in your scenes. Look for three or four places early in the second act where you can reveal the main character's internal and external problems through action. Cut dialogue lines that explain and replace them with scenes that reveal character through behavior.

- Are you showing or telling?
- Are there places where you can convert dialogue to action, and reveal character through behavior?

Dialogue is Emotion

There is a lot more to dialogue than just the words. Dialogue should reflect a character's emotional state. Something happens between two characters in a scene and they react emotionally through their dialogue. The audience does not need to be told how the characters feel, they pick up on the emotional exchange between the characters. Characters can also use words as weapons to attack and inflict pain.

Look to see if you are using your dialogue to express emotion in your scenes. Locate key emotional moments and review how your dialogue is enhancing the emotions expressed in the scene.

- Do your characters use dialogue to express their emotions?
- Do your characters use dialogue to inflict pain or attack another character?

Less is More

Don't overwrite your dialogue. It's a mistake to fill up your scenes with wall-to-wall dialogue. Long speeches and long sentences become monotonous and boring over an entire screenplay. Screenplays should have a rhythm, tempo, and momentum to them, and if every speech is filled with unnecessary words, it will slow down your screenplay, and bog down your scenes. Pauses, and lines left unsaid, can communicate more than an actual line. Silent pauses communicate a great deal.

Go through your screenplay and trim your dialogue to the bone. Look to cut entire lines, and even cut sentences in half. What does the audience need to know? Cut everything else. The first time you read a scene after cutting lines, you may miss some lines. Do you miss lines because they are familiar, or because something important is missing? There must be a specific reason to put a line back, and that reason cannot be, "Oh, but I liked that line."

- Are your speeches too long?
- How deeply can you cut a speech and still retain its purpose?
- Does your dialogue have rhythm and flow, or is it static?

Subtext

Subtext is implied or inferred dialogue. On the surface the dialogue is saying one thing, but the true meaning is something else. The characters speak without thinking and what they say reveals a great deal about themselves—what they talk about, as well as their attitudes toward a subject. The audience sees the characters act and react, and draws their own conclusions.

Seduction scenes and negotiation scenes are also good places to use subtext. Alan Ball, the writer of *American Beauty*, and the creator of *Six Feet Under* and *True Blood*, is a master of blending text and subtext. A good scene to study for subtext is in *American Beauty* when Lester tries to seduce his wife, Carolyn. The scene begins with Lester watching TV. Carolyn enters through the kitchen and stares at Lester. (*The parenthetical dialogue lines are subtext interpretations.*)

> LESTER
>
> What?
> (*What have I done wrong now?*)

> CAROLYN
>
> Whose car is that out front?
> (*You better not have bought that expensive car.*)

> LESTER
>
> Mine. Nineteen-seventy Pontiac Firebird.
> The car I've always wanted and now I have
> it. I rule.
> (*I'll buy anything I want. I'm in charge of me now
> and I'm going to get what I want.*)

> CAROLYN
>
> Ah, where's the Camry?
> (*What have you done, you idiot?*)

> LESTER
>
> I traded it in.
> (*It's gone and it's not coming back.*)

> CAROLYN
>
> Shouldn't you have consulted me first?
> (*Power struggle: I run this family and I make the
> decisions around here.*)

> LESTER
>
> Hum? Let me think. No. You never drove it.
> (*I make my own decisions about my life now, including which
> car I drive. I don't have to answer to you any longer.*)

While on the surface the dialogue is about the car, the scene is really a power struggle. Carolyn has always worn the pants in the family, but in this scene Lester declares his independence. As the scene continues, the dialogue switches from subtext to on-the-nose as they go on attack effectively smothering the dying embers of their failed marriage.

Independent films tend to work more in subtext than large Hollywood blockbusters. Since independent films are character driven, it's more interesting to let the characters reveal themselves slowly, one layer at a time. The phrase that is often used is to "peel back the onion one layer at a time."

Review your scenes for places to add subtext. Seduction scenes and negotiations are good places to use subtext. Try to make the scene appear to be about one thing when it is really about another. As in the scene above, you can blend subtext and on-the-nose dialogue in the same scene. Often the subtext leads to direct confrontation.

- Are there scenes that can be converted to subtext?
- If you have seduction scenes, are you using subtext in your dialogue?
- If you have negotiation scenes, are you using subtext in your dialogue?

On-The-Nose Dialogue

There is no rule that says all screenwriters must write subtext. It is not that subtext is good and on-the-nose is bad. It's a matter of which approach is more effective and appropriate for the scene. Aaron Sorkin is known for his blistering on-the-nose dialogue.

- In *The Social Network*, written by Sorkin, Harvard student, Mark Zuckerberg, explains to a young woman all the reasons why he is joining the Harvard Club. He also explains why she should be grateful to him for helping her social climb. The dialogue reveals many things about the main character. He's blunt and socially inept. He's insecure, wants to social climb, and be part of the "in" crowd. Although he doesn't reveal this directly, it is implicit in what he is talking about, and how he sees his social world.

Be strategic about when and where you use on-the-nose dialogue. On-the-nose dialogue usually works best during confrontations and high emotional scenes. A character may be blunt, but not all your characters should be blunt. Make sure your on-the-nose moments are emotionally motivated and consistent with the character's voice and attitude. You want to try to achieve a balance between subtext and on-the-nose. Dialogue tends to be more on-the-nose later in the second act.

- Are your on-the-nose dialogue moments motivated?
- Does your on-the-nose dialogue reveal more about the character than just the text of the lines?
- Are you using a blend of subtext and on-the-nose dialogue?

Confessional Scenes

In many films, a character needs to hit rock bottom before they can see things clearly and acknowledge what they have been denying their entire life. These are confessional scenes. The main character reaches their lowest point where everything appears to be hopeless. They find themselves alone with someone they trust, a confidant or best friend, and face the truth about themselves. Confessional scenes are on-the-nose dialogue. These scenes usually appear late in the screenplay and must be motivated by severe emotional setbacks or plot reversals.

There is an iconic confessional speech in *On The Waterfront* where Terry and Charley ride in the back of a taxi, supposedly to go to a boxing match at the Gardens. But unless Charley can get Terry not to testify to the Crime Commission, he is taking Terry to his death. When Terry realizes what Charley plans to do, he is shaken by his brother's betrayal. Charley starts to reminisce about Terry's boxing career and blames the manager for Terry's failure.

TERRY

It wasn't him, Charley, it was you. You remember that
night in the Garden? You came down to my dressing room
and you said, "Kid this ain't your night. We're going
for the price on Wilson." You remember that? This ain't
your night? My night. I could have taken Wilson apart.
So what happens? He gets the title shot out doors in
a ballpark and what do I get? A one way ticket to
Palookaville. You was my brother, Charley, you should
have looked out for me a little bit. You should have
taken care of me just a little bit so I wouldn't have
to take them dives for the short end money.

                              CHARLEY
            I had some bets down for you. You saw some money.

                              TERRY
            You don't understand. I could have had class. I could
            have been a contender. I could have been somebody
            instead of a bum. Which is what I am. Let's face it.
            It was you, Charley.

For confessional scenes to work, the character must be at their low point and important new information must be revealed. The audience must learn a key missing piece of the puzzle about a character or a dark secret. In *On the Waterfront*, the audience learns Terry threw a fight, sabotaged his dream, and his own brother sold him out to the mob. The final pieces of the character story come together and it all becomes clear.

Confessionals, used sparingly, are an effective way to reveal character insights. If you are getting notes that your main character is unclear or unmotivated, write a confessional speech for your main character to help you understand their internal story. You may not ever use it, but it would be helpful to know what your main character's inner voice is secretly saying. If you do have a confessional scene, make sure the main character is at their lowest point in the story and motivated to face the truth about their internal problem.

- Are you using a confessional scene to help reveal your main character's personal story?
- Is your confessional scene emotionally motivated?
- Is the main character at their lowest point in the story?
- Is there a missing piece of the puzzle or a dark secret that is revealed in the confessional scene?

Accusatory Dialogue

Early in your screenplay, it can be helpful to have a character confront the main character about their flaws or bad behavior. This is accusatory dialogue. Rather than have the main character tell us something about themselves, it is more effective to have another character, such as the best friend, accuse the main character of bad behavior or state their character flaw. Usually the main character rejects the accusation; they are not ready to face the truth. But, the audience, and the reader, gains a little insight into the main character's problem. In *Shaun of the Dead*, Shaun's roommate, Pete, has become exasperated by Shaun's emotional stagnation. When Shaun tries to stick up for one of his deadbeat friends, Pete confronts Shaun.

```
                        PETE
     Stop defending him, Shaun. All he does is hold you
     back. Or does it make your life easier to have someone
     around who is more of a loser than you are? Sort out
     your life, mate!
```

Accusatory dialogue is an easy way to state the main character's problem dramatically. The main character can deny the accusation, but the audience, and the reader know, that the supporting character has touched upon an important issue. These accusations cue the reader to the main character's problem as well as what the drama is about.

- Are you using accusatory dialogue early in your screenplay to establish the main character's issue?
- Is the moment motivated by the main character's actions?

Exposition

Exposition is dialogue which reveals plot details or character backstory information. The less exposition the better. Stay away from sit-and-talk scenes. The best way to reveal backstory and character is through emotion, attitude, and drama. In *Erin Brockovich*, when a new neighbor moves in next door, he asks Erin for her number.

```
                        ERIN
     How's this for a number. Six. That's how old my other
     daughter is. Eight is the age of my son. Two is how many
     times I've been married and divorced. Sixteen is the
     number of dollars in my bank account. 850-3943 is my
     phone number. And with all the numbers I gave you, I'm
     guessing zero is the number of times you're gonna call.
```

While Erin's response fills in blanks about her past, what is best communicated is that she has had a lot of disappointing relationships and the last thing she needs right now is another dead-end relationship.

Cut all unnecessary exposition. If you need exposition, be artful about how and where you reveal essential information. A little bit of information dropped here and there is more effective than dumping a boatload of information in one scene. Spread out revealing information across several scenes so the screenplay doesn't have to come to a complete stop. Let the plot unravel through action; use your dialogue to focus on your characters and their dysfunctional relationships.

- Do you rely upon exposition to advance your plot?
- Are you revealing exposition through scenes with conflict and tension?

Stage Directions

You can help your dialogue enormously by cutting the stage direction between lines. Let the lines play without constant interruptions. Dialogue is about fast banter and repartee, swordplay. The actors and the director will completely ignore your stage descriptions anyway. Excessive stage directions also will cause the reader to begin to skim through your scenes, and you do not want that to happen. Use limited stage directions only for essential movement within the scene and for emotional punctuation.

Go through your script and cut all stage directions between lines. Leave only those directions that are essential or are used for poignant pauses. There should be very few of them. Let the dialogue flow.

- Are you using too many stage directions between your dialogue lines?
- Are you describing the movement of the characters in too much detail?

Conversational Dialogue

Unless formal speech is part of a character's persona, or you are writing in period, dialogue should be conversational and contemporary. It's the banter, tête-à-tête, emotion, and subtext that matters most. Most people do not give eloquent soliloquies. Most people talk single sentences, sentence fragments, and contractions. They say: "Think so?" instead of "Do you think so?" Longer speeches must be motivated. Read your dialogue aloud and look for places to trim lines and words. Go for rhythm and flow, banter and repartee.

- Does you dialogue feel real?
- Are some of your characters speaking in fragments and half sentences?
- Are your longer speeches emotionally motivated?

Final Thoughts

Dialogue is one of many tools a screenwriter needs to master. Less is more. Don't try to do too much with your dialogue. Make sure all your dialogue has a purpose and stays in character. Your characters' dialogue must come out of their internal stories. Each character needs a specific attitude that is reflected in their actions and their dialogue. Don't be precious with your dialogue. Nothing improves dialogue better than a sharp pencil.

22

Consistency Pass

Quality Control

A character should be clear from his present actions. And his behavior as the picture goes on should reveal the psychological motivations. If the writer has to state the reasons, something's wrong in the way the character has been written.
                                                    Sidney Lumet, Writer/Director,
                                                    Dog Day Afternoon, The Verdict

For the writer, inconsistencies are often hard to see. But when someone else reads your screenplay for the first time, inconsistencies can leap out at them and derail your entire script. Character storylines, plotlines, subplots, relationships, and dialogue are key areas to review for inconsistencies. What you establish in the opening must be consistent scene by scene until resolved by the climax. In this pass, look at your screenplay with fresh eyes as if you have never seen it before.

There are a few apocryphal stories of screenwriters writing scripts over a weekend, but the majority of us rewrite our projects over years, not days. If your script is fortunate enough to go into production, there can be rewrites for producers, studio executives, directors, and actors. It is easy to lose sight of the big picture. Characters and relationships that were sharp and clear can become muddled and overwritten. The plot may be rewritten so many times that there are two or three competing plots. Eventually, it can get pretty mixed up and confusing. The Consistency Pass is the place to make sure your characters, scenes, and plotlines are all telling the same consistent story scene by scene, character by character, and line by line.

Objectives for Your Consistency Pass

- Make your screenplay cohesive and consistent.
- Ensure your premise, theme, and tone are aligned and support each other.

- Make sure the main character's story arc and main plot problem are consistent and recurring.
- Make sure your characters are motivated and their behavior is consistent.
- Use attitude, voice, and purpose to ensure your supporting characters are consistent.
- The antagonist must be consistent and relentless in their pursuit of their agenda.

Consistency Notes

It is rare that a reader will give notes directly about script inconsistencies. They are subtle and hard to pick up. They insidiously take the reader down a wrong path. Notes about inconsistencies are words like: confusing, unclear, or hard to follow. These notes suggest you may have serious inconsistencies with your characters as well as your overall storytelling.

Consistency Notes

The Note:	Potential Solutions:
The main character is inconsistent. They keep changing.	Internal Character Story*, Motivation, Attitude, Character Arc, Want*, Need*
I'm not sure who the main character is.	Internal Character Story*, Motivation, Attitude, Character Arc, Want*, Need*, Relationships
I'm not sure whose story this is.	Internal Character Story*, Character Arc, Motivation, Relationships, Main Plot Problem
I didn't believe main character would do that.	Internal Character Story*, Motivation, Want*, Need*, Character Arc, Relationships
All the characters sound the same.	Motivation, Attitude, Character, Relationships, Supporting Characters
I thought the story was about one thing but it ended up being about something else.	Premise, Theme, Internal Character Story*, Character Arc, Main Plot Problem
The plot was confusing.	Main Plot Problem, Antagonist, Four Major High Points*, Structure*
The screenplay seemed to wander.	Touchstone, Premise, Theme, Internal Character Story*, Character Arc, Main Plot Problem, Antagonist, Four Major High Points*

(Continued)

Consistency Notes (Continued)

The Note:	Potential Solutions:
I'm not sure of the tone of this screenplay.	Tone, Theme, Internal Character Story*, Main Plot Problem, Antagonist
I'm not sure if this is a drama or a comedy.	Premise, Theme, Tone, Main Plot Problem, Touchstone

*See index: concept found in other chapter.

Touchstone

The Consistency Pass is a good place to revisit your touchstone and reconnect with your original inspiration. You have been through several passes, and made many changes to your screenplay. In the fog of rewriting, it's easy to get pulled in different directions. It's always good to check in with your touchstone.

- Are you following your original inspiration?
- If not, are you clear about your new direction?

Premise

Your premise is the concept statement, and the basis of the central plotline.

- An honest son is seduced into the family's corrupt business and becomes corrupted: *The Godfather.*
- A selfish outsider learns to become part of a team: *Top Gun.*
- A dysfunctional family is forced to ride together across the state to a beauty pageant and reconnects: *Little Miss Sunshine.*

Your premise must be consistent throughout your screenplay, and cannot change direction. Establish the premise in your set-up, complicate and test it during your second act, and resolve it in the third act.

Review your original premise and make sure your screenplay adheres to it. If you have gone on a tangent, bring your screenplay back into alignment with your original intent. Your third act resolution should complete your premise. Review that your central plotline supports it.

- Can you state your premise clearly and succinctly?
- Is your premise consistent throughout your screenplay?
- Is your premise the basis of your central plotline?

Theme

Theme is the writer's underlying philosophy or truth about life and the human condition that runs under the surface like an operating system for your screenplay. Your theme should be restated in many different ways through character, dialogue, relationships, and scenes and situations. It is common to have several themes at work in a screenplay. But your main theme must dominate and be central to your main character's journey. It is also important not to switch themes mid-screenplay.

In this pass, look for theme consistency. See that you are stating and restating your theme through your character's actions and dialogue. The main character's journey should reflect the main theme. Do not change or drop your theme during the second act. Continue to project your theme until the final resolution of the third act.

- What is your main theme?
- Are you restating the theme consistently throughout your screenplay?
- Do you use action, situation, events, and dialogue to reinforce your theme?

Tone

An inconsistent tone is confusing to the reader. They need to know the tone of the screenplay right from the first page. Once the tone is established, it must be consistent throughout the entire screenplay. A comedy can take a serious turn, but it still has to remain a comedy. A thriller continues to deliver on its premise to be suspenseful. Shifting tone is a common problem for aspiring writers.

- Is your tone clearly established in your opening pages?
- Is your tone consistent from beginning to The End?

Character

Consistency is essential to creating great characters. You've heard the phrase: "That was out of character." Once you establish a character, they must stay in character unless they are motivated to change, or a secret reveal explains an uncharacteristic action. Either way, a character's behavior must be motivated by their story. This rigidity is what makes characters interesting. Characters cling onto their worst flaws, and only change "kicking and screaming" under punishing situations.

Be clear about each character's story, attitude, and agenda in your screenplay. Go through your screenplay scene by scene and review each character's story, attitude, want, and agenda to make sure each character has a consistent presence in their scenes. Characters should never act "out of character" unless there is a reason, or motivation, for them to break character.

- Are your characters consistent scene by scene?
- Do your characters stay "in character" from the beginning to The End?
- Are the main character's actions consistent with their personal story?
- Does the main character respond consistently to plot and relationship problems?
- Is the main character's growth and transformation motivated?
- Is the main character's growth consistent with your theme?

Motivation

The Method Actors in the fifties were known for the phrase: "What's my motivation?" They weren't wrong. A character must be motivated to act, speak, and move. There must be a reason for their actions—something they want or something they need. Their motivation must be controlled by the writer and communicated dramatically to the audience. Human beings are complex and have conflicting motivations, but screen characters need a single motivation that drives them moment by moment, scene by scene.

Each major character's motivation must be established early in the screenplay, and cannot waver unless significant events force a change. When a character changes, they immediately have a new motivation.

- In *On the Waterfront*, Terry's motivation is to stay out of trouble and just get by. But once his brother Charlie is murdered by the waterfront mob, Terry becomes highly motivated to seek revenge on Johnny Friendly.

Review your major character's motivation. This is your character's North Star and you cannot deviate from it unless something significant changes it for them. Track each major character to consistently motivate their stories, actions, dialogue, and scenes. You may find moments you like, but if they are unmotivated and out of character, rewrite them, or cut them.

- Is your main character's motivation consistent?
- Are your supporting characters' motivations consistent?
- Is each character's motivation established in your set-up and consistent throughout your screenplay?
- If a character changes, are they motivated to change?

Character Arc

The most important storyline in any screenplay is the main character's story arc. The main character has a want they are pursuing. Usually it is a false want that will not give them what they really need. In the end, they have an epiphany and embrace their need. Their character arc must be consistent and recurring. Failure to have a consistent main character story arc will result in a screenplay that feels vague and unclear.

Trace your main character's arc throughout your screenplay. If you are using index cards, mark the beats that constitute significant moments in the main character's arc. These beats and scenes should consistently pressure the main character's flaws throughout the second act.

- Is the main character's arc consistent and recurring?
- What specific scenes along the main character's journey pressure their story arc?
- Can you trace the main character's arc and events that lead up to their transformation?

Attitude

Assigning a character a strong distinct attitude is one of the most effective ways to create a consistent character. Once a character's attitude is established, it should not change unless there is a very significant reason. A timid character suddenly cannot become bold unless motivated by action and events. For supporting characters, a consistent attitude is their strongest characteristic.

Scene by scene, check each character's attitude. Make sure it is consistent unless something significant causes the character to change their attitude. A character's attitude should be reflected in their dialogue and action.

- Does each of your characters have a distinct attitude?
- Is each character's attitude consistent scene by scene?
- Is each character's attitude reflected in their actions and their dialogue?

Dialogue

Once you establish a character's approach to their dialogue, you must be consistent with the rhythm of how they talk throughout the screenplay. Dialogue should be motivated from character and attitude. If your character's dialogue shifts from scene to scene, they will be inconsistent and confusing. A character's dialogue pattern is like their fingerprint—once established it must be consistent until motivated to change. A quiet character can have a burst of dialogue when motivated by events to become insightful.

In your rewrite, when you move scenes to new locations, the dialogue may need to be adjusted for content and continuity. Review for orphan lines that are out of place and have lost their meaning. In addition to content, you should also be looking for story continuity. Your dialogue should reflect each character's story and attitude with a verbal presence in your scenes. Don't fall in love with your lines. They are either in character, or not. If they don't work, rewrite or cut the lines.

- Is each character's dialogue rhythm consistent scene by scene?
- Is each character's dialogue consistent with their story and attitude?
- If you moved a scene, have you adjusted the lines for content and continuity?

Antagonist

Just like the main character, the antagonist must be consistent and motivated. The antagonist is the immovable object that ultimately determines the plot. They must be single minded and consistent in their ambition, agenda, and goals.

The antagonist, or their minions, must be a consistent threat throughout your screenplay and not disappear for long periods of time. They must apply sustained pressure on the main character.

- Is your antagonist's character consistent?
- Is the antagonist's motivation clearly established?
- Is your antagonist one-dimensional or do they have a personal story?
- Is the antagonist a recurring presence throughout your screenplay?

Supporting Characters

Aspiring writers will introduce a supporting character with a strong attitude in their initial scene, but in later scenes the character fades, loses their attitude, or disappears altogether. It is important your supporting characters are consistent in their voice and purpose throughout your entire screenplay. To be effective and add tension, they must have a strong presence.

In this pass, go through each scene and make sure your supporting characters are consistent in their behavior, voice, and attitude. If a supporting character has lost their attitude and purpose, bring up their voice so they remain active. Stray characters that disappear from your screenplay should either be cut or combined with another character to create one strong character.

- Are your supporting characters consistent in their attitudes, behavior, and purpose?
- Are your supporting characters active and recurring?
- Do you have any supporting characters that disappear in the second act?

Relationships

Dynamic relationships are the core of great screenplays as well as great literary fiction. While the nature of each relationship must be consistent, your major relationships must be under pressure and in a state of flux. Once they change, and form new bonds, that change must be consistent. Major relationships have an arc.

In this pass, examine each major relationship to make sure the bonds that tie your relationships are clear and consistent scene by scene. Mark the places on your cards or outline where relationships change. Once reformed, the nature of the new relationship must be consistent. Note the scenes where your relationships arc.

- Scene by scene, are the bonds of your relationships clear and consistent?
- When a relationship changes and reforms, is the nature of the new relationship consistent?
- Do the major relationships have an arc?

Main Plot Problem

At the end of the first act, the main plot problem should be apparent, and the audience should clearly understand what the main character must do to solve it. Once established, the main plot problem must be consistent and recurring throughout the screenplay. It is not uncommon after multiple passes and drafts, for the main plot problem to get muddy, or even to have two competing main plots in a screenplay.

Trace the continuity of the main plot problem throughout your screenplay. It should be forcing the action and be recurring. The main plot problem you establish in the first act must also be the plot problem you resolve in the climax. If the main plot problem is going to change, it's only because the antagonist misdirected the main character and the audience. This major plot change is also a major plot reveal. Use the main plot problem to pressure your major character's stories and relationships.

- Is the main plot problem clearly stated at the end of the first act?
- Is your plot problem consistent throughout the screenplay?

Final Thoughts

A writer who writes a consistent screenplay is a writer in control. Writing consistent characters, scenes, and dialogue takes hard work. To master this skill, you need to take the time it takes to get it right. Once you succeed, you will carry this lesson with you on every script you write. In screenwriting there are no points for being close. Either it works, or it's just a pile of paper. Inconsistent characters, attitudes, motivations, dialogue, and plotlines are unacceptable. The deeper you go into your rewrite, the more you must pay attention to consistency and detail.

Screenplays must be set in tightly contained worlds. The characters living in these worlds must be consistent in their stories, attitudes, voices, and purpose. They cannot change according to the whim of the writer. They must be motivated and consistent from the first moment they appear in your screenplay until The End.

23

Polish Pass

Dialogue, Text, and Tightening

When your story is ready for rewrite, cut it to the bone. Get rid of every ounce of excess fat. This is going to hurt; revising a story down to the bare essentials is always a little like murdering children, but it must be done.

Stephen King, Novelist/Screenwriter,
Carrie, The Shining, The Shawshank Redemption

You built a spec house and you want the buyer to see that it's smartly designed and well built. You've laid a solid foundation, constructed the walls, put the roof on, put the plumbing in, and run the wiring. The windows are in place, the hardwood floors are in, and the walls have been painted. Now it is time to complete all the details and do the final touchups. You want the buyer to be impressed with the quality of your workmanship so they will buy your house.

It is normal to be sick of your screenplay at this point and feel like nothing works. You just want to get done with it already. Do not overreact. Have faith in your work. Stay focused on your objective for the Polish Pass. Focus on dialogue, text, description, scene tightening, consistency, spelling, grammar, holdovers, and orphans. Tie up the loose ends and add finishing touches. If major issues remain, then you need to do another pass before polishing. The polish should be your last pass before you send your screenplay out. You are near the finish line and you don't want to stumble when you are so close to bringing it home.

Objectives for Your Polish Pass

- Review character arcs and character development.
- Read for character and plot consistency.

- Track character storylines and subplots.
- Trim excess and repetitive dialogue lines.
- Thin out text descriptions for a better read.
- Cut stalled scenes and flat spots.
- Check for holdovers and orphans.
- Check for spelling and grammatical errors.

Polish Notes

You may still have minor notes to address, but for the most part this is a housekeeping pass. You're cleaning up your construction zone, and want to remove any leftover debris. Tighten whenever you can. Most drafts at this stage are long and need judicious editing. Professionalism and details are important. You are asking a studio to invest millions of dollars in your screenplay. What does it say about you if your screenplay is littered with misspellings and poor grammar? Producers and executives need to know you can be trusted. A sloppy screenplay doesn't build trust. Your screenplay needs to be tight and professional. "Nice try" doesn't cut it.

Polish Pass Notes

The Note:	Potential Solutions:
The script feels long.	Script Length, Tightening Dialogue, Trimming Text, Making Big Cuts, Stall Scenes, Trimming Heads and Tails
There are some really slow spots in the screenplay.	Script Length, Tightening Dialogue, Trimming Text, Making Bigger Cuts, Stall Scenes, Holdovers and Orphans
Some of the scenes feel really long.	Scene Length*, Scene Point*, Tightening Dialogue, Trimming Text, Stall Scenes, Trimming Heads and Tails
I got confused.	Internal Character Story*, Plot*, Structure*, Tracking Character and Story, Consistency, Making Bigger Cuts, Stall Scenes, Holdovers and Orphans
This character's name kept changing.	Holdovers and Orphans
There are spelling and grammar errors.	Spelling and Grammar

*See index: concept found in other chapter.

Script Length

Generally, your screenplay should be one hundred to one hundred and ten pages, but not over one hundred and twenty pages. Readers sense how long a script should be and there is "reader exhaustion" if a script is too long. You may believe you need every word, but you don't. You are writing your screenplay to get read. First and foremost, it must be a great read from page one to The End. A great read is a quick read. Excess words and dead scenes negatively affect the read and will color the reader's overall feel about the screenplay. You want to have a tight screenplay that gets passed up the executive chain. Better to have it shorter than longer. There are always places to trim.

- Is your screenplay a reasonable length?
- Is your screenplay a great read, line by line, page by page?

Established successful screenwriters can get away with longer screenplays because they have a track record and are in demand. Unless you are in high demand, keep your screenplay tight—under one hundred and twenty pages— because in today's market, one hundred and twenty pages is a long script.

The Polish Read

If you've ever taken apart anything mechanical, then you are familiar with the sick feeling of reassembling the machine only to find you have extra parts left over. Parts can be left over in your screenplay too. Some need to be put back and others you'll need to discard. To find loose ends, read your screenplay one more time cover to cover in one sitting. Once again, go old school and print out a new hard copy of your last pass. During your read do not skim a single word or line. Some writers read their scripts aloud to make sure they read every word. Do not edit your draft on your computer. First edit on paper, then edit on the computer.

Look to tighten, clean, cut, and trim wherever possible without harming the flow of the story. In addition to small trims, look for entire scenes to cut. Bigger cuts usually yield more dynamic results and often draw the entire screenplay together. Remember that scene you really like but in the back of your mind you keep wondering if you need it? You don't need it. Kill your darlings. In addition, look for ways to cut scenes in half, or cut a quarter page. Each small cut tightens the read. As you're reading, always ask yourself: "If I cut this will I lose anything?"

If you are not clear why you need a scene or a line, then you probably don't need it. My motto is: "When in doubt, cut it."

- Do you need this line?
- How can you trim this speech down?
- Can you get out of this scene quicker?
- Do you need this scene?
- If you cut the entire scene will you miss anything essential?
- When you make a cut, what is the cause and effect of that in later scenes?

Tracking Character and Story

In addition to reading for cuts and trims, you should be reading for character development and character arc. Remember, character work is never done.

- The main character should be front and center in your screenplay and the major action needs to revolve around them.
- Your main character must be constantly challenged by plot and relationship complications.
- Your storylines and character threads should be consistent and well spaced throughout the script.
- There needs to be a logical flow to the story and a sense of deepening the characters as you progress.
- Your plot should be clear and the main plot problem should be consistent and escalating.

If you have a serious character issue, better to fix it now, than to have your screenplay rejected because you failed to resolve a significant problem. One of the great lessons of rewriting is the more you do it, the more efficient you become at making surgical repairs.

- Does the main character's story track?
- Is the main character's arc clear?
- Are the major characters' attitudes, goals, and motivations clear?
- Does the screenplay intensify and build toward the end of the second act?
- Do the stakes continue to rise?

Consistency

Look for inconsistencies that still undermine your screenplay. Along with character issues, consistency is one of the critical elements of a successful screenplay. Not only must all the characters be consistent, but your subplots, storylines, theme, and tone must also be consistent. Inconsistencies can really sink a screenplay. You have to be a careful reader to read for the emotional links and connections—the character relationships—and thematic unity. A few cuts, some slight revisions, or a well-placed line can add clarity and set the script back on track.

- Are the characters consistent?
- Are the theme and tone consistent?
- Are there any glaring inconsistencies that you need to address?
- Can you fix an inconsistency by making a cut or trim?

Often, the best solution at this point is to cut problematic material. Cuts can usually solve the problem, unless the problem is systemic such as a character's motivation suddenly changes mid-screenplay without any reason.

Dialogue Review

Read each character's dialogue carefully to see that their voice and attitude is consistent in each and every scene, as well as throughout the entire screenplay. Dialogue change is motivated by story or events, such as an arrogant character becomes humbled, or a character acts one way around his friends and a different way around his parents. These inconsistencies must be woven into a character's story. Characters must be consistent throughout your screenplay unless motivated to change.

- Does each character's dialogue reflect their story and attitude?
- Is each character's dialogue consistent from scene-to-scene?
- If the dialogue changes, is the change motivated by story or events?
- Is each character's dialogue distinctive in some way?

Tightening Dialogue

You can improve any dialogue by cutting redundant lines and trimming excess words. Most screen dialogue is one or two lines. Screen characters talk in fragments and contractions. Longer speeches have their place, if they are motivated by a significant emotional moment or plot event.

Be on the lookout for dialogue exchanges in the middle of a scene that are dead space. They may be nice lines, but you don't really need them. If you cut them, your scenes will improve, and the overall pace and rhythm of the screenplay will pick up.

The challenge of trimming and cutting is to know when you have cut enough to improve the scene, but not so much that you've lost something. The hard part is knowing the difference between lines you assume you need, and lines that should be cut. Often, I'll cut a scene and then revisit it the next day to make sure the cuts work. I make deep cuts, but inevitably put a few lines back. You have to trust your instincts. Sometimes a line just works because it works. This isn't science—it's art.

- What is the purpose of this line?
- Does the line reveal character, plot, story, or entertain?
- If you cut it, would you lose anything?
- How does the cut affect the rhythm and flow?
- Have you cut the dialogue too tight and hurt the flow?

As an exercise, take a short scene and cut it to the bone. Enter later than you think you should. Cut a word, or a line from every speech. Near the middle of the scene, look for a few dialogue exchanges to cut. Exit the scene a line or two earlier. See what happens. One or two of the cuts may work. They all may work. None of them may work. See what you learn about trimming your dialogue.

Trimming Text Description

While you visualize each location down to the last detail, let the set decorator and the art director do their jobs. Only describe what is *essential* to understand about the setting and character action. Be economical. Remember, you are writing a blue print for a movie—not a novel. What *must* the audience know? All else should be cut.

The read is the thing. Your description sets the pace of your script. You want the read to be fast, visual, and a page turner. Detailed descriptions can grind your screenplay to a halt. Every reader has an in-box full of screenplays. The last script they want to read is the one with massive descriptive paragraphs—especially on the opening page. Make the opening page easy to read to get the reader quickly interested in your screenplay. Start with conflict and dialogue on page one. Every word you cut is one less word the reader has to read, which accelerates your screenplay.

- In the script for *Moneyball*, written by Steve Zaillian and Aaron Sorkin, there isn't a descriptive passage more than four lines. Each line of description has a specific purpose. The text is lean without fat.

Your description should produce *images* in the mind of your reader. The reader should see the movie. If you are writing an action movie, then use short sentences—even fragments—to make the read faster—staccato. The script should read with excitement and urgency. If you are writing an independent film, the text can be more detailed and nuanced.

Cut stage directions and text between dialogue lines. Nothing kills a scene faster than descriptions between each line of dialogue. Trust your dialogue and let it flow—get out of your own way. You may know exactly how the characters look and act, but it may be killing your scene. The actors won't act like that anyway.

Review your draft and cut as much description as possible. Defend each text line. Do not over "direct" your scenes. Staging is important, skip detailed directions. They may be fun to write, but they are work to read.

- What descriptive words and lines can you cut?
- Is your opening page easy to read?
- Are you letting your dialogue flow or breaking the flow with needless descriptions?
- How can you make descriptions more visual so the reader can "see" the movie?

Scene Polishing

You just completed a Scene Pass so your scenes should be in good shape. Still tighten your scenes as much as possible. Each scene needs a clear scene point, sufficient tension, and whenever possible, elements of suspense. Have many reveals and reversals. The intent and purpose of each scene should be clear.

On the Polish Pass, look for connections and threads between your scenes—cause and effect. Each scene builds upon the previous scene to take us further down the road. Your scenes tell stories, reveal information, and put your characters into increasingly difficult situations. In the back of your mind ask: Do I need this scene? Is this scene contributing something essential to the screenplay? If I cut this scene would it be missed?

Trust your instincts and emotionally react to your scenes. They should move you. You should feel the main character's arc. Tie up loose ends and make further connections.

- Do your scenes touch you emotionally?
- Are your characters' attitudes sharp and distinct?
- Does each scene contribute to the screenplay?
- Is the intent and purpose of each scene clear?
- Is there a logical flow from scene to scene?
- Is there cause and effect between your scenes?

Trimming Heads and Tails

A quick way to improve scenes and shorten your screenplay is to cut the heads and tails of your scenes. The first few speeches of most scenes are often unnecessary and slow down the flow. Cut "hellos" and start in action. In addition, you may find speeches at the end of your scenes that you do not need. Enter scenes late and exit early.

As you read through each scene, trim the first few opening speeches to see how it plays. Have you lost anything? Approach the end of each scene the same way. Trim the last few speeches and see if you miss them. Probably not.

- If you trim the head of a scene, what is lost?
- If you trim the tail of the scene, what is lost?

Stall Scenes

Stall scenes are scenes that do not advance the screenplay. Typically they are holdovers from previous drafts or scenes you think you need. They may be nicely written, but if removed, they do not affect the plot or the character. One good way to tell if you have a stall scene is to cut the scene and then read for flow.

When reviewing, look for places where the plot or the character development stalls and the screenplay comes to a standstill. If a scene has lost its original purpose, then cut it—be merciless. The flow and pace will greatly improve. Removing one stall scene can have a huge impact on the entire screenplay.

- Do you have any stall scenes?
- If you cut the scene, will you miss anything essential?

Making Bigger Cuts

Often the best way to cut pages is to cut entire scenes. Painful as that sounds, there are usually scenes you don't need but are emotionally attached to. Scenes that do not advance character or story should be the first to go. Either a scene has a purpose or it is a stall. Cut the scene, then go back and reread the scenes before and after the cut for rhythm and flow. Do you miss it? Big cuts can energize a screenplay. It's all about the read.

Another solution to reducing screenplay length is to combine scenes. Essential information can be moved to another scene which allows an entire scene to be cut. Be aware that a cut in one area may have an effect on a later scene or character. Track how your cuts affect the scenes and characters that follow.

- Do you need this scene?
- Can essential information be combined with another scene?
- By cutting the scene, does it help the flow and tempo of the screenplay?
- If you cut the scene, how will it affect the scenes and characters that follow?

Holdovers and Orphans

Holdovers are characters, dialogue lines, storylines, or scenes that are no longer relevant from previous drafts. They may have played an important role in previous drafts, but changes have rendered them unnecessary. Often you become so accustomed to a scene or a line of dialogue that you skip over it, and don't notice it is irrelevant. Not only is the line taking up valuable space, but it can also be confusing. This is why you need to read your draft *word for word* to ensure you are not missing any holdovers.

Orphans are characters and character names that have been changed, but for some reason the old name is in a description or still above a line of dialogue. These orphans can be confusing to the reader who suddenly encounters an entirely "new" character in the middle of the screenplay. You don't want the reader to stop reading and go back to eventually figure out this was a typographical error. Check dialogue headings and characters in scene descriptions. Run "search" on character names you have replaced to make sure one isn't hiding in your screenplay.

- Are you skimming or reading every word?
- Have you checked your screenplay carefully for holdovers and orphans?

Spelling and Grammar

Proofread your screenplay closely for spelling and grammar errors. Spell check can be a great help, but spell check doesn't always give you the right word. If you are not great on spelling and grammar, then you might want to enlist someone to proofread your screenplay. This is a screenplay, not an English paper. Sentence fragments are not only allowed, but also encouraged, especially in dialogue. Make sure you input the changes on your draft and agree with the grammatical changes. A comma can change the way a line reads.

A common mistake is the usage of "your," "you're," and "you are," as well as "its" and "it's." Another common error is the incorrect usage for "there," "their," and "they're." It is easy to make these simple mistakes, but they make your screenplay feel hurried and sloppy. You never know when you are going to run across a serious grammarian and you do not want anything to distract the reader. Remember, your screenplay is selling you as a writer, and sloppy mistakes reflect poorly on you. Take a few minutes to fix these errors.

Final Thoughts

Polishing is a reward for all the hard work you have done to get to this point. Take a deep breath and apply yourself. Tell your story as effectively and efficiently as possible. Cutting unnecessary scenes, repetitive dialogue lines, and excess descriptions will streamline your draft. The tighter the draft, the more your story and characters will shine. Check carefully for emotional links and storyline consistency.

Construction, deconstruction, and reconstruction are always challenging, but in the end, screenwriting *is* rewriting. You've been running a marathon and no matter how tired you are, finish strong. In long-distance running, athletes talk about the finishing kick. The Polish Pass is your finishing kick.

Sending Out Your Screenplay

Letting Go

There was no plan B. My theory was that eventually people give up, and the easiest way to make it here is just to outlast them.

Damien Chazelle, Writer/Director,
Whiplash, *The Last Exorcism Part II, Grand Piano*

There comes a time when the work has to stand on its own merits. You send out your screenplay because you believe in it and not because you are tired of it. You have done everything in your power to showcase your writing ability. If you have taken your screenplay as far as you can, addressed all the major issues, and believe this draft represents your best work, then it is ready to go out. All drafts have flaws and you should not expect perfection. Good is obtainable, but little, if anything, is ever perfect.

Note: This is Not a "How to Find an Agent" Book

The topic of this book is rewriting and not how to find an agent or a manager. There are books and websites devoted to breaking into the industry. The competition has always been tough, but it's even tougher than ever. While it should be all about the writing, there is a lot of self-promotion and assertiveness that is necessary to break out of the pack. You need to work your career. Part one: Write a great screenplay. Part two: Promote the hell out of your screenplay.

There is no one way to get your screenplay read, but the common thread in all success stories is the writer who was persistent and used every way imaginable to get their scripts to the right people. Networking is not just an annoying word—it's an essential skill and a full-time job. Use all your personal contacts, family contacts, friends, and ingenuity to get your work into the hands of people who can be helpful to you. Meet assistants who work at agencies. They are always looking for a great script to bring to their boss.

Many aspiring writers take production assistant jobs to find a mentor who offers guidance and support. Internships are a way to learn about the business and make contacts. Be the first to arrive, the hardest worker, that someone everyone can rely upon. Maybe then, someone will take you under their wing and read your screenplay. You need to earn your read. Send your screenplay to screenwriting competitions, read online industry trades, learn the names of up-and-coming agents and managers, and most importantly, be bold. The race is not won by the meek.

People who are persistent and stay in the game year after year, writing screenplay after screenplay, have the greatest chance of success. One screenplay is not enough. Create an *idea file* filled with concepts, characters, titles, scenes—anything that excites you as a writer. You should be constantly developing new ideas and producing new material. As a screenwriter, you must continue to generate ideas. That's why the business needs you.

Don't Take No For An Answer

You will get a ton of "no"s, but do not take them personally. If you try hard enough, and pester people nicely, you will get your screenplay read—eventually. That is why you must do everything in your power to take your screenplay to the highest professional level. If there is still work that needs to be done, you need to do it now. You will get a few reads, but you do not want a critical weakness to derail your efforts, especially after you have done so much work to get it this far. This is a business for fighters. There are no dilettantes or casual screenwriters. It's all or nothing.

I'm Worried Someone Will Steal My Idea

Aspiring screenwriters can be frozen by two fears. The first is your work is never good enough, and you never send it out. At some point you have to let it go. You want to do all you can, but eventually you need to let it go. Then start writing another screenplay. The second paralyzing fear is that someone is going to steal your idea. The best way to protect your idea is to register your screenplay with the Writers Guild of America, West, or ProtectRite. ProtectRite is an online registration company which can be found at www.protectrite.com. ProtectRite has one advantage over the WGA in that they offer an "eternity" registration. The WGA registration expires after five years requiring you to reregister with the Guild which is easy to forget. You can also copyright your work with the United States Copyright Office which is a department of the Library of Congress. See www.copyright.gov for more details.

Registering your screenplay will at least give you peace of mind if someone appropriates elements from your screenplay. An independent third party can authenticate your registration on a specific date and time. Register all your story pitches, too. Write them up as treatments. Keep a permanent log of all your meetings and conversations, as well as to whom you sent your screenplay.

Before an agent or production company will read your screenplay, you may be asked to sign a release form covering their development of similar ideas. By signing this release form, you release them of any liability. I am not an attorney and cannot offer legal advice on whether you should sign this or not. If you don't sign it, they won't read your screenplay. You took a chance when you put all this time and effort into writing and rewriting your screenplay, now you've got to take a leap of faith and put it out there.

Continuing Education

Learning never ends. The most successful people in the business are very bright, eternally curious, and never stop learning. No matter how successful you are as a writer, there is always something more to learn. The business is constantly evolving. What was hot last year is old news this year—audience's tastes constantly change. Don't be narrow and only watch current films. Great screenwriters watch all kinds of films and have a working vocabulary of virtually every major American and International film ever made. You need to be able to reference a wide range of films when in conversations with producers, executives, and directors.

Read screenplays—a lot of screenplays. You should be reading a screenplay a week, if not more. It's important to stay up to date on current styles and techniques. Plus, you will learn a lot from reading other screenwriters' work. Make sure you are reading the actual screenplay and not an internet transcription. Many scripts on the internet are transcribed copies made by people watching the film. In an original screenplay, the dialogue will differ from the actual film, scenes may exist in the script but not in the film, and the text descriptions and staging will be different. Reading transcriptions is counterproductive so make sure you are reading the genuine article.

Final Thoughts

Nobody likes rejection, but it's part of the game. You're going to hear "no" more often than "yes." Grow a rhinoceros hide and go with the punches. Send out your screenplay. Listen carefully to the responses and use them to grow. With each new screenplay you will grow as a writer. You will become stronger—but you must stay in the game, and keep writing and rewriting. There is no guarantee. Writing is not something you want to do—writing is something you have to do. Believe in yourself. Do the work. Send out your screenplay, take a break, fill the well, and then start in on your next screenplay.

Working With Directors, Producers, & Executives

Navigating the Executive Experience

You can win more arguments then you might think as a writer, even though you legally have no recourse, and your script can get muddied and altered in any way possible. You can use reason, logic, and passion to argue persuasively for a case in your favor.

Shane Black, Writer/Director,
Lethal Weapon, Iron Man 3

Very few spec screenplays actually sell. Your spec is your calling card and shows off your talent. The perfect scenario is a studio wants to make your screenplay, the movie is a huge hit, and you are an overnight sensation. Not going to happen. A more likely result is if your screenplay is really strong, a producer will want to hire you to write, or rewrite, one of their projects. Most screenwriting work in Hollywood is work for hire.

Getting an assignment to write a script for a producer would be a great break, but it means you will be working for someone else and have to execute their ideas and vision. You can't just write whatever you want; you have to satisfy their tastes—while at the same time retain your own integrity. They want to hire you because they believe you have the right sensibilities for their idea and are a good match for their project. So, they want you to be you, except when they don't. So, you are now in the tough position of bringing what you are really good at to the project while at the same time making the client happy. In addition to great writing, you must be a diplomat, a mind reader, and able to maneuver around all the egos and politics of the situation. Welcome to world of professional screenwriting.

Producers

There are all kinds of producers. Some are money people and their talent is to find the money. That's a great talent. Others are creative producers and help develop the script. If they have great instincts, they are great partners. Today, many producers are investors who get a producer credit in return for their investment. It's important to learn what type of producer you have on your project, so you know what to expect and how to maneuver. For this discussion, let's assume you are working with a strong creative producer.

Since producers are on the firing line daily, they know the temperature of the industry. They understand what studios are buying and what is possible or impossible to sell. Producers get paid when they set a project up at a studio, so it's in their best interest to get the project on the boards so they can get paid. There is no point in trying to sell tomatoes if the studios are buying oranges.

One of the more difficult aspects of the business is the amount of spec work demanded by producers and studios today. Unfortunately, it's become part of the industry. No one likes to do spec work, but you need to get something set up to advance your career. There is a point when a little exploitation is okay, but a lot of exploitation is not acceptable. It's a thin line, and you have to gauge when it's been crossed. It's been my experience that people do not value what they do not pay for.

Executive Notes

If your project gets set up at a studio or a production company another layer of bureaucracy is added. Instead of having only producers, you now have a studio executive attached to the project. That's a good thing. It means the project has moved into a position to get made and you are on the map. But it also means you have one more person to answer to.

Great executives, with great story sense, will partner with you to help get your project off the ground. They do the heavy lifting of maneuvering the project through the studio maze and getting the film green lit. That's a great skill, and a valuable partner. But writers and executives come from very different places and have different types of personalities. The corporate world of development and the solitary world of the screenwriter are vastly different. Some executives are great with creative people and some are not. If you have a "me" versus "them" attitude, you're not going to go very far. You do need to work with them—not against them. They don't need you—but you do need them.

Here's the core of the problem. Everybody thinks their ideas are brilliant, and you have to work with that. Not everybody can be brilliant all the time, so you have to pick and choose which ideas you can make work, which ideas you'll try to make work, and which ideas you'll ignore. You have to be subtle, diplomatic, and creative.

In working with executives, you need to try and see the logic behind their notes. Always look for "the note behind the note"—the intent of the note. Don't expect executives to solve your screenplay problems, but listen to their concerns. In the end, it's your job to find a solution to their problem. In other words, their problem becomes *your* problem and you need to either fix it using their solution or come up with a better one.

When meeting with an executive to get story notes, confrontation will not work. Be the diplomat, but *never* commit to a note in the room. When getting a questionable note say, "Yes, I see what you are getting at." "I see what's troubling you, but I want to play with it a little." Or, "These are good ideas. They really point me in the right direction." You need time to digest the idea. Let them know you are on board with the general direction and listening to them. You can throw up cautionary flags during a meeting, "I see what you are saying, but that might affect this part of the story. Let me spend a bit of time with it and see if there might be another solution to the problem."

Don't commit yourself to something that, at first blush, might work, but after closer examination, will unravel the entire story. Once you agree on something in a meeting, you've either got to write it, or work to reverse the decision. Better to leave it open ended and work on finding *your* solution to *their* problem. It's better when the executive points out a problem but leaves it up to you to find the solution.

Give Good Meeting

Nobody likes to get notes, but that is your job and you need to do it with great aplomb. Being on the receiving end of notes is the hot seat and you need to keep your cool. I tend to get very defensive in these situations and feel my blood boiling. Sometimes, I wonder if they even read the script! Breathe. You are not there to argue the merits of your screenplay; you are there to listen and engage in a creative discussion.

In all your meetings, be the writer in the room. They want you to be the writer, so think like a writer and talk like a writer. Be the expert on story. Be the creative force in the room, the person coming up with ideas and solutions. Be funny, be charming, be witty—come alive. But if you act as an obstructionist, or are argumentative and defensive, then they will be leery of your ability to "fix" the draft. They will begin looking for another writer. Show them they can work with you, and that you have a lot of good ideas.

Always partner with the strongest element on the project. The 800-pound gorilla initially may be the producer, and then that will shift when a strong executive comes on board, and then shift again when a director is attached. Be diplomatic, but strategic. Everyone else is being strategic, and so should you. It's not just about the words on the page, it's also about playing the game. You may not like it, but it comes with the territory.

Also, don't be late to meetings. This sends the wrong message. Be early and use that time to relax and get to know the assistants. Assistants have their own passions and ambitions, and one of them will end up running the studio one day—seriously. Where do you think these people come from?

Going Into Production

If you are fortunate enough to have a script go into production, you will find yourself working with studio executives, producers, and a director. Once a screenplay is slated for into production, the pace picks up and the rewrites become virtually nonstop. It's important you make a great effort to work as collaboratively as possible when interfacing with the director, producer, and the studio. It won't be easy. The pros suck it up, and get the job done no matter the frustrations or resistance to their ideas. You're *the* screenwriter and the goal is to stay *the* screenwriter on the project for as long as possible.

You have to be seen as collaborative while at the same time protecting the essence of the project. The more voices that join the chorus, the more different directions the project can take. You need to be the center keel and hold the project on line. The moment you are removed from the project, you no longer have a say in the direction of the screenplay, and a project can take a sudden 180-degree turn onto the rocks.

If you have lost faith in the direction of the project, given it everything you have, and can no longer support the project in good faith, it may be best for you to step away. Do it gracefully without recriminations. This is a small town and you do not want a reputation as a prima donna, or someone that is difficult to work with. Personally, I'd rather lobby to get a project back on track rather than abandon it as a shipwreck. When someone else comes on to do the revisions, it will change.

Directors Are Not the Enemy

Contrary to what you may have heard, good directors are invaluable creative collaborators. I have been fortunate to have had excellent experiences working with directors. Good directors are confident and offer great leadership. All collaboration is compromise; it's just a matter of how much a writer is willing to compromise. When the writer and director are on the same page, it can be a great creative experience. The director can be an excellent sounding board and give the project a clear decisive vision. When the writer and the director see two different movies, it's a disaster and a divorce in the making—and the writer will lose.

You want to form a solid relationship with the director and have them see you as a confidant who will help them during production. Once you have the director's trust and confidence, you are in a better position to affect the outcome of the movie. The director must see you as their ally, but if you cast yourself into an adversarial position, the director will seek someone else for support and script changes. Stay engaged with your director. Listen and try to work together. There are usually a lot of big egos involved, and it takes self-discipline and a sense of the big picture to put everything into the proper perspective.

Timing and Diplomacy

A good director will not shoot a scene they do not believe in. Either you must make the changes, or they will hire someone else to make the changes. But the changes *will* be made. The worst-case scenario is when the director starts handing you pages the next morning. You don't want the director to do the rewrites. The key is to stay on board as long as possible to keep the vision consistent and retain what is essential. It's hard to have clarity during the fog of production, so it's better if you can hang in there and offer support whenever asked. This is why a lot of writers become directors—to protect their work.

This does not mean you should belly up and cave in on every suggestion. Good directors listen and know the best idea wins. If you have a difference of opinion on the direction of the screenplay, put together a strong logical argument based on character, theme, story, and motivations. Also, choose your battles carefully. Timing is everything. If the director is having a bad day or battling a difficult actor, this may not be the right moment to approach them with your ideas. Timing and diplomacy are critical to getting people to listen. There may never be the "right" moment, but there may be a better moment.

The Writer Always Loses the Power Struggle

Once the director comes on board, it's a completely different game and your allegiance shifts to the director. The director becomes the 800-pound gorilla who is actually making the film, and final creative decisions will rest with them. The studio and the producer will acquiesce to the director. Your job is to form a strong creative partnership with the director and work together to get a draft they are confident to shoot. Good directors want your ideas—up to a point. Eventually, they will make a decision you will have to execute—like it or not.

Never get between the studio and the director. The director will win every time, and you will be the sacrificial lamb. Stand on the sidelines, or align yourself quietly with the director. Once preproduction dollars start flowing, no one is really going to challenge the director very seriously. At that point the train has left the station and you want to be on board as long as possible.

Pick your battles carefully. Give up on the small stuff but fight for the big things like theme, character, motivations, relationships, and story. Know what to fight for. It's a unique negotiation—a dance. A good director will respect your passion and your ideas if you support it with dramatic references from the script.

You've Been Replaced

Eventually, if you write enough screenplays that go into development, at some point in the process, you will be replaced. Welcome to the club. It's infuriating, frustrating, and humiliating. Even though you might like to pick up the phone and give someone hell—don't. Not only do they not care what you think, the ship has sailed. More importantly, you can also do yourself irreparable harm.

You've taken the script to this point—don't destroy your relationships. You may ask what kind of relationships can these be if they just replaced you on your own idea? It's Chinatown, Jake. Don't try to make sense out of it. Take a long walk, get out of town for a few days and clear your head. Time to move on. The love affair has ended. Let it end nicely. Hope for the best. You may even be brought back and asked to do more work. Maybe even fix the mess the next writer makes. Never close a door or burn a bridge. It's a very small town and everyone has a long memory. Complain to other writers, but don't take it out on the director, producer, or executive. Be professional, hold your head up and get back to work.

How Do You Become A Script Doctor?

A script doctor is a rewriter extraordinaire—someone who can see the major story and character issues, and then revise them quickly and surgically. Script doctors are adept at dialogue and character, and have a good sense of how to streamline and clarify a convoluted plot. Script doctors are like relievers in baseball and are often brought on for a specific purpose. It's not rare these days for a studio to bring in three or four screenwriters on a high-profile project.

You can't apply to be a script doctor. You are hired based on your reputation. Most script doctors have had several big hits, or have previously done rewrite work for a producer or the studio. If you can fix a mess under pressure, then you are suddenly in high demand. You are a knight to the rescue, but it's also high pressure. A film might be weeks away from production, so the costs are mounting daily. As a script doctor you have to be able to assess the problems and have clear solutions that you can achieve in days or weeks.

Robert Towne is one of the most successful and well-known script doctors. His work on *Bonnie and Clyde*, *The Godfather*, and *Mission Impossible* is legendary. He earned his vaulted position by writing outstanding original screenplays as well as saving many pictures at the eleventh hour. His dialogue, character, and scene work are remarkable, and he can deliver overnight. When Towne comes on a picture, there is a collective sigh of relief.

Final Thoughts

The saying that "too many cooks spoil the broth" is especially true in screenwriting. As the screenwriter you will find yourself in the difficult position of being in the middle and executing conflicting notes and ideas. In addition to being able to do the work, to succeed at the highest level of screenwriting, you also have to be a diplomat and be able to read the political winds. While it should be all about the writing, this is a business. Your ability to work the room and maneuver between the political battles is critical to staying on the picture and getting your vision on the screen. In addition to being a great writer, a screenwriter must also be a Secretary of State. You need to understand shuttle diplomacy between the director, the studio, and sometimes, the actors.

You are not the director and you are not the producer. You're the writer and it's important to continue to create characters and stories, and let the business sort itself out. Hollywood is the school of hard knocks. It's essential you have your head screwed on straight, and keep a positive attitude toward your work. Ups and downs come with the territory.

Work to achieve disciplined daily writing habits. Be consistent and approach your work like a job. Self-discipline is the key to turning out quality, as well as a quantity of screenplays. Those who stay in the game and give it all they've got, have the best chance of succeeding. It takes a long time, and a lot of hard work, to become an overnight success.

Part Three

Screenwriters on Rewriting

Robert Towne

Speaking purely as a professional, you've got to accept the fact that rewriting is probably going to be your job the majority of the time. So, it is critical.

Robert Towne

Robert Towne has arguably had more influence on American screenwriting in the last forty years than any other writer. He is best known for his Academy Award®–winning screenplay, *Chinatown*. In addition, he has written screenplays for *Shampoo*, *The Last Detail*, *Personal Best*, *Days of Thunder*, *The Firm*, *Without Limits*, and *Mission Impossible I & II*, to name a few. He has been nominated for four Oscars® and a number of other awards, including The Golden Globes and BAFTA Awards. Towne is also known for his script doctoring work. He is uncredited but much heralded for his work on *Bonnie and Clyde*, *The Godfather*, and *Heaven Can Wait*.

Jack Epps, Jr.: When writing your first draft, what are the important screenwriting elements you're trying to get down?

Robert Towne: In writing a first draft, I try to imagine some sort of structure bearing in mind that I'm not going to be so specific that I can't discover things along the way. Because if a screenplay is working at all, what's going to happen is the characters are going to start dictating structure and you have to leave room for that. You don't want to hamper them in your own mind by saying this has to be accomplished by page 30, this has to be accomplished by page 40. You can do that, but what you're going to end up doing is saying maybe the character wouldn't do that. He wouldn't zig, he's going to zag. And so you have to feel free to follow a character at that point, but to have enough of a structure for the character to argue it, if you know what I'm saying.

I generally start with some sort of loose structure, outline it, and then see how the characters react to that structure. In other words, having some idea of who they are, some idea of what the structure is, and between the structure and your idea of the characters, you find what they are and what the story is.

Epps: When you say structure are you talking about structuring the character's development or are you talking about plotting structure?

Towne: Plotting structure actually. And then as I said, let the characters, and you, deal with it in some way. Starting a script is always difficult. It's a pain in the ass. You feel like you've gone out onto the dance floor and you don't know the steps.

Epps: We've done this so many times before. Why is this still so hard?

Towne: Yes, and you say, "What the . . . man?" But at a certain point, you've been leading, and if the characters start working, they'll start to lead, and then you'll follow. I think that's when you know something is beginning to work—when they're sort of dictating to you. That's what you hope for anyway.

Epps: Let the characters tell their story, tell you who they are, and tell you what is happening to them. Even though you preplan, you pre-think it, in the end it's their movie.

Towne: That's right.

Epps: In terms of planning you said you use an outline. Is it a rough outline? Is it a sequential outline? Do you use index cards?

Towne: No, I don't use index cards. I did at one time. I use a rough sequential outline and it's sort of a combination of character notes, and structure notes.

When I was writing *Without Limits*, I had outlined it, but there's a sequence in it where Prefontaine had lost the Olympics, had come in fourth, and he's miserable. He's working in a bar and Bowerman goes to see him. That scene took place actually in life. But I didn't know quite how it was going to go. When I got there I realized as I was working on it that Bowerman's goal was to try to talk Pre into coming back to working out and starting over again. And Pre was saying, "I'm just no good. I thought I could do anything, and I can't." And Bowerman gives that speech of "That's your conceit, Pre, that it just doesn't take talent. Guts is misleading. So you just think that if you lose you don't have enough guts, but the fact is . . . ." And he goes through those natural gifts that he had—his lung capacity, his feet—everything else. What I didn't realize would happen is that Prefontaine turns on him, and calls him a manipulating old man and a son-of-a-bitch. I'm sure he felt that way about Bowerman, but that was a nice surprise. His voice came up and that's what came out. So, that's what I mean by a change. There is a point where they're going to come together, but just how they come together can change so completely that it's not only a different scene, but it even changes the structure.

Epps: The change comes out of the relationship and the things that had been laid in beforehand. I think it also comes out of knowing the character so deeply that he has a freedom inside you when he talks.

Towne: Yes. In that case, I spent time with Bill and it was very helpful. I had done a movie there years before called *Personal Best* which created a big controversy up at Oregon, and Bill was mad. He first thought the movie was well done and then the more conservative elements at this school said, "Those two women together!" So, he was embarrassed about it, and he thought the coach was not nice. I started working with him and I said, "Bill, that was about a bad coach. I'm not writing about a bad coach now; I'm writing about you." And we got along great. That was good. But, there's a sense in which rewriting is something of a misnomer, because all writing is rewriting.

Epps: When you are starting a first draft do you expect to rewrite it?

Towne: Oh, absolutely. I mean, I don't think I could start writing if I didn't know I had the capacity and freedom to rewrite it. In fact, one of the problems with computers is that tendency to rewrite too quickly. When I had my IBM Selectric and I couldn't shift dialogue around within the context of a scene, I just kept going. I sometimes think that we were better off.

Epps: I make my students print a hard copy and work from it for that reason—to make sure when they start to think and read through it, they don't start playing with their script. It's so easy to make little changes, but I think you have to think your way through your rewrite before you start making changes.

Towne: That's right. You get caught up making the little changes.

Epps: When you write a first draft do you show it to anybody before you do a set of changes, or do you have a general idea of how you want to revise it?

Towne: I suspect I'm no different than all of us. I have about 3 or 4 people whose opinions I really trust and I show them the draft. On the basis of that, I will or won't make certain changes. Sometimes somebody will say something with which you don't agree. But it does stimulate you to say, no, I don't think that's right, but I think this is right. One of the things I've experienced over the years with producers, and sometimes directors, is they don't know what is wrong with it. Or putting it another way, they say something is wrong, but their solutions on how to make it right are very often wrong. It behooves you to pay attention to the fact that they do feel something is wrong, but they just can't articulate it. You can't expect them to, but you can't dismiss it out of hand because they're saying something is wrong. But if they can't say what would make it right, you still have to pay attention to it.

There's a favorite story of mine about Winston Churchill who was an amateur brick mason. He used to love to make little portions of a brick wall. A friend of his came up to him one day and he said, "Winston, that wall is all crooked." And Winston said, "Any blockhead can tell me what's wrong with this wall. Can you tell me what's right with it?" With friends, this is invaluable because they see something that's really right with it. That can make you realize you were really on the right path, that you just hadn't gone far enough.

Epps: I think it's important, especially in rewriting, to make sure you know what is working.

Towne: Yes.

Epps: The process can be so negative. I know that with studio notes they tend to pile on all the negativity. So, I think it's important to be able to say, no, here's what is working. You have to protect what's working because it can get trampled and get lost in the process.

Towne: I think arguably the most valuable criticism is the criticism that points out what's right.

Epps: After you receive notes is there a "Robert Towne" approach to rewriting? This is my process, here's how I go through it, and this is how I begin to work?

Towne: No. As you know, each problem is different. For example, when I was doing a rewrite on *Godfather*—it was the garden scene between Al and Marlon. There had been no scene between the father and son in the book. Francis found himself in the position of having to come up with a scene while he was shooting, and he couldn't do it. So, he called me, and I flew back from L.A. and I saw the footage for the first time. I was knocked out by what I'd seen. Everybody had been telling Francis how bad it was. I couldn't believe it. In fact, I praised it so much that Francis got worried. He thought, "This kiss ass. I'd flown him in from L.A." He thought I was pulling his leg.

They had tried things and it didn't work. I met with Marlon, and Marlon said, "Just once I would like this character not to be inarticulate." I said, "In other words you want to talk." He said, "Yeah, I want to go 180 degrees in the opposite direction" from what he'd been doing which was so self-contained.

That was basically the only instruction I was given the night before I had to produce this scene the next morning. But it was a good instruction. In other words, "let me talk." Then I constructed the scene which was about a man who knew he was passing onto his son a very heavy burden and wanted to apologize for it, and yet not apologize. He'd done everything he could. Francis's initial request for me was "I want to have a scene where they say they love each other." I said, "Francis, you can't write a scene like that."

Epps: It's the subtext.

Towne: Yes, it's the subtext. I said, a man who struggles to tell his son everything he tried to do and how it had fallen to him—Santino was killed, Fredo couldn't do shit. So, that's how it began to take shape. The novel of *The Godfather* had on the cover an embossed design of a puppeteer holding a puppet. That's where I got the image, "I refuse to be a puppet on a string for the big shots." That's how that came into being.

The only other thing I would say about rewriting is that I take it to be my job not to write differently from the novelist or the previous screenwriter. Generally speaking, the better the writer you're rewriting, the better you can write, because you can work at that level, bearing in mind, that you're trying to do something that doesn't stand out, that isn't glaringly different within the context of that author's world and his characters. You're able to expand it a little and illuminate it but have it not be different. That was one of the fascinating problems with rewriting *The Firm*.

Epps: You are trying to seamlessly improve the script rather than put your stamp on it. You're trying to bring out what's already there.

Towne: You are in somewhat of the position of an actor trying to work your way into the role of the author, and do it the way he would do it, working at his very best.

Epps: Going back to originals. You have a first draft and you're starting in. Are you working on character improvement, structure, or plot?

Town: It depends so much on the story. Each one is so different. I mean in *Chinatown* I rewrote with Roman. We would talk and I would write. What we were trying to do was work out details of a structure which was very maddening. Our approach was interesting. I did it on *Bonnie and Clyde* and on almost every script I've written. I do an outline of the script, but try to confine my description of each scene, each segment, to one sentence. It's both a factual description of the scene, but also a distillation of the essence of the scene simply by describing it, not saying what it's about, but by choosing details of it. Suggest what it's about, but very briefly. That in itself starts to suggest that there's something wrong if you can't do a cogent, accurate, simple one-sentence description of the scene. I mean, if it gets long, there's no point in the exercise. It's a distillation.

Epps: It tells you there's something wrong at the core—which may not be the scene you are working on. It might be several scenes before that scene, but the problem shows up there.

Towne: That's exactly right. In the case of *Chinatown* we did that, and then we took a scissors and cut each one down. It was about 80 or 90 little strips of paper. We put it up on the door and stood there, you know, the equivalent of a monkey on a typewriter moving it around. Will this work there? That one won't work there. The final structure came out of that like the confrontation with Evelyn Mulray where she says, "My sister, my daughter," because Gittes pulled the glasses out of the pond. He found out it was salt water when he had learned earlier Mulray had salt water in his lungs. Then Evelyn just looked at the glasses at the last minute and she says, "Those weren't Hollis." And he said, "What are you talking about?" She said, "He didn't wear bifocals." That came out of that moment, and that's when Gittes called Noah Cross, had him come by, had him read something, saw the bifocals, knew they were the same, and knew he had his man. You know details like that can work out. In the case of a highly structured piece like that, that was very valuable.

Epps: Then once you and Roman had worked out how you wanted it to flow, did you go off and revise the script?

Towne: The script was complete at that point. I don't remember whether he just left me alone and let me write the scene, and then came back into the room. That's how we did the final draft on *Shampoo,* in a not dissimilar fashion. Five horrifying days with Warren, who you know. That's how we worked that.

There were basic things very early on in *Chinatown,* long before Roman was involved. It seems absurd now to talk about it. But I was trying to think, well, what mystery do I want to unravel first? The water scandal or the incest? I actually worried about that. Of course, I was just stumbling around, but after a while then it was obvious to me it had to be the water scandal. Once I realized that, that made a huge difference. That was early on in the development of the script.

Epps: It is amazing when you're struggling to find the pieces. You have them all, but you don't necessarily know how they fit yet. It's interesting when one piece just fits into place, how the rest of it falls together.

Towne: That's right.

Epps: If you've done your work properly, you have the right elements. Suddenly it's all going to fall into place and become clear. Something very confusing can suddenly become very clear.

Towne: That's right.

Epps: It takes a lot of struggle. That's what a lot of young writers don't realize, how much struggle it takes to bring all the pieces together.

Towne: Yes. You have to be prepared to be humiliated. It's such a humbling experience. You feel like such a fool so many times because you do so many dumb things before it goes right. The only really thrilling time in writing a script is when you don't know what's going to happen next, but you don't care because you know something's going to happen. Then, the story is dictating itself to you.

Epps: You've done the groundwork with the characters. They have free will.

Towne: And they'll help you out.

Epps: How many drafts do you need before you start to feel a script taking shape and you're comfortable with the characters?

Towne: Well . . .

Epps: I know everything's different, but in general terms.

Towne: Totally different. I think because you're talking about two things: an overall draft, and certain sections of it, and sometimes certain scenes. I mean, I've written certain scenes 30, 40 times until I've got it right. Sometimes it's very tough to move on. An overall draft? Three or four drafts I would guess. Depends on it. For example, in *Chinatown* there were three drafts. Three major drafts, but within the context of those drafts there was tremendous rewriting.

Epps: In a script like *Chinatown,* did you work around the scenes you liked or did you start running the script through a typewriter a second time?

Towne: There are certain things that you know will stay the same. For example, in *Chinatown* the first scene with Curly—you knew there was going to be a reprise at the end where, "Hey, Mr. Gittes. Hey, honey. This is the fellow that . . ." "I know who it is." So, there are certain constants that are going to stay there. They may change a little bit, but their placement is pretty much dictated by the draft that you've already done. But aside from that, very often, you change things quite a bit.

One of the most interesting problems I ever had to deal with was in *Mission Impossible II* where John Woo was the director. They had a bunch of writers on it and scripts that didn't work. But John went his merry way and did his storyboards. He outlined the action. Location people and production people had begun to design and construct, but John really didn't have a story. So, he gave me his storyboards and he said, "Would you write the story? Use the story boards for whatever story you come up with. I need these scenes." That was interesting. I think there was a movie of Sly Stallone's about mountain climbing right about that time.

Epps: *Cliffhanger.*

Towne: Yes. So, John had an early scene on the mountain. Cruise was climbing the mountain, and they were trying to make it suspenseful. I said, "No. Let's make it a busman's holiday. He's out there. This is his idea of relaxation. He's out there just to have a good time." That was sufficiently different but I could utilize that scene. We were on a mountain and it satisfied all the production requirements, but it was basically an entirely different scene.

Epps: Yet it informed Cruise's character, who he was, and what he was enjoying. His idea of a good time.

Towne: There was another scene in an airplane where the villain, Dougray Scott, was talking to the doctor he rescued. It was the guy who had developed this chimera. He killed him on the plane, and then he took off the mask, and it was Dougray Scott. I said, "What the hell is that?" Who knows who Dougray Scott is and who cares? If you're going to make this work, it's got to be Tom who supposedly is rescuing this guy. Tom kills him, then the mask comes off, and it's Dougray Scott. That will work. That changed so many things structurally, it subsequently invented a lot of scenes. It was a reprise to that scene when Dougray was with Tandy and he pretended to be Tom. It's silly, taking off the mask, but it worked.

Epps: It's an interesting challenge having to write around existing scenes and sets that are already built while trying to make a story of it. Each situation is different which means as a writer you're going to face all sorts of different challenges. But it all comes down to character, the story you are telling, and how you keep that character consistent all the way through.

Towne: Exactly.

Epps: As a writer/director it's a different situation when you're giving notes to yourself. How do you keep your objectivity about the screenplay?

Towne: You have to depend to some extent on a couple of people you trust. That's really invaluable. When the Producer comes in, there's someone you can turn to. I think your most valuable assets are your actors. Because if they're having trouble with a scene, you've got to think, if they're any good, then the problem is with the scene.

In *Without Limits*, Billy Crudup helped me with the love scene with Monica Potter. The love scene between them wasn't working. I realized his difficulty with the scene made me have to rewrite it on the day that we were shooting it. Billy was nervous about acting in a love scene with a girl who wasn't his girlfriend at that moment. Felt disloyal. So this is more of a director's instruction. I said, "Billy, I want you to play this scene. All you're trying to do is sleep with this girl. You don't really care about anything else. You'll move heaven and earth to do that. Don't worry about anything else. It will look sincere." And it did. And it was.

Epps: How important is it to learn to rewrite as a screenwriter?

Towne: Well, speaking purely as a professional, you've got to accept the fact that rewriting is probably going to be your job the majority of the time. So, it is critical. It's absolutely critical to be able to work within somebody else's vision and expand it. Of course, when you're rewriting you're working with other people, rarely with another writer, but with the producer and sometimes with the actor. You know, I don't think anything is much more important.

Epps: I've always enjoyed working with directors.

Towne: Yes. Me too.

Epps: You hear about the antagonism which I don't find. Working with a good director can be a great creative experience. I find their thoughts really helpful and I always like knowing the vision. As a writer it's hard because you get notes from executives and producers. But when it comes to the director, suddenly you're on target, and you feel like you know exactly the direction you are heading.

Towne: Listen, I've been working with Fincher. It's a joy because he's so smart. You're worried that a scene is taking too much time and a really good director may come along and say, "The problem is you're not taking enough time." That's a wonderful note to get. And you go, he's right. No, I've had great experiences with directors.

Epps: It depends on how good the director is and how confident they are. A confident director is always a good experience. And a director who is somewhat insecure becomes a tough experience.

Towne: I've had that too.

Epps: What last advice might you give aspiring writers who are struggling with rewrites?

Towne: There are certain things—it's amazing how often they're ignored. If the character seems a little stiff or stilted, or is not working well, I think one of the most critical things you can ask yourself is what is that character afraid of? Because nobody's not afraid. Fear humanizes everybody—humanizes heroes—if you just bear in mind to always ask yourself, what is this character afraid of?

Epps: Internally, not just externally. What are they not facing within themselves?

Towne: Oh no. I don't mean externally. I mean internally. Because that will inform the dialogue of everything. As you and I both know, it's not the text we're looking for, it's the subtext.

Epps: You can't write subtext unless you know what's going on inside—the turmoil inside the character.

Towne: I don't think there's a more important question from my point of view. It's surprising how often that helps.

Epps: Robert, thank you.

Towne: My pleasure.

Frank Pierson

You know if God were a screenwriter he'd be looking at it and saying, "Oh, shit! I've got to do another six days work on this." So, that's the pain of rewriting. You are constantly undoing what took enormous amount of effort to do.

Frank Pierson

Frank Pierson started his professional career writing for television on such iconic shows as *Have Gun Will Travel*, *The Naked City*, and *Route 66*. But Frank's greatest impact has been as a writer/director of feature length motion pictures. Frank won the Academy Award® for his remarkable screenplay for *Dog Day Afternoon* and was nominated for two more Oscars® for writing on *Cool Hand Luke* and *Cat Ballou*. He was also nominated for Emmy Awards and DGA awards as well as a host of other awards. In addition to the above films, his writing credits include, *A Star is Born, Presumed Innocent, In Country*, and as a consulting producer on *Mad Men*. Frank Pierson served two terms as President of the Writer's Guild of America, West, and was also President of the Academy of Motion Picture Arts and Sciences.

Jack Epps, Jr: Before we start talking about rewriting, I have some questions about writing in general. When you start a project what are you trying to accomplish with your first draft?

Frank Pierson: In a philosophical sense, the difficulty with the first draft is that you have all the possibilities of twists and turns in the universe. You have to try to get to the heart of what the truth is. What is it you are trying to get across with this movie? You've boiled it down. OK, I know how it's gonna end. I know how it's gonna begin. I know there is this scene, and this scene, and this scene, and those are the things that I want it to be. Everything else, at that stage of the game, is like a bridge—how I get from this beginning to that essential scene—from that scene to this other big scene, and gradually it begins to take shape. It takes quite a long time for me to get that sorted out. For me that first draft is the equivalent of what a muralist would call a cartoon. It's the sketch. The shape of what it's going to become.

It took me a long time before I realized the first draft was nowhere near where we were eventually going to get with the movie. The difficulty with the first draft is you know in your heart of hearts that half or maybe even two-thirds of what you're writing is just going to go in the garbage can. That's very disheartening. Once you have achieved the first draft, you have brought some order out of the chaos of all the possibilities. That's what art is all about—to find a design that is satisfying, that explains something about the world we live in, emotionally, psychologically, and even politically. Then you put the first draft aside. I'm looking at it and I'm saying, "This is pretty good!" So, I'll send it off to a friend of mine, Alvin Sargent. I'll drive over and stick it in his mailbox. By the time I get home I'm on my phone calling him and saying, "Don't read it, because it's no good." The mere idea of thinking of what it is going to look like from another person's perspective that somehow I see all the flaws in it, where it is unfinished, and one thing and another.

What you're doing when you break it open again is undoing that basic task where you've brought a kind of order. Now, you're back in psychological territory, which psychoanalysis was invented to only nibble at, and that is, it is chaos again. You know if God were a screenwriter he'd be looking at it and saying, "Oh, shit! I've got to do another six days work on this." So, that's the pain of rewriting. You are constantly undoing what took enormous amount of effort to do. That is the work of an artist in bringing order to chaos, and it is a psychological process in which you are putting demons to rest. If you've gotten into it deeply enough, you have brought up all kinds of things that are very frightening in a purely psychological sense.

Bruno Bettelheim was a great psychiatrist who worked with children and wrote about the function of fairytales. If you look at Grimm's Fairytales, they were very frightening. People were dismembered, but at the end, everybody lived happily ever after. So what was the function of those tales? If we are successful with pictures, we are doing a version of the same thing. We are bringing people close to the fundamental fires of their psychological universe. The film's psychological function is to teach the audience, "Yes, I can handle this." It's ok to open these doors, think about these terrible things and experience them in an emotional way. And it will be alright in the end.

Of course, very few filmmakers ever get that deeply into it. Fellini took us there. But Fellini's monsters, while they are monstrous, are not really very frightening. They are like figures in a Grimm's Fairytale. We know that they are not actually going eat us. But at the same time, he's touching emotions in us that are potentially destructive. The function of art is to plunge you into those fires, that it's ok, it's alright, and you can handle it. You're going to be alright. That's a highfalutin' way of looking at the whole process, but it's what I think about.

Epps: When you start a project, how much time do you devote to planning? Are you an outline person or a treatment person? Do you use index cards? Do you like to prep before you actually begin writing?

Pierson: I don't use index cards. I just start typing into a file that I call "first thoughts." Those are literally by association—just this, that, and the other thing. I'm not thinking of any plan for it at all. Then I go to a legal pad and a pen, and begin to think about what's the order of these things. I'm beginning to think about how I am manipulating what I want the audience to think, where I want the audience to be in the story. Do they know everything the hero knows? Do they have more information than the hero? Do they have less information? Are we talking about suspense here? Are we talking about surprise? And who are we surprising: the audience or the hero? All of those rather mechanical, craftsman-like things begin to come into play.

I know what I am putting down at that point, I'm going to throw away completely. It's like when you're directing something, you come in with a shot plan and by ten in the morning it's all gone. And you're rethinking it. That's how I grope my way into it. Eventually I get to the point where I'll have a step outline. Literally, what I try to get is basically twelve movements, because each one you can break down into maybe two or three scenes. There are roughly about 120 to 140 scene numbers in the average screenplay. I don't try to detail every one of them, but I know that it is this location, these characters, and what's happening. I start to write from there—I start to write the screenplay. I write from the beginning to the end. I'm not the kind of person who will just write the end, and then go back and write a scene in the middle. I can't do it that way because I'm constantly thinking this is a journey I'm taking the audience on, leading them through, and I need to think about what that journey is. If I just scattershot things, I'm going to wind up with a whole bunch of scenes. That's not what a screenplay is all about. Basically, the structure is probably more important than the quality of the dialogue or a great many other things. The structure is the first major thing that I'm trying to figure out.

What happens when I start to write and I get to page fifteen, and already the outline is not working? I have to stop, go back and re-outline because I have learned so much about the journey that I didn't know in the writing of those first fifteen, twenty or thirty pages. That makes most of what I was planning to do invalid. I've got to reorganize and go on from there. It's two steps forward and one and a half steps back. It's unpredictable. I've written some screenplays that have taken me a couple of years, and I wrote one screenplay in ten days.

Epps: Every script is different. Every idea is different. Every experience is different. You've mentioned structure when you're doing a first draft. What about character? What are your thoughts about finding and developing the characters when you are starting a project?

Pierson: My first thoughts are all about the characters—character outlines of all the people, descriptions of the locations, where are we, what time period it's in.

Sometimes those turn into little essays about the whole subject matter. I'm trying to find out for myself what I think about it, and by putting it all down in that fashion, I'll know more about that character. Those character sketches—one or two sentences—will be incorporated into the introduction of the character, when the character first comes on stage. It would be in the stage direction where we introduce that character. Then I keep the larger explanation of the character as an addendum to the screenplay which I give to the director, producer and casting director.

Epps: So they have a deeper sense of the character going beyond just the script.

Pierson: When I'm putting down first thoughts, they are always the character sketches and the sketches may be three or four pages about the character. Where he was born, what happened to him, why he did that, and one thing and another.

Once it went so far that it got into the actual screenplay. My first draft of *Cool Hand Luke* was about 140, 150 pages. I needed to know just for myself what it was that Cool Hand Luke had been through that day that took him to the point where he was cutting off the heads of parking meters. He gets up in the morning, has a fight with his wife, and goes to his mother who's sick, and another thing happened, so he had a fight with his boss. There was like 60 pages of the screenplay that was just Cool Hand Luke's bad day. Then when it came to the actual movie, I suddenly realized we don't need that. But in the end I gave that to Stuart Rosenberg, the director, and he was grateful for it. So I helped him understand. I don't know whether Paul ever actually read that material or not.

Paul Newman kept saying to me, "You're not writing this part for me, are you?" I knew exactly what he meant. He didn't want something that was sculpted to be Paul Newman. He wanted a part he was going to have to figure out how to play, and that's how he was going to make the character his.

Epps: He didn't want to be Paul Newman on the screen; he wanted to be Luke.

Pierson: That comes down to what do you show an actor? When I'm directing I try to say as little to the actors as possible because I want to see what they're bringing to the part—how they interpret it. Then if we're lucky enough to have real rehearsals or discussions, if they go way offtrack, I'll gently guide them back to where I think they need to be.

But by letting the actors practice their art rather than simply telling them what to do, you get so much more in terms of spontaneity and real feeling. In that way, it's directing, as opposed to writing. It's kind of like surfing, you know, the energy wave—the actors are the wave. And as the director, I am surfing along, and sometimes you fall off the board.

Epps: Working with actors is a creative collaboration and the best of the actors want to be part of that process.

Pierson: The thing you have to guard against is the writers and directors who want to change the script. Rather than digging deep and saying to themselves, "Why am I afraid of this? Why does my mouth get all twisted up when I try to say this line? What's wrong?" It's much easier to simply change it. That is a childish tantrum. It's vandalism, that's what it is—artistic vandalism. But at the same time if you reach a point where an actor cannot or will not do the line, George Bernard Shaw wrote about this and said you have two choices. One is to fire the actor, and nine times out of ten it's too late to fire the actor. Or, you change the line. You find a way to make it work. But you change the line, not the actor.

Epps: Is there a "Frank Pierson" approach to rewriting? "Here is my big picture approach to how I like to think about rewriting."

Pierson: Gosh no. I try not to think about it too much. But you know one thing that's always interested me about my particular history is that there are some people to whom the art of motion pictures just comes. It did not come easily for me. I had to figure it out. I had to teach myself and find out for myself what worked and what didn't work. This has been something I have struggled to figure out for myself, and it works pretty well for me. Whether it would work for anyone else, I haven't the faintest idea at all.

Epps: Rewriting is something you just have to find how it works for you.

Pierson: The question is when do you know when you're done because most screenwriting is work for hire. When you need to get paid, you've got to turn it in. That helps a lot. The thing is—nothing is ever really done. Nothing is ever finished. You can always find something to do that might work. But there comes a day when you simply have to walk away from it. That day for me comes when I realize I send it to Alvin, or I turn it in. That is when I realize I can't stand this goddamned thing anymore. I don't understand it anymore.

The other great danger in rewriting is everybody spends so much time with the script that they begin to talk it to death. I remember there's a certain joke in *Cat Ballou* and Harold Hecht, who was the producer, looked at it and said, "You know, I think I've heard this joke before." I said, "Yes, you did, Harold. It was yesterday." You tend to forget when you first heard it, it was funny, or it was shocking, or it was just absolutely right. Now, six months down the line, a hundred people are looking at it and saying, "Jeez, you know, couldn't we do something better here?" That's when the producers call in somebody to punch the script up. I hate that.

Epps: We've seen more and more of that. There are more hands on a project. They tend to throw writers at it, and a lot of times the original idea, which is strong, gets weakened, and the focus of the movie gets very vague.

Pierson: Television dramas which are now all written in the writer's room with ten or twelve people, always have one personality dominating it: David Chase on

The Sopranos; David Milch on *Deadwood;* Matt Weiner, genius, on *Mad Men.* The danger in rewriting is different in that you begin to second guess: "What will Matt think?" "What will David think?" You can't anticipate that. So you really have to get a group of people who will stay focused on what the story is all about. In the writer's room, when we begin to wrangle about something, and people are a little lost, "Wouldn't it be better if we did this or did that?" People are pitching this idea and that idea, and I'm saying, "Wait a second, what's the problem we're trying to solve here? What is it that has to happen? What is the outcome of this scene? What are we looking for that's leading into something else later on?" To clarify the direction and stay focused on the story in that way really does work. Those television series are so complex with three or four threads in each episode that are interwoven and part of threads that extend through 13 episodes over a period of a year—that's Dickens.

Epps: It absolutely is Dickens.

Pierson: But Dickens didn't have to cast; he didn't have to argue with the networks; he didn't have to do the editing; he didn't have to choose the director; he didn't have to worry over the costumes and the sets and the god knows what all. There's only one way to do these things as complex as they have become and that is in the writer's room. Matt, as brilliant as he is, could not possibly have made *Mad Men* all by himself. It's just too much.

Epps: When you start each draft, are you thinking about something you're trying to accomplish specifically? Like on this draft I want to focus on the characters, or structural issues, or my dialogue needs some polishing.

Pierson: All of that. As far as the dialogue is concerned, you just look at the page. You say, "Wait a second. I can write a better line for this character. It doesn't seem right. Anybody could have said that line. What does this line need to make it so only that character would say it in that particular circumstance?" That comes towards the end. At the beginning it's a matter of getting the order of what happened. Where we are going and what stage of the journey are we in, and trying to understand it.

One thing we haven't talked about is the matter of writing every day. I probably spend two hours a day actually putting words on paper. All of the rest of the time it's clicking away in my head. There may become a moment when I suddenly will say to my wife, "Excuse me, honey, I've got to do something." I've just thought of something I don't want to forget. But for the most part, it's just a matter of sitting down everyday at ten o'clock working until twelve, then getting up and having a life.

Epps: It's not about how long you can sit in the chair, but the quality of the time you're there. And knowing what you're there to do.

Pierson: If I can't think of something to write, I don't sit by idly. I start to think ok, why can't I write this? Why are the ideas not coming? What is it? Nine times out of ten it's because I don't understand enough about the character and the situation. So I sit down and just do exercises, and become a dog with this character. "What kind of dog would this character be if he was a dog . . ." you know.

Epps: That's very interesting. You take him out of the screenplay and look at the character in a different way.

Pierson: Put the character in a lot of different situations. How would he get change for a hundred dollar bill at two o'clock in the morning in the black section of Detroit? How would he change a tire on the freeway at rush hour? That kind of thing.

Epps: That's great because each character would do it a very different way. What's interesting is you're taking yourself out of the confines of "I have to get this perfect" to "Let's be playful."

Pierson: The analogy is the exercises they do at the Stanislavsky School of Acting. You're asking the actors: This scene, you're being asked to do something. What does that remind you of? Is there something you can think of in your past? How do you feel about that? Try to bring that feeling to what you're doing in the context of the scene. It's exactly analogous to taking us out of the fictional world of the story that we are telling and searching for the parallels or the origins in real life.

About half of what we do in the writer's room is finding ourselves talking about "Well, you know, I remember when I had an aunt who was bi-polar, and she's a drunk too and so then she turned out just like Betty." This is fictional. But what if Betty became a born-again Christian? What would Don's reaction be? Then we begin. Everybody at the table talks about their aunt or the uncle or somebody who had a similar kind of thing happen and what happened in the context of their family, how it made them feel. All of that goes into the screenplay.

Epps: How many drafts do you go through before you feel like you really know the script, until you've got it pretty close to where you think it's working?

Pierson: Twelve to sixteen.

Epps: That's a lot of drafts. Is that full drafts, or do you go in and work on sections?

Pierson: Every time I do that, the whole thing falls apart and has to be reassembled. Once you get down from draft nine to draft twelve, the differences get smaller and smaller as you go along. But between draft two and draft five the differences are going to be enormous. They will be restructured, scenes will be changed and reordered.

Epps: When you finish a draft, do you say here are things I'm gonna keep in the draft rather than starting all over again on page one?

Pierson: I'm not sure I'm going be able to answer that. I don't know. Movies to me have more in common with music than they do with anything else. You know, the rhythm, and all of that, is a really important thing. That's when you're getting down to draft ten, eleven, twelve, and thirteen—around in there. A feeling of how does this feel as music? I don't know how to explain it. For that I have to start reading it on page one. I'll read through, and come to where—wait a second. This needs to slow down a little here, or I need a pizzicato there. I need a montage. How can I do this in a montage rather than . . .? So, every day when I sit down at that point, I start at the beginning and read, read, read, read until I hit a bump, and then I try to fix the bump until I get to the end.

Epps: It is like bringing in the winds—I need some more violins here. There is an orchestration to a script, because it's so dimensional. So many different levels at work all at the same time.

Pierson: It's closer to opera than anything else.

Epps: Does any script come to mind, any project that was really difficult to rewrite?

Pierson: Every one is so different. There's a huge difference between those scripts that have actually been made because once a film gets in the hands of the director and the actors, there are a whole set of new writing problems that arise dealing with the director's particular interpretation of the material and how strongly he insists on taking it over. You know, deviating from whatever you intended, the strictures of budget, you can't do this scene in a castle, we're going to have to do it in a hut. The actors—what they are capable of doing and willing to do, or are good at. Or somebody comes up with an idea that you say, "Holy shit, I wish I thought of that. Let's put that in." So that becomes a whole different set of issues and makes it very particular. The difference between the writing experiences on a picture like *Dog Day Afternoon* as opposed to a picture like *A Star Is Born* are enormously different. You're dealing with a star vehicle as opposed to an ensemble piece.

You know, somebody asked me the other day what my favorite screenplay was that I had done, and they thought it was *Dog Day*. I said no, actually not. My favorite screenplays are the ones that have never been made because they unspooled in my head exactly as I saw them, without all the compromises that have to be made in the actual making of the film, and all the accidents, because it is an accident when it all comes together.

Epps: With *Dog Day Afternoon* was there any special rewriting in that process that comes to mind?

Pierson: No. We never got any notes from the studio. We never got any notes from anybody. There was a joke or two the director, Sidney Lumet, felt he had heard before, so I wrote him a different joke. We were all on the same page except for one particular thing. We were lucky because the whole cast was hired for the run of the show. We had three weeks of rehearsal and by then we worked out pretty much everything by talking. The idea was that Sidney would rehearse with the cast for maybe ten days, then I would fly in and sit in on a rehearsal. Then we would do whatever seemed to be needed to finish up the screenplay. So about three days into it I get a frantic call, "Get your ass on a red eye and get here quick."

So, I arrive in New York and go to Al Pacino's house. I walk in and there is Al and two extremely unhappy producers, and Sidney, who is steaming mad. I said, "Uh-huh. So I guess we have a problem here." One of the producers said, "Well, I think Al is talking about a dialogue polish." At which point, Al got down—this is literally true—got down on all fours and ran around the room barking like a dog. I didn't have the presence of mind to ask him if he needed a walk in the park. I said, "I think Al is saying that it's more than a dialogue polish. So what is it?" Al said, "Well listen, I don't know where to begin." I said, "Why don't you begin with what is it you don't like." He said, "Well, I'm not gonna appear in any scenes with Chris Sarandon." I said, "Then you mean the scenes have to be played on the telephone?" And Al said, "Yeah. But no split screen either. I don't want to be in the same framework with him." Then he said, "I don't want any discussion of sex." At that stage of the game the script was a lot funnier. There was a lot of description of the sex life between the two of them and the nature of it, some of which was funny and some of which was really terribly, terribly sad. Al said, "That's all out. I don't want any of that."

I said, "Well, anything else?" He said there was one moment in the real bank robbery that we all agreed was absolutely wonderful, and Al did too when he first read the script. They got his gay wife to actually go to the front door of the bank and talk to the bank robber inside. This was the moment they had to say goodbye to each other. Two people who had loved each other for quite a long time. They had to say goodbye where the bank robber is inside this door and his gay wife is out on the sidewalk with a two-hundred-pound policeman holding him by the belt so he can't be grabbed and pulled into the bank, and made another hostage. The two of them have to play this scene which is the ultimate scene of saying goodbye to each other—both of them by now knowing that this is a disaster, and it's not gonna come out well. They had to say good bye to each other. This was the one scene between the two people that most cried out to be played in private, and they have play it there with cops and crowds screaming obscenities, and people throwing empty beer cans at them and all the shit. At the end of it they kissed each other on the lips, goodbye. Al said, "That has to go."

There was silence for a moment and Marty Bregman, one of the producers, said "What do you think?" I said it's time to send the script to Dustin Hoffman. Al said, "Listen, you know, Dustin would be wonderful, really, truly wonderful in the part. But maybe you would just think about this for a second. In the course of your life with all the love-hate relationships, when the big things happen: the first time you decided to move in together; the first time you had a big fight; the first time when you finally decided you couldn't live with each other anymore and you moved out; all of those things. How often does sex come into it?" I said, "Never." He said, "Well, I think that it's possible to make this movie about two people who love each other and can't find a way to live with each other, and that's what it's about—rather than about two gay men robbing a bank"—which the movie had intended to be up to that point. It was funnier, and it probably would have been successful, but it would have by now aged out. It would be just bad taste jokes and so on. Like *Les Cage Aux Folles* is no longer funny. So Bregman said, "What do you think?" I said, "What I'm thinking is, you know, why didn't this son of a bitch say this to me four months ago when I had some time to really think it through." Al said, "Well, I wish you'd think about it and try." So that's what we did. It took about two days.

Epps: Two days to write and change all that?

Pierson: It was a matter of just lifting out the jokes. It required a little bit of restructuring, but very little restructuring. Some of it was just taking a line out of a scene. It concentrated the story between Al and his gay wife into two big long scenes to be played on the telephone. One, when he first comes and Al won't talk to him. Then they talk on the phone. The second move is more important because in the course of the eight minutes I wanted the scene to take the same journey that the two of them had taken in their lives. It begins with them meeting, tentatively, and they're not sure about what the other one is thinking, and then they begin a discussion. There's a moment when they've almost forgotten about where they are and their circumstances. They're able to joke about it a little bit and so on. Then all of a sudden the realization of the Pacino character is that he's being lured into saying something, that his gay wife had nothing to do with this thing. Then he gets pissed off and it's another betrayal. "Look you've done it again! Goddamn it!" That's the way things go. Then the rapprochement, and then the tender goodbye. All of that had to be built into that scene.

So what I did was I imagined that each character was talking to a psychiatrist or a good friend they really trusted who asked the question: "You really liked this guy. What went wrong?" "Oh, you don't know what it was like. He was arguing with my boss. He was so invasive. He was so infantilizing. He was all over me all the goddamn time, and so on." The other one is saying the mirror image of that, and I put all that down in four pages.

Then we went down to the soundstage. We sent everybody away. I gave Al a microphone and Chris a microphone. I handed them the pages and said, "Ok, read off the page or improvise off the page. Whatever. just let it flow. Rave on." So they started reading the page. Then they would go off the page. They'd come back to the page. Then they began to interact. We recorded that for about thirty-five, forty minutes, which is a hell of a lot. We gave that to a fleet of stenographers and out of that I distilled it into the scenes that were in film.

Epps: It's remarkable, especially the structure of the scene. It is the whole nature of their relationship.

Pierson: It was the greatest gift an actor could give to a writer. Al revealed to us all. He didn't know there was another depth to go to in the screenplay when he started out. So, that was the creative process. That's another step in the rewriting, isn't it? But if up front somebody had said, you know, you can only play these scenes on the telephone, I would have said, I think we all would have said, "Oh shit. You can't do that."

Epps: How important is learning to rewrite as a screenwriter?

Pierson: Essential. I mean, it's what it's all about.

Epps: Are there any thoughts you would share with writers who are struggling through a rewrite?

Pierson: Don't give up. There are those projects where you finally reach a point of saying, this doesn't work. I don't know how to make it work. Some years ago I tried to do a Lifetime story for Brian Grazer, not just the monkey trials, but Clarence Darrow as a whole big biopic. I couldn't solve it. And we tried like hell. There was just something unsatisfying about it, and there came a time when I said, "You know, this ain't working. Let's walk away from it. Maybe another writer can unlock it, but I don't know how to do it." For me, those have been rather rare. I can think of a couple that I wish I had quit. But it's really just a matter of not letting yourself get discouraged, and it's very hard not to get discouraged, as you know. The only people I know who are doing what they want to do are the people who never stop trying.

Susannah Grant

The biggest part of my own revising process is figuring out what I don't need, and winnowing it down to something specific and clear, rather than saying everything there is to say about it.

Susannah Grant

Susannah Grant first came to national prominence with her brilliant screenplay, *Erin Brockovich,* which earned her an Academy Award® nomination and the 2001 PEN Center USA West Literary Award. Long before *Erin Brockovich,* Susannah had written *Pocahontas, Ever After: A Cinderella Story, 28 Days,* and for the television show, *Party of Five.* Her further credits include *In Her Shoes, Catch and Release, Charlotte's Web,* and *The Soloist.* In 2011, Susannah was the cowinner of the WGA's Valentine Davies Award. The award is given to Writer's Guild of America, West members whose "contributions to the entertainment industry and the community at-large have brought dignity and honor to writers everywhere."

Jack Epps, Jr: What are some of the important things that you try to accomplish when you're writing the first draft?

Susannah Grant: You know it's a funny thing because I rewrite as I go along. So by the time I get to the first draft of the third act, I'm on about the twentieth draft of the first act. So, I'm really revising constantly. I have a bunch of friends who do what they call the Vomit Draft where they just churn the whole thing, beginning, middle, end. Don't get it right; get it written. Just blah it out on the page. I guess I must have done that at some point, but it's not my preferred way of working. I often end up with first drafts that are pretty close to where I want them to be.

That said, every scene definitely has a first draft feel or every section suffers from what I call "first draft-itis," which is, it accomplishes the intentions. Then I try to get myself out of it and pull up the intentions of the characters so you don't see the outline there so much. I mean, the worst of a first draft, you watch or read a scene and say, "Ah, I know exactly what this looks like on the outline." This is when this character goes from here to there, and that character opposes them. I like to get it to a point where the mechanics of it are invisible or are at least less visible, less interesting, less noticeable than the humanity of the people, or the uniqueness of the situation, or the memorability of the scene. I try to do something that surprises me in the scene so that the scene is surprising to others. That rarely happens for me in the first draft of a scene. Sometimes it does; sometimes you look at something and you have a great idea how to do it the first time around and it just sticks. But usually I need to get a little hardware down there before I play with it.

Epps: In terms of your approach, is it the characters you're looking to find? Get their voices as you're going through?

Grant: No, it's rarely the characters for me, because usually I have a pretty good sense of who they are before I start writing. Sometimes I don't bring those qualities out as much. So, I go back and I'm missing who that person is. But characters rarely reveal themselves to me as I go along—at least the primary characters. The stuff that usually bubbles up initially before I start writing anything is who they are and what their dimensionality is. It's how to dramatize something in a way that obviously isn't boring, how to use what's unique about those characters to dramatize the situation in a particular way.

Honestly, a lot of times it's cutting. I overwrite tremendously. I keep a file when I'm writing a script and when I write three scenes and think, oh, I'm not sure I need them. I take them out and put them in a separate file. I build a trash file for a script as I'm building the script. By the time I finish the script the trash file is at least twice as long as the script. So, I've written three times as many pages, minimum, by the time I've finished the script as the actual script. So, that's a lot of editing. Sometimes I'll write four pages on a scene before I get to the sort of surprising way of dramatizing something, and then I realize, well, I don't need those first three pages, so they go in that trash file. But I'm never sure I'm not going to need them. I rarely pull things out of there, but I save it all. I'd say the biggest part of my own revising process is figuring out what I don't need, and winnowing it down to something specific and clear rather than saying everything there is to say about it.

Epps: You cut as you're going along.

Grant: Yes, you have to keep moving the ball forward. There's a way of working in which you just revise and revise and revise and end up with the same 15 pages, which I don't do. I understand the inclination to do that, but that's really just noodling. What I usually do is sit down and print out the work I did before, and read that on a hard copy and make edits. Then I sit down on my computer and type in those edits and usually end up making a whole bunch more as well. By the time I get to the place where I've run out of ideas, I'm sort of ramped up to move forward again. That tends to be my process. I write moving forward from that. Then the next day, I'll print out that first draft work, and sharpen it. Sometimes, every four or five, six, seven days, I'll print out the whole thing and read it straight through again. So, it's a lot of going over, and over, and over.

Epps: My students are so computer oriented, I always tell them to print out a copy and work off a hard draft because it forces you to focus on the page, and not just start making those little changes on your computer as you're reading. Is that what you find?

Grant: Maybe it's because that I started out reading on paper, but it reads differently to me on paper. I suppose the inability to change it right then makes you think a little bit harder about it. But I don't really feel like I know what it is and what it feels like until I read it on paper for some reason. I can read other people's scripts on a screen and feel like I read them thoroughly. But when I'm trying to figure out where the glitches are in my own work it's easier for me on paper. I'm not even sure why.

Epps: There's something tactile about it. There's just something about having the page; it's there, you can feel it. There's a whole different relationship.

Grant: Yes, it's a transitional document anyway. It's not the finished document; the film is. In terms of moving chunks of script around, taking half a page from one scene and realizing you can put it four pages early—that kind of thing is easier with a pen to me. There's a lot of that kind of thing. I end up doing a lot of that.

Epps: But you're still working off the basic outline. It sounds like you're very free and loose with it which allows you to make changes, if that's what the story wants you to do.

Grant: Yes, but I'll revise the outline as I go along. I would love to be one of those people who can write a perfect outline, then sit down and write a script from it, and it all fits perfectly. Actually, I say I would love to be that kind, but the truth is I actually have a lot of fun with the fluidity of it as you're building it and the surprises.

Epps: That's part of the process. It's important, especially for aspiring writers, to realize that you create your own process. You take little bits from here and there, and figure out how it works best for you and how you find the heart of things.

Grant: That is the really, really important thing. Everybody I know, whose work I admire, works totally differently from each other. There really is no right if you can just get enough quiet time to figure out what environment creates the best fertile ground for you.

Epps: Your characters are really strong and vibrant. How do you accomplish that?

Grant: Thank you. That's nice of you to say. That comes fairly instinctively to me. That's goes back to really imaginative play as a kid. Seriously. I think I just never stopped doing it, so that's the fun for me. That's sort of what my brain does, and then I get to make it my work, which is great.

When I finish a script—because you can easily kid yourself that it's good enough—one of the things that I always do, and I do this for every character in the script, is I say: "If I'm an actor with choices, am I going to take this role over another one?" It sounds like a strategic packaging question to ask yourself, but it's really not. It's a writing question. Because if the answer is no, the answer is no. As an actor, if I could do this, or any other romantic comedy, and the choice wouldn't be that different, then you probably haven't done your job as a writer. You haven't found enough dimension to make the character something that someone can't say no to just because it's rich and vibrant, and somebody says, "Oh, I've got to spend four months of my life playing that character."

Epps: You've been around great actors. You know that they really want to dive into something. They're very talented, creative people, and they're looking for a challenge.

Grant: Yes, and if it's anything like writing, it's really hard to do if you're not in love with it. I can't imagine as an actor going into a job everyday and trying to play a character you didn't understand. I do it for minor characters too. That always enlivens a scene. If you have one scene that a cop is in, give the cop something because everybody's interesting. I had a Shakespeare teacher in college, and one of the first things he commented on was that every character in Shakespeare has a fascinating inner monologue, and you get a little glimpse of it. If you remember that about everyone, it just enlivens the whole scene.

Epps: Humanity is a hallmark of your movies. You see what your characters are going through—their lives, their struggles, their crises. It's messy. Life is really messy. But yet we identify with your characters.

Grant: Every now and then people say I write strong women. They're not strong. They're often a total mess. But they're alive and living it. That's her strength.

Epps: Erin Brockovich is a wonderful character.

Grant: Yes, she's struggling, though. But she finds her strength.

Epps: Now you've handed in your script, and the traditional rewrite process begins. What is that like for you?

Grant: Before I hand it into anyone in the work life, there are two people I show it to, other writers that I met in film school. We show each other everything we're doing. I know they will stop me from turning in anything hideous. I know I can show them hideous stuff, and they know that good writers write bad stuff sometimes. They're the people I don't have to feel embarrassed around because everybody writes bad stuff sometimes.

It's not about getting their okay, it's just you can lose a little perspective. Am I accomplishing what I mean to accomplish here? It really depends on the reception and the path to perfection which has so little to do with writing. If you've written a really solid first draft, often you don't do any more work until there's another element involved, a director or an actor or somebody else with whom you're going to be collaborating with, aside from the producers and executives. Lots of times people don't want to wait to invest in that second draft until they've got a couple more voices in the mix.

Then it really just varies according to the personalities you're working with. In my experience, there were two times in retrospect where I felt like I protected my job more than I protected the script, and those are the two movies I am least proud of. Where I feel like, I should have just said, "You are doing something else with this. I don't understand what you're doing. I don't see." Instead I tried to make it work. I tried to satisfy them and tried to satisfy me. I guess you never really know because lots of time a gnarly collaboration can lead to a great movie. But I do think your job is to protect the intentions of your script. I actually feel like it's important to write them down. Write it down really clearly, what the movie is about. Not just know it in your head, but have it on a piece of paper and, give it to your producer. Say, "As we go forward and we're making all these choices, this is the one thing we're going to protect. Let's protect this."

Epps: That is a great way to make sure everyone agrees they're making the same movie. It's not some agenda that you weren't in on that suddenly gets hijacked, and it's now something else.

Grant: Right. If it does get hijacked at least you can call it that. You can say, "You know what, this director has come on board and wants to make a different movie. I don't endorse that." Obviously, if you're a writer for hire it's not your call. You can fight but you can lose. At least nobody's under any illusions that it isn't changing. That said, I've had great collaborations. I am not a huge whiner about the development process if I'm working with smart people. I've had people make my work better all along the way. So collaboration can be good, it can bring out the best in you if you're working with good people. Those are usually fun collaborations. Even if they're hard, they're fun, and then sometimes you just lose. That's all there is to it.

When I was working with Joe Wright on *The Soloist,* I wanted to be as factual as possible. There was a character in Steve Lopez's life that Joe said was an extraneous character in the movie. If you look at the script, and take out the fact that it's real, this character wasn't pulling its weight in the script. He said, "Well, let's just not make him married." And I said, "But he has to be married, because he's married. Let's try and do something with that character." We also had the strike looming, so we didn't have tons of time to really dig in. I ended up losing the battle, and Robert Downey plays a single man and Steve Lopez is a very happily married man. He and his wife have a real partnership. I felt bad about that, and yet it probably made for a more solid script, because there wasn't this stray character that wasn't feeding the plot. But, you don't always win. I liked working with him. I liked fighting with him. But I didn't like losing.

Epps: When you do get a set of notes, what's your process?

Grant: I try not to leave the room if I don't understand how to approach something. In fact, I don't. I just say, "Let's talk about that one, because I don't get it." If it makes sense to me, it's not really that big of a mystery. You think, ok, I can do that there and there and there. Usually by the time you've finished a script you have the whole thing in your brain. If somebody says, "I'm not feeling his fear," you go, "I can pull it up here and there." You know the places where there's flexibility in this script for that. If I don't understand a note, I just stay with it, because the last thing you want to do is think, oh, I'll figure that out later, and then you don't figure it out or you execute it badly.

Then there's notes I flat out disagree with, and that happens. There are two kinds. One is being worried about, oh, is she going to seem unlikable or is he going to seem weak? But those are not internal ways of looking at a character. I try to say, "You know what, let's wait until we get a director; let's wait until we get a star. If you like it, let's just stick with it for now and let's worry about the marketing later." Unless it's like, "Look, I read this and I hated her, and I don't think I'm meant to hate her," then that's a note I want to hear. But if it's just sort of a cautious note, "I don't know; I'm nervous." I try to put those to bed.

Sometimes there's another note I just disagree with. The constructive thing I say is, "Why don't you tell me where in the script you've got a bad feeling and what that bad feeling was. Don't give me the fix. We'll work on the fix later, but let's try to diagnose the problem, because if I know the problem, the fix is usually very easy." But people will give you a fix that doesn't make sense to you. You think, well, I don't want to do that. That's doesn't feel right to me.

There's no point in arguing your fix versus my fix, because people get very invested in their fix. I find it much more constructive to say, "I really respect your point of view, and if you're having a problem with the script, that's a really important thing for me to know. Let's find out what that is and then maybe I'll do my job of fixing it, and you tell me if that does it for you." That tends to feel more constructive. So, when getting notes I try to get as clear as possible before leaving the room. Then I find executing notes to be the easiest part. I mean, it's fun because you have your landscape. You're just adjusting things and enhancing things unless you just rip apart the whole thing. But I don't think I've really experienced that.

Epps: You're lucky.

Grant: No, that's not true. I did. You know, I suffer from selective amnesia and when experiences have been very bad, I knock them from my memory bank. I just remembered one that was a legitimately bad collaboration where somebody wanted to make a completely different movie, but they didn't come out and say that. Things can just go totally south too. If the other person has more juice and equity, they're going to win. My desire is like, kill me quickly. Don't put me through two drafts if you're not actually invested in this. Just knock me out of the game and move on if that's what' it's going to be, because, doing a rewrite, trying to please someone who isn't even invested is really bad. You don't often know that until after the fact.

Epps: Until after the fact when you figure out what happened.

Grant: Yeah. Here's the thing. For students or for any writer, you can't go into it anticipating that sort of scenario. You just can't because bad things will happen. But if you go into every relationship anticipating bad things, they're all going to suck. You have to assume that you're working with people of goodwill who want to make a good movie. If you don't have that, I don't know what my advice is then.

Epps: Do you have a specific approach to rewriting? Do you go to character first, then structure?

Grant: It really depends on where I've not done my full work on the first draft. It can vary. But, it's rarely in character. The hard stuff for me is structure. That's the stuff that is work for me, which is fine. You know it's hard to finish a poorly structured script. It's easy to get halfway through a poorly structured script, but by the time you reach the end you know if you have a leaky vessel. So often, if there's something wrong structurally, I'll end up stopping on page 75, page 80, and do a big revision. If I feel like I don't have momentum driving me toward the ending, I can't finish it. Why bother? You know it's not going to last.

Epps: How long does it take you to complete what would be a first draft, which for you, is many, many drafts?

Grant: It's usually within the twelve-to-fifteen-week window. But you know how deals are. It takes you three weeks to get a job so that adds three weeks, because you're thinking about it. You have to virtually have an outline to get a job now. I try to be a reliable partner and deliver on what I promise. The last script I wrote was a very structure-dependent romantic comedy. I had it almost finished after the twelve weeks, but I wasn't in love with it. I called them up and said, "You just got to give me another three weeks here because if I gave it to you, you'd say it's not done, and I know it." So, I've done that. When you just feel like it's not there yet, that you're not dying to see this movie yet. But I try. I've never had one of those ridiculous jobs where you've been on it a year and everybody's saying where is it? That would make me miserable. That's a pressure.

Epps: What's your daily routine?

Grant: When I'm doing a first draft I have this weird routine of getting up at like 4:30, primarily because I have a family. If I get up and start the day with forty-five minutes of talking to kids and making lunch and figuring out who has cleats and who needs to be picked up where, I'd never ever get out of the gate. But if I get up really early and get two good hours of concentration in before all that business it's easy to go back for me. I get more done in the first four hours of the day when I get up at 4:30 than I do in an eight hour day when I get up at 7:00.

Epps: That's really a lot of self-discipline.

Grant: But it's desperation. I also like working late at night, but if I get up at 4:30 I'm asleep at 10:00 at night so that doesn't work as well. I don't do that when I'm rewriting, because I've been working on it long enough that I know it really well, and it's easy to drop back into it. That feels more compatible with life than a first draft. A first draft you're sort of excavating something from deep underground and trying to find out what it is and that requires more of me than revisions. So, yes, it's crazy. It's all dependent on a really good coffee machine.

Epps: Yes, caffeine is definitely the writer's friend. You are also a script doctor.

Grant: I only take those jobs when I look at the script and know exactly what I think it needs, and know that I can deliver it. Usually by the time they're coming to you for a rewrite they really want to make the movie. They're looking for a movie. They're not looking for another draft of a script. So, if I feel like I know how to turn this into a movie you can cast, you can get a director on, and you can make, I'll take that job. If I feel I can make this a little better.

Honestly, most of the work that comes my way for rewrites is because they're having trouble casting it. It's usually character based work or actor friendly assignments for somebody that I may have worked with before who has a certain level of comfort with me. Again, if I see it right away, if it's like one of those, you know, "magic eye" things, if I automatically say, oh, I know what that is: that's an airplane. You just can't see it yet. I know how to make it into that. If it's going to be really hard, and I don't know how to do it, then there's got to be someone out there who's better for the job than me. You only want to take those jobs if you know everybody's going to be happy with the outcome. It doesn't do you any good otherwise.

Epps: The good news is they're usually a little desperate at that point. Which is sort of fun because you're the rescue person.

Grant: Right. People also want you to be realistic if they're actually making the movie. You both have to have a sense of what can change and what can't. You know obviously you can't relocate it to Paris if everybody's prepping in New York. You know stuff like that. But again, the only reason work like that comes my way is if it comes naturally. It's just character work. Often I'll see something that is a great idea but the characters are still a little thin. So I'll look at that.

Epps: Character is really what most people struggle with, especially young writers. What do you bring to the characters?

Grant: The most important thing to think about is dimension. It's really important to be very clear about characters, but you can be clear and also have them to be complex, have somebody be incredibly vulnerable and incredibly arrogant. Maybe it's just a matter of understanding people. One of my favorite characters of the last decade was the character Ryan Gosling played in *Half Nelson,* who was the crack-addicted school teacher. He was such a great character. He was really good and he had a really big problem. That's the kind of dimension that people don't think about having because there's a pressure to be really clear and really specific. Sometimes it can end up being a bit thin. There's room—there's a lot of room on screen for characters to have complexity.

Epps: The audiences really like it. That's what pulls them into your movie, and that's why they bond with it.

Grant: I was talking to somebody about a script lately and there was a main character that was mean and bombastic, and dangerous and violent. I thought, the only people I know who are like that are terrified of something, you know. My feedback was go ahead and show us what he's scared of. The scariest dog on the playground is the one that's the most fearful. So, open that up a little. There's usually a shadow side to everything. If it doesn't come naturally to you I would say just study. Study people and movies that do it really, really well. Look at iconic performances and find out what makes them so good.

Epps: One movie I reference a lot is *On the Waterfront.* When you look at the movie, not much happens. It's about a man making a decision. But Terry's got this dark, dark shadow that he carries around with him.

Grant: Those are the characters I get excited about. If I were an actor those are the characters I'd want to play. Any situation is more interesting if there's somebody who feels that much more engaged in it. Even if people don't consciously know that there's a shadow side to everything, they feel it when a character is real. That old "ring of truth" thing.

Epps: When you are brought in to rewrite do you often have a specific problem to solve?

Grant: At times I've been brought into work on a specific character, and then it's going well, so you hang around and work on the other characters too. Because, as with any script, if you work on one character, everything works except for the daughter. So, I'll just work on the daughter. You work on the daughter and realize nothing else was good enough, so then you have to work on everything else too.

Epps: Screenplays are a house of cards. If you fix one thing it affects something else.

Grant: You make something better and you realize it wasn't as good as all the other stuff. You bring that up, and you think, oh boy, now look the dog is boring; I've got to make the dog better. I have a friend who when she's done with a script she prints out the title page with her nemesis's name as the author, the person whose work she wants to hate, and she tries to read through it looking for things. If her enemy had written it, what are the things she would seize on with glee as being shitty? That's her test for herself. If she can find anything in there that she is delighted to hate, thinking it's the work of somebody else, then she realizes she's not done yet. That's a particularly vindictive way of rewriting, but for her it works.

Epps: That's very funny.

Grant: I don't think I've ever come in on something that's really broken because I feel like for that much effort, I'd just as soon write my own script. It's like a home remodel. Sometimes it's just easier to take it down—just gut the whole thing and start over.

I'm very much a gut writer. You just know when it's right and you know when it's not good enough—if you're really honest with yourself. Sometimes you can be tired enough to think it's good enough. I always try give myself a week to let it sit, to just recharge, because I get very tired at the end. I work long hours and I get sort of dizzy and don't have a lot of perspective. Ideally it would be a week of putting it away. It's usually about three days of putting it away, trying to get a little perspective and trying to be invested in being finished rather than in it being as good as it can be.

Epps: It's always hard to do because you're tired and the simple fact is that you want to just get rid of it.

Grant: Yes, I mean you're so dying to be finished. If you're working for someone they're pressuring you to be finished. But nobody cares if it's late, if it's good. Nobody cares if it's on time, if it sucks. So, as long as you're still working on it, people don't care if you're a week or two late. As soon as you've turned it in that stops mattering. Unless there's a start date, there's no reason to turn it in if it's not really ready. That said, don't be disrespectful to your partners who've paid you money and expect the product. But I know the desire for it to be done can sometimes exceed good judgment.

Epps: For young writers they're so excited they've written something that they just to want everybody to see it now. They don't realize that they need to go through a process. Take a week and get away from it, then go back to it. See things with fresh eyes.

Grant: Exactly. Don't show it to mom, for instance. My mom, you know, she'll love it. She's not a writer. It's not something that comes naturally to her so she thinks that's great that I wrote something. A lot of people who are starting out feel insecure, and I understand that. I feel hideously insecure to this day when I finish a draft. So there's an instinct to look for feedback that's going to address your emotional needs, that desire to feel less insecure and less vulnerable and all that, and that's not going to make your work better. You really do have to sort of toughen up and look for the people who are going to give you the hardest time. You can easily find people who will tell you that you did a good job. Seek out the people who will be rigorous.

Epps: I think that's a hard thing for a lot of writers. Who do I get notes from? Who do I trust?

Grant: You just find them over time. I was lucky. The person I primarily go with is somebody I met in film school, and she and I are both screenwriters. She's the easiest person to show anything to. We just laugh if it's terrible. But I certainly had people whose feedback has been less helpful over the years.

Epps: What would you say about rewriting to an aspiring writer who's just finished a draft. They've got some notes and they're facing the need to do more work on it.

Grant: One thing I think it's good to be clear about what your intentions are with the script, and ask your readers if you're achieving those. Somebody can say, "I love it; it was funny, and I really like the ending." But if you know what you want the entire script to be about, ask questions. Say, "Did you like this?" Ask people to be critical. I ask people to read with a pencil and when they're happy, write a check and when they're unhappy write an X, and they're both important. Be bold, be brave, be tough. Because scripts don't get better if you worry about making yourself feel less vulnerable. The horrible, vulnerable, exposed, nauseating feeling—that doesn't go away. That's just your partner for life.

In rewriting, for a lot of people when they're getting feedback, they're looking for somebody to make them feel better. But you're not going to feel better; you're going to feel shitty because that's what the deal is. So, instead, just look for someone who isn't going to worry about your feelings. I mean eventually the script will go out there, and it will be read by people who neither know nor care about you, and your feelings will be irrelevant. So, don't worry about making yourself feel better about your work, worry about making the work better. If you're getting the same note from a lot a people it's probably a good note. If you're getting a million different notes from people you probably need to stop and rethink what you're doing. It probably means you're not being clear.

Epps: Absolutely.

Grant: That said, if you really know what you want to say and you're clear about that, the notes are there to help you do that. That's where the good writing is when people say, "I'm not actually worried about this being funny, because I have a bigger vision for this, and this is what that vision is." Have a clarity of vision and a really clear sense of the story you want to tell. If you have that, then you can be the one driving the conversation with notes. You can say, "Did I do this? Am I achieving that?" If the answer's no, then you know what to do. It's not mysterious.

Epps: I think it's very important for the writer to also be asking questions about their own work.

Grant: You're the writer. It's your thing. You're responsible, and if you don't have a clear vision out of the gate of what the movie wants to be, then no amount of notes are going to help you. You're just going to be herded towards somebody else's idea of what it should be. There's no substitute for a clear vision. I know plenty of people who had scripts with a clear vision that get into a situation where everything but the clear vision is what somebody wants. Like, we want everything about this story except your intention. And we'll pay you for it. Then you've got a hard decision to make.

Part Four

Examples

Studio Script Notes

Turner & Hooch Notes

My writing partner, Jim Cash, and I had worked with Jeffrey Katzenberg while he was Head of Production at Paramount on *Dick Tracy* and *Top Gun*. When he moved over to Disney, he reached out to us to rewrite *Turner & Hooch*. Tom Hanks was committed to star in the film. The picture was green lit, but the main character was still vague and his motivations were unclear. We were brought on primarily to add more character for Tom to play. During the development period, Tom was intimately involved and attended the majority of story meetings. At that time, having the actor involved in development was highly unusual, but it was great having Tom involved. He was always generous, funny, had great ideas, and threw out amazing lines.

I've included these notes because they are from Tom, and show his depth of understanding in creating the character of Scott Turner. Even more importantly, they show his insight about his relationship with Hooch. Tom laid out an excellent relationship arc that we used as the basis of our rewrite.

Memo

12/5/88

To: Turner & Hooch Team
From: Tom Hanks
Subject Notes to be considered for the upcoming rewrite

The following are comments regarding the character of Turner as well as a few story points with which I have problems.

1. WHY IS TURNER LIVING IN CYPRESS BEACH

I would like to think that Turner has recently been promoted out of uniform and been made an Investigator. He likes the prestige but he could still want more. He needs a DRIVE, a DESIRE to be somewhere else doing something more important than finding stolen rototillers and lost rubber boats. Turner's desire could be to parlay a good career as a police officer into a shot at the Chief's job, then the Mayor's, then he could run for state senate, and then Governor.

We could then make use of his *choice* to be a public servant, seeing that it means more to him as just a nice job in a nice town. He is actually dedicated to the idea of serving the public, but he also has some solid dreams of his own. He is also a meticulous guy, and this kind of long haul, twenty-years-down-the-road thinking is right in character for Scott Turner.

I think we should lose the idea that Turner was married and his ex-wife wanted to live in Cypress Beach, in which case he is there by accident and his being a policeman is the result of nothing. What if his father had been in the Army and it so happens that the Turner family was stationed at Fort Ord just as Scott was finishing high school, so he went to a cheap college nearby and joined the police force after toying with the idea of going to law school? Any character in any movie who has made the decision *not* to become a lawyer is *instantly* likeable.

Turner should desire a romantic involvement and have some sort of visible, hard-luck sexual past. Could there be a former girlfriend around town who Turner pursues even though she is obviously not meant for him (maybe a new take on Katie the dispatcher)? This could make Emily even more attractive to Turner, and get the audience rooting for a Turner/Emily coupling.

2. TURNER IN HIS COCOON

I think that Scott Turner was an only child and he is used to having things his way. The life he has built for himself is based on the fact that he has no responsibilities—no wife, no kids, no pets, no plants. It is a "low maintenance" lifestyle over which he is god, but his meticulousness should not cover the fact that he is *lonely*. His house is very neat, but it is also quiet. He has the patience to build his own stereo equipment, but he has nothing better to do. His kitchen is well organized and has all the right doo-dads, but he still only cooks dinner for one. His wardrobe can be fashionable (in subtle contrast to the rest of the town), but he still irons those shirts on Saturday nights instead of being out somewhere.

His cocoon is self-imposed because Turner is a product of his childhood environment and doesn't know anything else. When Hooch invades this cocoon, it is a shock to Turner but the audience should see that this is exactly what the guy needs. As the movie progresses and Turner becomes less meticulous, it is not just because the dog is a slob, but because Turner has actually adapted to Hooch's presence. He has not had the time to spend on himself because he has had to look after Hooch and all the trouble caused by Hooch, just like a brand new set of parents have their lives completely changed when their first baby comes home from the hospital.

3. RELATIONSHIP OF TURNER AND HOOCH: HOOCH AS A CHARACTER

I think the arc of this relationship is as follows:

> PART ONE Total reluctance on the part of Turner to take Hooch.
> PART TWO Turner and Hooch go through their version of Hell Week.
> PART THREE Turner adapting to Hooch's presence and loosening up in the process.
> PART FOUR Turner relying on Hooch as a partner.

Part One That Turner and Hooch don't like each other is obvious, but I think when Turner finds the dog back at the boat yard after his escape from the pound, Hooch should make his peace with Turner and actually *like* the man. This would get the audience emotionally rooting for Hooch and give us something to play with other than just the repulsive aspect of his character. This *does not mean* that Hooch then does everything Turner tells him, of course. Hooch is still his own boss (just as Turner views himself) and the dog will still do as he pleases, but what could be achieved by having Hooch throw himself happily all over a horrified Turner may be an invaluable source of empathy. And, Hooch could still hate everyone else, including Cortez.

Turner should not speak to the dog at all through the early going, other than a few ignored commands. We should save any real conversation until they are together in the apartment.

Part Two I think more needs to be made of Turner and Hooch both *in the apartment at the same time.* As it is, Hooch destroys the place while Turner is gone, and I think that makes for lost opportunities. Hooch's first night in the apartment could be a long night of hell for Turner, instead of him just coming home to discover a mess. In which case we are just redoing the kitchen scene from E.T. The food shopping scene is funny, and if we work in Captain Hyde we will save some time, but wouldn't the movie be better if we spent more time on the comedic possibilities of Turner and Hooch as opposed to Turner and the Dog food aisle? I think we are ignoring a gold mine.

Other moments could be the various ways Turner tries to tie Hooch up, always meeting with some kind of misfortune. This could pay off later when Turner doesn't even bother.

Part Three When Turner finally realizes that Hooch is a witness to the crime (somewhere around Scene 162) things change. Turner starts talking to his dog just like regular dog owners do. He becomes oblivious to other people's complaints. He becomes disheveled and sloppy. He gets laid. He could begin to enjoy Hooch, letting the dog run rampant on the Golf Course during the confrontation with Boyett. This stuff is in the script already, but more needs to be made of it.

Part Four Once the bomb goes off, I think Turner and Hooch become a team. Something could be made of this, such as Hooch, sensing that something horrible has happened after the explosion, hesitates before going with Turner, until Turner hollers "Hooch! Car!" I think the audience could get a big charge out of this, raising the stakes for the end of the movie.

When Turner carriers the wounded Hooch into Emily's office he could even say something like " . . . look what they did to my dog . . ." Somewhere in Part Four Turner comes to think of Hooch as "my dog".

4. GENERAL NOTES

—I am concerned that our chosen crime, the laundering of money, has no consequences to the audience, and that hiding the cash in the blocks of ice will only confuse them. Yes, Amos and Cortez is killed, but over what? Frozen money? Where does the money come from? Who wouldn't take such an easy shitload of cash? Who is it really hurting? None of this means anything to the audience. I don't mean that we need drugs or guns to be the object of Boyett's operation, but we need to have some other aspect of the crime be accessible to the audience's sensibilities. How rich is Boyett getting? What are his future plans? What new jeopardy will the town be in because of all this?

— I still have a problem with Hooch finding a brick of *ten thousand dollars*. The bad guys make no mention of the lost money, but surely they would miss it. And surely such a find would cause an immediate ruckus amongst the police. Right now *ten thousand dollars* is held as evidence as though it were a rock thrown through an old lady's window.

— The cards in Scene 162 should say all the things connected with a police investigation EVIDENCE, MOTIVE, WEAPON, SUSPECTS, WITNESSES, M.O., and whatever else we can think of. There should then be other cards grouped with these cards, like KNIFE, MONEY, AMOS, BOYETT, ZACK GREGORY, etc. Under WITNESSES of course, there is only one card. HOOCH.

— The vomit sketch. This scene could be funny if the punch line is something other than Turner and Cortez bolting for the door. I've seen that too many times. I like the idea of Riker *expecting* to make the two cops vomit, but having trouble doing so. Maybe Turner and Cortez can *pretend* to be unphased by the autopsy only to have to make a very quick stop in the bathroom. This could be a scene for the construction of their relationship.

Sister Act Game Plan and Studio Notes

After our work at Disney on *Turner & Hooch*, Jim Cash and I were hired to do a rewrite on *Sister Act* which at that time was being written with Bette Midler in mind. Eventually, Bette passed on the project, Whoopi Goldberg was cast, and film history was made.

Included are a set of notes and a simple game plan. The game plan is for our first pass on the script which in turn triggers the August Memorandum. These notes are a good example of the complexity and detail of studio notes. The challenge is to satisfy the needs of the studio while at the same doing what you think is best for the project.

"SISTER ACT"

GAME PLAN

1. This is a character story about people. Each and every character needs a personal story. They must be committed. This is a story about people's lives and how people affect each other.

   (Bette's life is in crisis and transition. She has hit bottom and this is a story about how she comes back on top. She's a cynic, and like Terry Malloy, her philosophy is "Get the other guy before he gets you". Everybody's out for themselves, it's a dog eat dog world.)

2. Base the story in a sense of reality.

3. Make Bette's character as outrageous as possible without crossing the line. Katzenberg calls her "The Mouth". That's a great way to think of her. Her mouth has always gotten her into trouble. She can't stop it.

4. Create several new, funny, sensitive and warm nun characters. These are very important because these are the people that ultimately the story is based on.

5. Create a good new subplot at the convent to carry the second act. The convent needs to have some sort of complication that Bette helps to solve.

6. Make the script funny.

7. Finish it in four weeks. We start writing on Monday, April 16th and finish it four weeks later.

THE TAPES

1. David Hoberman tape—This was the first meeting and lays out our approach and what Hoberman is looking for. This is a very important tape and helps focus our task.

2. Jeffrey Katzenberg tape—Jeffrey always has good ideas, we just need to pick and choose carefully what we want. He has a good vision of how "Disney" sees this project. I always like to satisfy Jeffrey.

3. Mary Pat Kelly—the technical advisor—This is our research tape that gives us background information about the life of nuns. There is a lot of good material here, and as you will quickly see, Mary is too concerned with reality. Ignore her concerns about the way we portray the convent. We are not doing a documentary.

There is a lot of character and comedy that comes out of truth, such as Bette being awakened the first night at 2:00 a.m. to pray. As one of the sisters explains to her, "People are sick in the middle of the night and they need our prayers".

The first tape is the most important one, and so far, the best.

Get some rest, shoot some hoops and let's knock this baby off. Thanks for all the hard work. I think it really turned out much better than we both thought it would.

Best,
Jack

[Redacted]   Memorandum
To: SISTER ACT TEAM   Date: AUGUST 13, 1990
From: [Redacted]
Subject: SISTER ACT—Summary of Meeting with Jim Cash, Jack
Epps Jr., Scott Rudin, and [Redacted]

The following notes summarize our meeting of 8/10/90.

CHARACTERS

- **TERRI**

Maintaining Terri As the Focus of the Movie

- This draft may have shifted too far toward becoming a
  "save the convent" story. In general, we would like
  to focus the through-line of the movie more clearly on
  Terri and her transformation. Through revitalizing the
  choir and breathing new life into the convent, Terri
  becomes a hero and restores her faith and belief in
  herself. When we are introduced to Terri at the hotel,
  perhaps we can find ways to emphasize the fact that she
  is on a "loser track", and most of all that no one has
  ever appreciated her true talent. Perhaps when Eddie
  waylays Terri in her dressing room, he can refer to
  how far down she's fallen.

Defining Her Turning Point

- We would like to more clearly define the moment where
  Terri, motivated by her relationship with the nuns,
  begins to "come around" and take an interest in the
  other nuns and the convent's endangered future. One
  point where this might logically occur is when Terri
  returns from her night out with Frank. The awakening
  she's been building toward could be motivated by the
  way that the sisters reach out and help her even though
  she's betrayed their trust.

Terri's Impersonation of a Nun

- At times it seems that Terri isn't trying to
  masquerade as a nun. This, and the fact that the nuns
  seem oblivious to her bizarre behavior, occasionally
  makes the other nuns seem a bit dense. To protect her
  identity, Terri could make a greater effort to devise
  outrageous lies about her past, handing a different
  line to each person who asks her. For example, after

her night out with Frank, she might invent a wild
story to explain where she's been.
- Although we like waiting until the concert to reveal
  Terri's true identity, the nuns should sense earlier
  on that something is not quite right with Terri.

- **THE MOTHER SUPERIOR**

Building and Clarifying Her Role

- The Mother Superior currently seems to take a back
  seat to some of our other characters. We suggest
  reworking her role in the story so that she is
  clearly our antagonist.
- We would like to look for ways of playing out the
  relationship between Terri and the Mother Superior as
  a contest of wills. The Mother Superior represents
  deeply conservative, traditional religious values
  which are in sharp contrast with Terri's wild,
  irreverent and uncontrollable style. As the Mother
  Superior takes on a larger role, we may need a
  clearer sense of where she's coming from. Is she a
  traditionalist who's holding on to the old ways?
  Is she personally afraid of the threatening world
  outside? Has she experienced some crisis of faith? We
  discussed looking for points of conflict in surface
  issues that reflect the woman's basic values.

Some Ideas We Discussed:

- The choir is a natural battleground for Terri and the
  Mother Superior. We should consider ways of bringing
  Terri's involvement with the choir into the story
  earlier, and emphasize their need to wear one face in
  public and another in private.
- We could also further explore the Mother Superior's
  response to the changes taking place around the
  neighborhood.
- Perhaps when Terri goes AWOL, the Mother Superior
  should call Eddie, or the Bishop and try to have her
  thrown out of the convent.
- We discussed the idea that, as Terri seems to be gaining
  the upper hand in their struggle for power, the Mother
  Superior could reach a point where she resolves to leave
  the order. Perhaps she asks the bishop for a transfer.
  At this point, Terri, having realized the Mother
  Superior's worth, could intervene. She might blackmail

her into staying by threatening to stop singing, or leak
word to the other nuns and rally their support.

- Although she is generally an antagonist, we also feel
  that the Mother Superior could show Terri some moments
  of wisdom or humanity.

- As in Terri's case, we would like to highlight the
  emotional beat where the Mother Superior sees Terri
  in a new light. This might occur when Terri shows
  up at the concert, ignoring her own safety, so that
  the choir can have its moment of glory. After Terri
  is kidnapped, the Mother Superior could emotionally
  reveal Terri's true identity to the other nuns.

- We all love the humor when the Mother Superior
  disdainfully watches Terri undress and the scene where
  she picks up the rat. We'd like to give the Mother
  Superior more moments like this.

- **THE NUNS**

Differentiating Their Characters

- We like portraying the nuns as "real" people, but in
  the next draft, we would like to find ways of making
  them more distinct from one another. Without going
  over the top, perhaps they could be more comic and
  quirky. Within the group, there could be one slightly
  wacky nun. Another character we might highlight is
  Mary Timothy, "the snitch". Perhaps she could more
  persistently spy on Terri. There could be a show-down
  scene, where Terri shows her true colors and puts the
  sneaky nun in her place.

- Having Terri lobby so actively for Mary Robert to
  forgive Frank may make Terri seem irresponsible or
  presumptuous. Perhaps Mary Robert should come to Terri
  and ask for help having made her own life decision,
  rather than the reverse.

Heightening the Emotional Bond Between Terri and the Nuns

- In the next draft, let's emphasize the emotional
  moment where Terri has bonded with the other nuns,
  knows she is leaving, but can't blow her cover by
  saying goodbye. Perhaps after their success in driving
  the crack dealer from the neighborhood, the women
  gather at night for a kind of "slumber party" to
  revel in their victory. Terri knows that it is her

last night in the convent and experiences the festive
moment with melancholy.
- In between the time when Terri is unceremoniously
dragged away from the curb by Eddie and the final song
at St. Patrick's, let's consider adding a scene to
resolve the relationship between Terri, the Nuns and
the Mother Superior.

- **EDDIE**

Keeping Eddie Alive
- We discussed several ways of having Eddie and Terri
interact more consistently throughout the story.

Ideas We Discussed:
- Perhaps Eddie watches the convent to keep an eye on
Terri.
- Eddie might contact Terri to warn her that the mob is
closing in.
- Terri could try to reach Eddie when she learns he's
left her in a convent that's about to close down or
after the serious attempt on her life.
- After Terri has her night out with Frank, The Mother
Superior could call Eddie and demand that he remove
Terri from her convent.
- Also, the Mother Superior might contact Eddie when
Terri begins to really insinuate herself into the
neighborhood (i.e., confronting the crack dealers and
rapping in the street). This is another point where
Eddie might have a serious confrontation with Terri
about her rebellious behavior.

Love Interest
- Let's consider heightening the romantic angle between
Eddie and Terri. As we build their love relationship,
we should try to maintain some of their feisty, verbal
sparring as currently written in the dressing room.

STORY CHANGES
- **DIMINISHING SECONDARY CHARACTERS AND STORYLINES**

Frank and Mary Robert's Story
- To help us focus the story more clearly on Terri's
relationships with the Mother Superior and Eddie, we
discussed various ways to diminish the prominence of

this subplot and integrate it into our main storyline. For example, the debate over Frank and Mary Robert's relationship is another arena where Terri and the Mother Superior can lock horns. Mother Superior is all too aware that Terri's stay in the convent is only temporary, and resents her for stirring up problems that she will have to deal with later. Perhaps Mary Robert is her favorite. This could be a moment for the Mother Superior to display some insight and wisdom. Perhaps she could suggest to Mary Robert that a woman shouldn't become a nun to hide from the world or run away from a love affair. Terri, on the other hand, might give Mary Robert the wrong advice.

Gina and Mario

- We all agree that the classroom scene with Gina and her friends is terrific, but perhaps we should consider scaling back some of the scenes where Gina interacts with her boyfriend, Mario. Two areas we discussed reworking are: Gina's rejection of Mario (p. 52); Gina giving Mario the cold shoulder (pgs. 92-93).

- **INCREASING THE JEOPARDY**

The Mob

- In order to intensify our perception of a threat looming over Terri and make the danger more viable, we should explore ways of keeping Vince or his goons more visible in the second act. It might be funny if they've zeroed in on the neighborhood and Joey actually passes Terri and the nuns on the street without recognizing her. Perhaps it could be Joey who rescues the nuns from the mugger.
- Perhaps we should consider making Bates more of a threat and allow him to get closer to Terri early on. We also discussed the possibility that as Bates zeroes in on Terri, he might keep the mob at arm's length, slowly feeding them information as he drives up the price on her head.
- Finally, let's consider making the FAX device more humorously covert.

The Cathedral Performance

- We would like to amplify the perceived danger of the choice Terri makes when she agrees to perform at the

cathedral, as well as heightening the importance of the
event itself. We feel this will help clarify the notion
that Terri's decision throws her own life into complete
jeopardy, and is motivated only by the desire to see
the nuns realize their dream. Depicting the concert
as a huge media event could increase Terri's risk of
blowing her cover as her image is splashed across
newspapers and airwaves.

Student Annotated Pages

In my rewrite class, one of the first assignments for my students is to print out a hard copy of their draft, read it in one sitting, and write notes to themselves on their draft. It's important for the writer to respond to their material as a reader and not as the writer. *Suicide Girl* is a screenplay written by Ivy Pruss, an alumnus of the School of Cinematic Arts' Writing for Screen and Television graduate program. While reading her draft, Ivy had a great conversation with herself and created an invaluable document to guide her rewrite. She stars things that are importance and draws arrows connecting ideas. Ivy is honest about what is working and what needs work. She also jotted down quick ideas for potential solutions. Ivy was recently accepted into the Universal Pictures Emerging Writer's Fellowship and is glad to be writing full time.

Suicide Girl

By Ivy Pruss

Logline: After an accidental overdose, an opiate-addicted suicide girl pin up model gets a chance for redemption when she moves home to live with her estranged mother and pursues a cut-throat apprenticeship at a straight-edge tattoo shop.

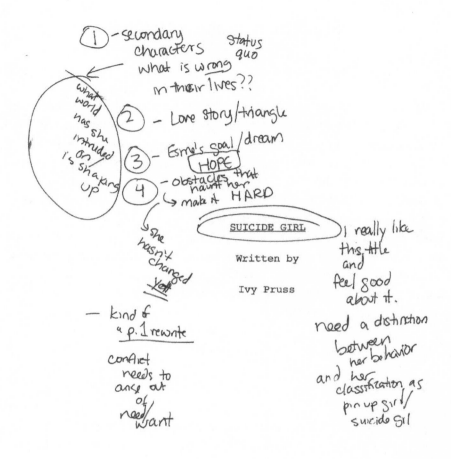

① - secondary characters — status quo
what is wrong in their lives??

what world has she intruded on is shaking up

② - Love story/triangle

③ - Esme's goal/dream
HOPE

④ - obstacles that haunt her
↳ make it HARD

↳ she hasn't changed *yet*

SUICIDE GIRL

Written by

Ivy Pruss

I really like this title and feel good about it.

— kind of "p.1 rewrite"

conflict needs to arise out of need/want

need a distinction between her behavior and her classification as pin up girl/suicide girl

→ what gives Esme hope?
↳ give something for the reader to latch onto.

what if Esme doesnt overdose but just
kind of moves back home, an uninvited house guest??

19.

like in Hesher

SASHA
You made your choices, and I'm
confident you will find a solution.

she overdoses in her apartment??

The nurse taps her pen.

NURSE
It's time to go, ladies.

no one saves her.

Sasha pulls the nurse aside.

SASHA
Can I speak with you a moment?

she's not literally a "suicide" girl, she's just dark and flawed + bad

she wakes up.
devoted. comes home

INT. NURSE'S STATION - CONTINUOUS

The nurse sits calmly in a chair while Sasha paces.

NURSE
Since she is uninsured, legally, I
can send her to the state hospital,
or I can release her to your care.

it's a choice.

SASHA
It'll have to be the hospital.

The nurse points to the hallway, crammed with beds of
drooling, hopeless people, many talking to themselves.

NURSE
I'm going to be honest. I used to
work at the state hospital. This
place is paradise compared to it.

This scene is not working
↳ got bored

SASHA
It can't be that much worse.

NURSE
They're severely understaffed.
She'll be chained to a bed, lying
in her own filth, listening to the
screaming raving madness of the
truly insane. When they can, maybe
in a day, maybe not for weeks, a
psychiatrist will evaluate her.
Since she's cogent and can wipe her
own ass, they'll release her.

shakes up the lives of her family... what are their stories??

SASHA
But she'll have nowhere to go.

A thought: Tonally this script is somewhere between Sherrybaby and Secretary

20.

NURSE
They can put her in touch with a
social worker, but there's a four
month wait for women's shelters.

I'm pretty sure this whole scene needs to go except

Sasha paces, covering her face with her eyes.

SASHA
I can't do this anymore.

NURSE
The patients I've seen recover are
the ones who have family support.

Sasha gets hope for the first time that

Sasha stops.

SASHA
Recover? As in get better?

Esme could recover—She's not hardened anymore./It

The nurse nods.

NURSE
Borderline Personality Disorder is
tough, but with a good support
network, her chances are better
that she could recover.

makes something loosen in Sasha.—that

SASHA
All the psychiatrists, they gave
pills to manage her condition.

Still boring. Where! the conflict?

NURSE
The pills are to manage symptoms,
but the underlying condition can
improve, sometimes remarkably, with
the right emotional support.

SASHA
She's been in and out of hospitals
the better part of ten years. No
one ever said she could get better.

hope that her daughter could be okay.

NURSE
Like I said, there are no
guarantees.

SASHA
But there's a chance?

The nurse nods, nudging the release papers toward Sasha.

Better if BPD is unstated but informs behavior

Nurse trying to guilt them seduce w/ idea of recovery?

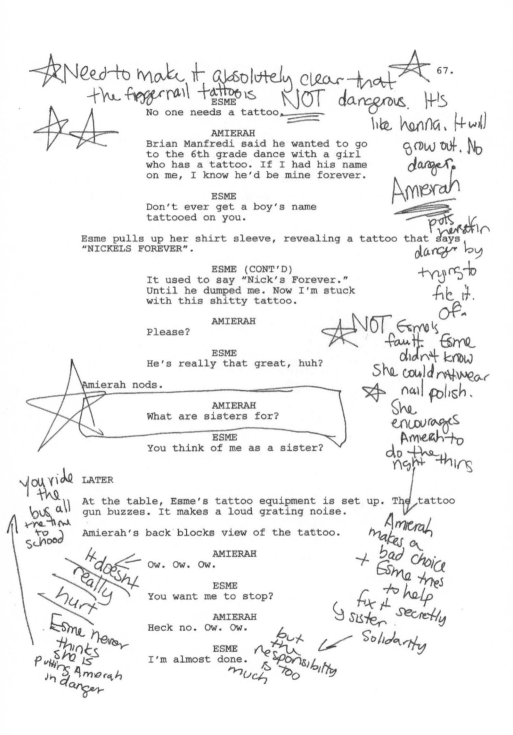

Need to make it absolutely clear that the fingernail tattoo is NOT dangerous. It's like henna. It will grow out. No danger.

67.

ESME
No one needs a tattoo.

AMIERAH
Brian Manfredi said he wanted to go to the 6th grade dance with a girl who has a tattoo. If I had his name on me, I know he'd be mine forever.

Amierah puts herself in danger by trying to fix it.

ESME
Don't ever get a boy's name tattooed on you.

Esme pulls up her shirt sleeve, revealing a tattoo that says "NICKELS FOREVER".

ESME (CONT'D)
It used to say "Nick's Forever." Until he dumped me. Now I'm stuck with this shitty tattoo.

AMIERAH
Please?

NOT Esme's fault. Esme didn't know she could not wear nail polish. She encourages Amierah to do the right thing

ESME
He's really that great, huh?

Amierah nods.

AMIERAH
What are sisters for?

ESME
You think of me as a sister?

LATER

You ride the bus all the time to school

At the table, Esme's tattoo equipment is set up. The tattoo gun buzzes. It makes a loud grating noise.

Amierah's back blocks view of the tattoo.

Amierah makes a bad choice + Esme tries to help fix it secretly

AMIERAH
Ow. Ow. Ow.

It doesn't really hurt

ESME
You want me to stop?

AMIERAH
Heck no. Ow. Ow.

sister solidarity

ESME
I'm almost done.

but the responsibility is too much

Esme never thinks she is putting Amierah in danger

Student Notes and Game Plans

David Ngo is an alumnus of the USC School of Cinematic Arts' Writing for Screen and Television Division graduate program. David was a student in my MFA Thesis class, and did excellent work on rewrites of his screenplay, *Take Your Grandma To Work Day*. His notes and game plan are detailed and specific.

TAKE YOUR GRANDMA TO WORK DAY
By David Ngo
© 2015

NOTES OVERVIEW

LOGLINE: Alex, on the verge of a layoff at a women's cable network, crashes a company retreat to impress senior management and save his job. And his grandma is coming with him

OVERALL LIKES

- Alex's dilemma is introduced well. The reader understands he is stuck and frustrated.
- Lana has all of the great scenes. And she is the strongest character.
- Terry, Reyna, and Autumn are really good characters for Alex to deal with.
- Well drawn story with consistent, believable characters. A look behind media and corporate America.
- The end of scenes pop on a high note.
- The pitch fest is a fun idea, along with Alex's intentional bad idea becoming a great idea that will benefit from rewriting.

OVERALL CONCERNS

- Needs clarity, especially the first sequence. Allow us to empathize with Alex and his problems early. Consider use of voice over or flashback. Make it his story.
- Identify a specific goal for Alex. He wants to move up as an executive.
- Not enough highs and lows. Get the first act more active for Alex.
- There are a lot of characters introduced in the beginning.

- Overall, scenes need better staging and less talking heads. The scenes need more crisis, energy, pressure, and movement.
- The screenplay should take more chances and push more, but not to the point of stupid and absurd, but bigger moments that pressure Alex.
- There could be more Alex and Autumn character scenes. *Need to develop chemistry*.
- The character voices need to be more distinct. They all sound alike.
- Could there be a bigger time clock element to the trip?
- Good resolutions, but the final scenes are lengthy. The ending needs rewriting to keep voices active.
- Several important moments occur off-stage and could be in the script Show Alex quitting. Show Lana talking to daughter.
- There could be more planting of character elements throughout the story.

THE PLOT

Firing the Janitor
- Slows story down and might confuse tone. What if I replace the janitor with James?

Performance Review
- Could I move Alex's review into the first ten pages to put him in immediate crisis?

Road Trip
- Alex getting his work done on the road is good, but his obstacles could be even tougher. Could the road trip scenes be less episodic?

Hotel Room
- Alex and Lana leaving the hotel because the power is out feels contrived. Instead of a power outage, what if the room has broken outlets? Or, what if Alex's computer breaks and he needs a new computer to use?

The Off-Site
- Alex's arrival should be a bigger deal, especially with Terry.
- Reyna leaving due to the spreadsheet error is vague, and Alex's actions aren't extreme enough.

TONE/THEME/THE WORLD
The tone of the first act seemed to waver at various points. Keep up the comedy.

The Off-Site
- The off-site can be satirized more and be more over-the-top. There is not enough going on at the off-site. Amp it up.

CHARACTERS

ALEX

Personality/Character

- Alex is passive and part of his transformation is to take-charge. He should be put into situations where he has to react.
- Alex is the least interesting character in the story at times, but does have frantic problems to solve, like on pg. 58.
- Make it clear that Alex wanted to be in TV because he saw his grandma succeed in it.

TERRY

Personality/Character

- Makes you want to scream. She could be even nastier though.
- Love this character. Could she be played by Sigourney Weaver?
- Terry hiring Reyna without Alex is a great example of passive-aggressiveness.

AUTUMN

Can we see Autumn stressed more at the off-site?

She needs a real connection moment with Alex.

Autumn defends Alex

- Autumn sticking up for Alex is a good scene that shows she has guts, but is naïve.
- We need to see Autumn's arc, so that it is earned when she speaks up to defend Alex.

REYNA

Personality/Character

- We understand why like Alex hates this nice girl. She is a good opposition force.
- Can we see that Reyna is out of her league at the off-site? This would allow Alex to swoop in actively and show her up to the H.R. rep.

MR. RIVERS

Personality/Character

- He is an executive ass. He has the right mix of con man and politician.
- Mr. Rivers is smarter than expected at the end. Can Mr. River's smarts be planted earlier?

PAGE NOTES/MISC FEEDBACK

Pg. 4—Separate out the characters in stage descriptions for clarity.

Pg. 5—End scene before Alex asks how to send it out.

Pg. 8—What if Mr. Rivers was in a video conference, to make his entrance impactful later? Also, we can focus on Alex and the other characters more in this scene.

Pg. 20—Tweak female nurse about how she loved Lana's show?

Pg. 25—Save Alex's backstory for later in the script?

Pg. 36—What does Alex tell James to change his mind about?

Pg. 45—Nice visual of Alex helping Lana in the SUV. Maybe compress this scene into the previous scene with the You Tube clip?

Pg. 62—Opportunity for Alex to recommit to his love of television, and convince Lana to help him.

Pg. 74—Repeated dialogue by James that needs to be fixed.

Pg. 88—Check for typos with Mr. Rivers' lines.

PITCHES

- What if James and Autumn are the same person?
- Consider using voice over or a flashback in the beginning to tell Alex's want.
- Possibly consider a different setting because this TV world is hard to follow.
- Is part of Alex's struggle that he doesn't have a pitch?
- Can there be a moral element to this job? Is Alex by the book?
- Let's see a scene of Alex at his apartment.

TAKE YOUR GRANDMA TO WORK DAY
by David Ngo
© 2015

GAME PLAN FOR THE NEXT PASS

1. ALEX WILL BE ACTIVE AND HAVE A CLEAR POINT-OF-VIEW

Alex, the main character, comes off as the least interesting person in the script. To readers, Alex's story is vague. Readers aren't sure what Alex wants, what he desires, and what type of person he is. For example, does Alex want his own show on The Breathe Network or does he hope to climb the executive ladder? Alex's voice, tone, and personality need more distinction. There is a lack of character development with Alex in the first forty pages of the script. Consequently, readers are not as invested in his plight.

In the script, Alex is too passive. He is not dictating the course of action. Alex's flaws need to play a bigger role in the next pass. Alex is a believable character, but his quirks need to be exposed. I plan to revise scenes so that Alex drives the action.

I need to work on establishing Alex's character. From the beginning of the script, it should be obvious that Alex has a clear internal problem that manifests itself through his actions. Essentially, Alex is the guy that plays it safe. He's the person who would rather pass the ball than take the last shot. Alex takes risks, but only when he's calculated them to not be risky.

I plan to spend a lot of time revising Act 1 to ensure that Alex's story is clear. I want to include new scenes that show off Alex's personality and life outside the office. These new scenes will help inform Alex's life inside the office. For instance, there could be a scene where Alex plays basketball (as the best player on the court) and passes the ball to a teammate instead of taking the game-winning shot. I want to show that Alex is risk adverse because he is afraid to appear vulnerable.

2. THE PLOT: ADD ROLLER COASTERS

The plot is even-keeled, with slight deviations of highs and lows. It is like a ride at *Disneyland,* when it should be a roller coaster at *Magic Mountain.* The highs need to be higher, and the lows need to be lower. With this lack of deviation, the story is bordering on dramedy, when it should be a clear comedy. The stakes need to be higher for Alex, the cast, and the Breathe Network. The plot needs more pressure.

There is a consensus that the script becomes interesting once Alex and Lana start their road trip. At this point, the plot drives forward and Alex becomes more active as a character. Once at the off-site, the story forges ahead, but not with the sense of grandeur expected by readers. I need to increase the sense of pressure in the story. The Breathe Network is in a state of crisis. Employees fear losing their jobs in a tough economy. Everyone is looking over their shoulder and worried about job security, especially Alex.

My plan is to significantly revise Act 1 to fully establish Alex's story. In doing so, I'll also work to heighten the sense of fear at Breathe. I intend to make a major change in Act 1 by having James get laid-off. I want to "kill off" the best friend early to put fear in Alex's heart and force him to act, especially after Terry hires Reyna. Alex is afraid of losing his job, and consequently, crashes the off-site to prove his worth and save his career. In Alex's personal life, Lana fears the fatality of cancer and Vicky worries that she can't take care of her kids (and Lana).

Once on the road trip, I want to make time a bigger factor. Alex has to get to the off-site by a certain time, and obstacles stand in his way. These obstacles need to be more extreme without becoming absurd.

I also intend to amp up the spectacle of the off-site. It needs to have a carnival-like atmosphere. The off-site is the culmination of the script, where we root for Alex to finally take the game-winning shot. This shot could be pitching at pitch fest, which Alex is hesitant to do because he is afraid of being vulnerable.

3. THEME: TAKING CHANCES (AKA "THE SQUEAKY WHEEL")

The first draft is a successful look behind the doors of a cable network and corporate America. Alex is a guy who is stuck in a rut and needs to take charge of his life. However, since Alex's story isn't clear and established in Act 1, there isn't a clear theme in the story. There are several central themes a reader can take away from the first draft.

For the next pass, I would like to establish a theme that is apparent in all of the core characters. A phrase that stuck out to me when I was working in corporate America was, "The squeaky wheel always gets heard." To me, this phrase revolves around the idea of taking chances, which I want to feature as a core theme of this screenplay.

4. STRENGTHEN TWO RELATIONSHIPS

Build Alex and Autumn's chemistry

I only touched the surface of Alex and Autumn's relationship in the first draft. I need to develop this relationship further and build on the sexual tension I was trying to create. Alex and Autumn need a deeper connection that extends beyond physical attraction. As I work to revamp Alex in Act 1, I can also strengthen his relationship with Autumn. I plan to add a scene to show that Alex and Autumn have a deep connection and are truly star-crossed lovers.

Establish Alex and James as best friends, and then "kill off" James

When James gets laid off in the first draft, this was supposed to be "the straw that broke the camel's back" for Alex. However, this moment may have come too late in the script and was not as impactful as I hoped. As a result, I need to give James and his friendship with Alex a fuller arc earlier in the story. In general, James needs his own story. In the first draft, he serves as a chorus for Alex without an arc of his own.

5. STRUCTURE

For the next pass, I would like to trim fifteen pages (or so) out of my script and get my page count to around 100 pages. I can do this by addressing character issues regarding Alex and revising scenes for better action, movement, and staging. In the first draft, there are too many "talking head" passages. I will look to start scenes later and leave scenes earlier to keep the script compact, concise, and forward-moving.

Student Notes and Game Plan

Romi Barta is an alumnus of the USC School of Cinematic Arts' Writing for Screen and Television Division graduate program. Romi wrote a dark romantic comedy set in Chicago, *F@#% The Knot*. Her bullet point approach to her notes and game plan make for easy access and rewriting. With each pass, she continued to get closer to her original intention until she finished with a tight character driven comedy.

F@#% The Knot
by Romi Barta
© 2015

COMPILED NOTES

LOGLINE: Best friend Sara is dating this "vanilla" guy Dennis. He's about to propose, which is not okay. Friends don't let friends marry the wrong man. So, Carly is going to break them up. And for the record, her inability to commit or be close to anyone has nothing to do with this.

OVERALL
- Core is working. Vibrant characters. Rings true and insightful.
- Carly and Dennis, and Carly/Max relationship need the most work.
- Needs to be Carly's story. It is at the end, but not through most of the beginning and middle.
- Cut 30 pages. Lots of long scenes, unnecessary scenes, set-up, world's longest night.
- Don't lose funny, character, or sense of dating in new millennium (esp. when cutting one long night scene).
- Paint a stark but true picture of the challenges of finding someone.

SETTING & LOCATIONS

- Use more unity in locations; seems like there's a lot of exposition to establish why everyone is going to a new place. Reuse locations to get to scenes faster.
- Too much description in scene settings.

STRUCTURE

- Make clear that they have a plan, will do X, Y, Z. Pull these things into the middle of the second act and reach a crisis at the end of Act II.
- Things are happening too late in the film.

SCENES—in general, they go on too long. Start later, end earlier.
- Get rid of some scenes with minor characters.
- Dialogue is fluid and comfortable.

CHARACTERS

CARLY

- We need to see her in more personal crisis, running away from her decisions and projecting her problems onto Sara. Yes, she's a mess, but we don't sense it until she falls apart.
- Need to add to Carly's personal problems and expand out the complications.
- Not sure what Carly wants. Not sure what she's running away from.
- Add campfire scene in middle of movie to learn about why Carly has issues with men.

MAX

- Max seems just as nervous as Carly does about the ring, but not sure if he's earned it yet.
- Max gets off the hook too easily.

CARLY & MAX

- Need to know more about Carly & Max during first half of the movie.
- Why does Carly need Max? Not sure why Max is there. Need more from him.
- What are the stakes for Carly and Max as a team?

SARA & DENNIS

- Clarify why Dennis is bad for Sara at the top so we are onboard with Carly breaking them up.

SCENES

OPENING

- Four characters introduced quickly.

CARLY TELLS MAX THEY CAN STOP THE ENGAGEMENT

- Maybe Carly says she's been thinking about it for a while. Right now, it's out of the blue for us, which is good, but it feels like it's out of the blue for her, too. Or treat it like an epiphany and get her really visibly fired up.

DECISION TO BREAK THEM UP

- Make it more clear. Carly says, "We are saving them from themselves. It's for a noble cause. Are you in?" Make it more clear.

GOING OUT DISASTER SEQUENCE

- Cut bar scene in half.

POST BAR MCDONALD'S

- We should get a sense of Max/Carly chemistry here.

CAB RIDE TO THE RING

- Cut scene, Jimmy doesn't need to comment too much.

STEALING THE RING

- The doorman scene shows how capable Carly is. Can plant this before so we get a kick out of seeing a heightened version of this here.
- Sara seeing Carly and Max is more of a slapstick moment and sticks out from the rest of the script.

POST BREAK-UP

- By destroying the other couple, they become a couple, and then it destroys them. How can you be together when they came together by destroying their best friends? How can we be happy now?

ENDING

- Hoping to see one more scene between Carly and Sara to close out the story. Sara should end things with Carly, instead of having Dennis act as a buffer. They are close friends and Sara should have at least one more word with her
- Seems like it ends before it ends. Carly & Sara's relationship is left too open-ended. Feels unsatisfying.

- If Sara's friendship is so important, need them to have a rapprochement at the end.
- There is potential for fulfilling emotional connections at the end. Need to really resolve them and earn that.

F@#% The Knot
by Romi Barta
© 2015

GAME PLAN—FIRST PASS

CHARACTERS –
CARLY

- This needs to be Carly's story from the very beginning. I want to make sure the first act focuses on her. We need to see and understand that she is in crisis from the top—not just when she learns about the engagement.
  - **Relationships with men:** I want to establish Carly's past relationships with men. Carly doesn't seem to think there's anything wrong with her love life. I also want to establish that Carly is put off by how her friends have been treated by men, so we understand she subconsciously keeps them at a distance to avoid heartbreak.
  - **Establish other pressures in Carly's life**
- **Character flaw:** Emotionally sealed off. Fear of commitment . . . fear of getting hurt.
- **Need:** To have trust and faith in love and the people around you. Expand this need into the entire story and the friendships, particularly between Sara and Carly.
- **Capacity:** Art of persuasion. A saleswoman, literally and figuratively.
- **Carly's dream:** Cut the lawyer stuff. Carly and Sara want to open their own boutique. This has been their plan since they were in high school.
- **Understanding Carly:** The audience needs to be on board with Carly's plan to break up Dennis and Sara—at least, at first. This, in large part, will come from the changes I plan to make with Dennis.

CARLY & MAX

- **Create lobster moment**: We see Carly & Max as a couple before they do.
- Bring them together in the first half of the movie.

DENNIS
- **Make Dennis a person:** I plan to completely re-write Dennis' personality and attitude. He's pretentious, uncompromising and controlling. I want to show that his opinion has a huge affect on Sara.
- **Friendship with Max & reasons for marrying Sara:** It's important to understand why Max doesn't want Dennis to propose to Sara. I am considering having Dennis tell Max that he is going to propose in the first act. It's all very unromantic and should almost be like Dennis is checking off boxes of his ideal wife. Maybe that's a theory he has for liking online dating, you can literally search for qualities you want in a spouse. I want him to be likeable in his unlike-ability; everything he says should have some kind of truth in it.

PLOT –
RE-STRUCTURING AND CUTTING
- **General:** Start scenes later, end earlier. Cut set-ups. CUT 30 PAGES (yikes . . . maybe 20 on this pass . . .).
- **Going out sequence:** Chop in half, at least. Cut sushi scene. Streamline cuts
- back and forth between the girls and guys nights.
- **Cut blackmail:** Too much happening at the end.
- **Cut Carly's mom & divorce:** Okay to have divorce come up once as a piece of information about Carly, but no need to make a big deal about it.

THE ENDING
The main things that need to happen:
- **Sara and Carly resolution scene:** There needs to be a scene between Sara and Carly after everything has happened. I still don't think Sara forgives Carly, but this needs to be established in person.
- **When do Carly & Max get together:** Does it comes earlier? Does Max kiss Carly after the charity event?
- **Carly and Max own up to what they did:** Do they do this together with Sara and Dennis? Get them together so they can say, "What you don't know is we ruined your life? I messed up and I'm sorry?" and, in doing so, the friendship is over?

Areas to Address:
- Carly family life—we all get frightened of being hurt.
- Let's see Carly in her current state. It's messy.

- One relationship ending, and now look what happened, we weren't gonna get tied up, etc.
- Carly decided doesn't want emotional attachments, set boundaries and doesn't want to get attached. She had her heart broken and believed. Love catches you unprepared. You can't control love, as much as she tries to control it, doesn't want to be two years down the road and a statistic.
- When Sara's gone, she's alone. She's looking for company, but not a relationship, show that she's actually looking for the attachment, not willing to emotionally open up to something else. Find beats for that in the existing scenes.
- Accusatory scene: "Look at Dennis, he's nice. There are guys out there. David likes you." "Oh please. I've been there." Throw away lines. Less is more.
- Write out a beat sheet for the ending. Now it's about how and where.
- Write Dennis scene.
- Want fun in the opening. Don't do too much at once.
- Note: Set-pieces. A couple of big comedy pieces. *Bridesmaids*—what's the big scene that's hilarious? Don't get slapstick, but is there a scene I can blow up a little more. Want a couple of those big ones.
- More with the apartment—is that the lobster scene? That scene seems under-staged. More complications there can be funny, embarrassing situations.

Essential Three Act Questions

ACT ONE

The Set-Up

State your premise in two or three sentences.

Use one word to describe what your movie is about.

Where does the movie take place?

What new world are you examining or creating?

Describe the current status quo of the story.

What is the theme of the screenplay?

What is the main character's internal character story?
  (It's the story about a man/woman who... They need to...)

Use one word to describe the main character.
  (Ambitious, defeated, defiant, etc.)

What does the main character want?

What is the main character's dream?
  (This does not mean a sleeping dream. All characters need a dream—"In a perfect world this is what I would like my life to be. . . ." A character's dream should reflect elements of their personal story.)

What is the main character's character flaw?

What is the main character's personal dilemma?

What is the main character's defining scene?
  (A defining scene is an early scene that reveals key information about the main character. A strong defining scene establishes a strong character. It also reveals hints of the internal character story.)

How did life turn out differently for the main character from what they expected?

Describe the main character as the world sees them.

Who is the antagonist and what is their internal character story?

If you do not have a classical antagonist, then who or what is your main opposition force?

Describe the antagonist in one word.

What is the antagonist's want?

What is the antagonist's goal?

Who is the love interest?

What is the love interest's internal character story?

Describe the love interest's character in one word.

What is the main problem that keeps the lovers apart?

Describe each major supporting character in one word.

What are the major supporting character's personal stories?
  (It's the story about a man/woman who... They need to...)

What are the major relationships established in the Set-Up?

What is the crisis that sets in motion an irreversible chain of events?

What is the overall plot problem that must be solved by the end of the movie?

For the main character, where is the point of no return from which there is no turning back?

What is the dramatic event that clearly marks the end of the first act and thrusts your characters into the second act?

ACT TWO

Complications and Obstacles

At the beginning of the second act, what is the immediate plot problem the main character has to solve?

  (This is different from the overall plot problem. This is an immediate problem that propels the main character forward for the first few scenes of the second act.)

At the beginning of the second act, what is at personally at stake for the main character?

At the beginning of the second act, what is at stake in the overall plot?

At the beginning of the second act, what are the major questions being asked in your screenplay?

At the beginning of the second act, what is the main conflict facing the main character?

How has the status quo changed for the main character and what is the new normal?

What is the ticking clock for the second act?

How does the love story complicate the main character's want?

What is keeping the lovers apart throughout the second act?

What does the antagonist do to thwart the main character from accomplishing their want?

List the many elements of complication that help deter the main character from reaching their want in the second act.

Which relationships "help" and which relationships "hinder" the main character from reaching their want?

List the major subplots throughout the second act.

What are the sequence tensions throughout the second act?

What are the major character reveals throughout the second act?

What are the major plot reveals throughout the second act?

What major obstacles must the main character navigate throughout the second act?

What major reversals or setbacks does the main character suffer throughout the second act?

What is your mid-point plot turn and how does it intensify the back half of the second act?

How does your mid-point plot turn affect the main character's personal story?

How does your mid-point plot turn affect the overall plot?

How are you using the antagonist's plan to create plot events?

In the second act, where do the personal stakes rise for the main character?

In the second act, where do the plot stakes rise?

What other significant character, or characters, will suffer dire consequences should the main character fail to resolve the main plot problem?

What are the high points and the low points of the main character's journey throughout the second act?

What scenes or events specifically pressure the main character's internal story?

At the end of the second act, what is personally at stake for the main character?

At the end of the second act, what is at stake in terms of the plot?

What is the event that ends the second act and places the main character into a dangerous situation either physically, emotionally, or psychologically?

(This can also be a combination of physical, emotional, or psychological.)

At the end of the second act, what are the major questions being asked in your screenplay?

(There should be personal character questions as well as plot questions that need to be resolved in the third act.)

What are several possible third act resolutions to ensure the ending is not predictable?

ACT THREE

Resolution

At the beginning of the third act, what dilemma faces the main character?

At the beginning of the third act, why is the antagonist more powerful than the main character?

What is the ticking clock for the third act?

In what ways has the main character grown and transformed from their experiences in the second act which make them capable to overcome the antagonist in the third act?

What brings the love interest together in the third act?

How is the main character's internal story resolved?

How is the main character's need satisfied?

How is the main plot problem resolved?

How does the main character earn the ending?

How does the antagonist get what they deserve?

What makes the ending satisfying and unpredictable?

At the end of the story, what is the new status quo or new normal?

At the end of the movie, what is the hope for the main character?

Acknowledgments

In writing *Screenwriting is Rewriting*, I am forever indebted to my wonderful wife, Cynthia, who first edited my film reviews while we worked on, *The State News*, the Michigan State University newspaper. She became my trusted reader, and subsequently read all my screenplays written with my partner, Jim Cash, before we sent them out on the town. From the first moment I mentioned I wanted to write a book about rewriting, Cynthia enthusiastically encouraged me to write it. I could not have written *Screenwriting is Rewriting* without her constant support and guidance. She played a critical role in shaping and editing this book. In addition, I greatly appreciate the support and encouragement of my two remarkable children, Liza and Kerri. They are great cheerleaders and helped me get to the finish line.

Special thanks to my friend and Writing Division colleague, Paul Foley, who gallantly jumped in and gave me a slew of invaluable notes on how to structure and focus the book. With a growing family and his own career to manage, Paul was remarkably generous with his time and ideas about rewriting. Like any writer receiving rewrite notes, I fought them as much as I could until I surrendered to their truth and insight.

I am indebted to all my colleagues at the Writing Division for contributing to a culture of openness and collaboration, as well as the free flow of ideas and methodology. One of the great rewards of being a faculty member at The USC School of Cinematic Arts Writing for Screen and Television Division is being surrounded by so many accomplished and supportive writers. In addition, I greatly appreciate the School of Cinematic Arts' Dean Elizabeth Daley for her enthusiasm and encouragement. *Screenwriting is Rewriting* is the result of a project I began during an academic sabbatical.

What makes teaching at USC special is working with so many talented and dedicated student writers. Special thanks to my former writing students, Romi Barta, David Ngo, and Ivy Pruss for sharing examples of their work. Each of these students was a delight to work with, and their generosity is greatly appreciated. Additional thanks to Writing student, Tommy Waas, for helping prepare documents for the book while balancing a heavy writing load.

I would also like to thank Katie Gallof at Bloomsbury Books for believing in this project from the start and enthusiastically shepherding it through Bloomsbury. Also, I would like to extend a thank you to Mary Al-Sayed at Bloomsbury for her support. In addition, I would like to thank Grishma Fredric of Deanta Global Publishing Services, and all the members of her team, for their hard work and diligence in copyediting, proofreading, and typesetting the manuscript.

And last, but not least, a huge thank you to my first screenwriting instructor, and subsequent writing partner for over twenty-five years, the late great Jim Cash. When I was an undergraduate at Michigan State University, Jim was teaching the only screenwriting class. When I tried to register for the class, I was distressed to learn it was full. By talking my way into the class, I took my first step in learning to be a screenwriter. When I moved to California, Jim and I began a long-distance writing relationship that included over thirty commissioned screenplays, and eight produced motion pictures. Jim was simply the most remarkable writer I have ever met, and I continued to learn from him every day. Jim touched so many lives through his writing and teaching at MSU, that everyone who was fortunate to have met Jim was better for it.

Works Cited

Frontispiece Quotations

Engel, Joel. *Oscar®-winning Screenwriters on Screenwriting: The Award-winning Best in the Business Discuss Their Craft*, 86. New York: Hyperion, 2002a.

Engel, Joel. *Oscar®-winning Screenwriters on Screenwriting: The Award-winning Best in the Business Discuss Their Craft*, 102–03. New York: Hyperion, 2002b.

Mackendrick, Alexander. *On Film-making: An Introduction to the Craft of the Director*. Edited by Paul Cronin, 40. London: Faber and Faber, 2004.

McCurrie, Tom. "Aaron Sorkin Gives A Few Good Tips On Writing." *Hollywood Lit Sales.com*. August 9, 2011. http://www.hollywoodlitsales.com/cf/journal/dspJournal. cfm?intID=2720.

Introduction

Brady, John Joseph. *The Craft of the Screenwriter: Interviews with Six Celebrated Screenwriters*, 347. New York: Simon and Schuster, 1981.

Fowler, H. W., and R. W. Burchfield. *The New Fowler's Modern English Usage*. 3rd ed, 779. Oxford: Clarendon Press, 1996.

How To Use This Book

Gilroy, Dan. "On Writing: Rules Made To Be Broken." *Los Angeles Times*, January 1, 2015, The Envelope sec. S15.

Let's Talk About Rewriting

Iglesias, Karl. *101 Habits of Highly Successful Screenwriters: Inside Secrets from Hollywood's Top Writers*, 108. Avon, MA: Adams Media, 2001.

The Pass Method

Faraci, Devin. "Exclusive Interview: William Broyles, Jr. (Jarhead)." *Chud.com* Exclusive Interview Williams Broyles Jr Jarhead. Comments March 7, 2006. http://www.chud. com/6087/exclusive-interview-william-broyles-jr-jarhead/.

Johnson, Rian. Interviewed by Jack Epps, Jr. at the University of Southern California. September 16, 2012.

Movies You Need To See

Truffaut, Francois. *Hitchcock*. 6th ed, 71. New York: Simon and Schuster, 1967.

Chapter 1—Notes

Fahy, Thomas Richard, ed. *Alan Ball: Conversations*, 36. Jackson, MS: University Press of Mississippi, 2013.

Chapter 2—Interpreting Notes

Used by permission of Bob Cooper.

Chapter 3—Annotated Draft

"Francis Ford Coppola Reflects On His Film Career." *NPR*. November 22, 2011. www.npr.org/2011/11/22/140870590/francis-ford-coppola-reflects-on-his-film-career.

Chapter 4—Game Plan

Iglesias, Karl. *101 Habits of Highly Successful Screenwriters: Inside Secrets from Hollywood's Top Writers*, 133. Avon, MA: Adams Media, 2001.

Chapter 5—Character

Blake, Meredith. "Marks of Character." *Los Angeles Times*, April 5, 2015, Calendar sec. E9.
Petit, Zachary. "13 Stephen King Quotes on Writing|Quotes From Stephen King." *WritersDigest.com*. March 9, 2012. http://www.writersdigest.com/editor-blogs/there-are-no-rules/13-stephen-king-quotes-on-writing-your-moment-of-friday-zen.

Chapter 6—Foundation Pass

Lumet, Sidney. *Making Movies*, 10. New York: Vintage Books, 1996.

Chapter 7—Character Pass

Bauer, Erik. "Method Writing: Interview with Quentin Tarantino." *Creative Screenwriting Magazine*, accessed May 2, 2015. http://creativescreenwriting.com/method-writing-interview-with-quentin-tarantino.

Chapter 8—The Set-Up

As Good As It Gets. Copyright © 1997 Tristar Pictures, Inc. All Rights Reserved.
Crowe, Cameron. *Conversations with Wilder*, 357. New York: Knopf, 1999.

Chapter 9—Story & Theme Pass

Iglesias, Karl. *101 Habits of Highly Successful Screenwriters: Inside Secrets from Hollywood's Top Writers*, 133. Avon, MA: Adams Media, 2001.

Chapter 10—Structure

Brady, John Joseph. *The Craft of the Screenwriter: Interviews with Six Celebrated Screenwriters*, 115–16. New York: Simon and Schuster, 1981.

Chapter 11—Structure Pass

Engel, Joel. *Oscar®-winning Screenwriters on Screenwriting: The Award-winning Best in the Business Discuss Their Craft*, 22. New York: Hyperion, 2002.

McNamara, Mary. "So, Writers, Why Must All Men Die?" *Los Angeles Times*, June 16, 2014, Calendar sec. D5.

Chapter 12—Plot

Callaghan, Dylan. "Casanova Re-writ." Accessed June 15, 2015. http://www.wga.org/content/default.aspx?id=3240.

Chapter 13—Plot Pass

"50 Great Screenwriting Quotes—ScreenCraft." *ScreenCraft*. January 23, 2013. http://screencraft.org/2013/01/23/50-great-screenwriting-quotes/.

"Writing Advice from South Park's Trey Parker and Matt Stone." Accessed June 17, 2015. http://www.aerogrammestudio.com/2014/03/06/writing-advice-from-south-parks-trey-parker-and-matt-stone/.

Chapter 14—Feedback on Your Interim Draft

Callaghan, Dylan. "Jarhead Knowledge." Accessed June 15, 2015. http://www.wga.org/content/default.aspx?id=3254.

Chapter 15—Opposition Characters

Blair, Iian. "Director's Chair: David O. Russell—'American Hustle'" *Post Magazine*. January 1, 2014. http://www.postmagazine.com/Publications/Post-Magazine/2014/January-1-2014/Directors-Chair-David-O-Russell-American-Hustle.aspx.

Chapter 16—Obstacles, Complications, Reveals, and Reversals

"Toronto 2011: Pearl Jam Comes out of Its Shell."—*Latimes.com*. September 13, 2011. http://latimesblogs.latimes.com/movies/2011/09/pearl-jame-movie-vedder-crowe-toronto-tour-dates-air-canada-centre.html.

Chapter 17—Obstacles, Complications, Reveals, and Reversals Pass

"Aaron Sorkin on Theme, Intention & Obstacles." *Screenwriting from Iowa.* January 11, 2011. https://screenwritingfromiowa.wordpress.com/2011/01/11/aaron-sorkin-on-theme-intention-obsticles/.

Chapter 18—Relationships

Engel, Joel. *Oscar®-winning Screenwriters on Screenwriting: The Award-winning Best in the Business Discuss Their Craft*, 45. New York: Hyperion, 2002.
McIntyre, Gina. "A New Glimpse of Tim Burton's World." *Los Angeles Times*, December 22, 2014, Calendar sec. D4.

Chapter 19—Relationship Pass

Ordoña, Michael. "Oscars 2014: With 'Her,' Spike Jonze Gets into Relationships." *Los Angeles Times.* February 13, 2014. http://articles.latimes.com/2014/feb/13/entertainment/la-et-mn-spike-jonze-her-20140213.

Chapter 20—Scene Pass

Engel, Joel. *Oscar®-winning Screenwriters on Screenwriting: The Award-winning Best in the Business Discuss Their Craft*, 23. New York: Hyperion, 2002.

Chapter 21—Dialogue Pass

http://m.imdb.com/name/nm0000519/quotes.
American Beauty. Copyright © 1999 Dreamworks, LLC All rights reserved.
On The Waterfront. Copyright © MCMLIV Columbia Pictures Corporation International. Copyright secured. All rights reserved.
Shaun Of The Dead. Copyright © 2004 WT Venture, LLC. All rights Reserved.
Erin Brockovich. Copyright © 2000 Universal Studios and Columbia Pictures Industries, Inc. All Rights Reserved.

Chapter 22—Consistent Pass

Lumet, Sidney. *Making Movies*, 37. New York: Vintage Books, 1996.

Chapter 23—Polish Pass

Petit, Zachary. "13 Stephen King Quotes on Writing|Quotes From Stephen King." *WritersDigest.com*. March 9, 2012. http://www.writersdigest.com/editor-blogs/there-are-no-rules/13-stephen-king-quotes-on-writing-your-moment-of-friday-zen.

Chapter 24—Sending Out Your Screenplay

Rottenberg, Josh. "Damien Chazelle's Wild, Crazy Ride to the Oscars with 'Whiplash.'" *Los Angeles Times*. February 15, 2015. http://www.latimes.com/entertainment/movies/la-et-mn-ca-damien-chazelle-20150215-story.html#page=1.

Chapter 25—Working with Directors, Producers, and Executives

Rabin, Nathan. "Shane Black." Interview, *The A.V. Club*. November 9, 2005. http://www.avclub.com/article/shane-black-13960.

Annotated Draft

Suicide Girl. Copyright © 2015 Ivy Pruss.

Script Notes and Game Plan

Take Your Grandma to Work Day. Copyright © 2015 David Ngo.
F@#% The Knot. Copyright © 2015 Romi Barta.

Index